A
Lyme
Miscellany
1776-1976

A
Lyme
Miscellany
1776-1976

Edited by
GEORGE J. WILLAUER, JR.

With an Introduction by
JOHN P. DEMOS

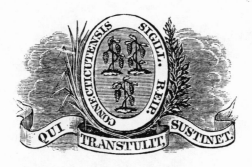

WESLEYAN UNIVERSITY PRESS
Middletown, Connecticut

"The Reverend Stephen Johnson and the Stamp Act in Lyme: Religious and Political Thought in the Origins of the Revolution" first appeared, in a slightly different form, in *Perspectives in American History* (Cambridge: Charles Warren Center for Studies in American History, Harvard University, 1971). Copyright © 1971 by Bernard Bailyn.

The publication of this work has been supported by grants from the American Revolution Bicentennial Commission and the Town of Old Lyme, Connecticut.

Endpapers: *Connecticut and Parts Adjacent* (Amsterdam: Covens and Mortier and Covens Junior; K. Klockoff, *Sculp.;* 1780). From the Map Collection, Yale University Library.

Library of Congress Cataloging in Publication Data

Main entry under title:

A Lyme miscellany, 1776–1976.

Bibliography: p.
1. Lyme, Conn.—History—Addresses, essays, lectures. 2. Lyme, Conn.—History—Revolution, 1775–1783—Sources, I. Willauer, George J., 1935–   II. Bailyn, Bernard.
F104.L95L9   974.6'5   76-41483
ISBN 0-8195-5009-4

Manufactured in the United States of America
First edition

To the citizens of the Town,
past and present

Contents

Contents

Editor's Preface

In the summer of 1972 Mrs. John Crosby Brown, then president of the Lyme Historical Society, asked me to work on a project in recognition of the bicentennial observance of the American Revolution. I accepted enthusiastically. When the Old Lyme Bicentennial Commission was appointed and Mrs. Brown became chairman, it assumed sponsorship of the project and obtained a federal grant from the American Revolution Bicentennial Commission which the Town of Old Lyme graciously matched. Connecticut College also contributed several grants in aid to support research.

Once launched by Mrs. Brown's initiative, a book gradually evolved. Upon consultation Bernard Bailyn endorsed the idea of compiling essays about and documents of crucial years during the revolutionary period and provided the first essay. He also recommended potential contributors who might explore the religious and political activity of the town, the lives of its prominent men, the relation of the town to the colony, and civil rights then and now. The hope was to produce a volume of interest to the community today as well as to students of American history throughout the state and nation.

In its completed form the book has two parts. The first contains seven essays and the second approximately fifty items from primary sources. Each selection has been treated as an entity in itself so there is some duplication and even contradiction, but ideally this should accommodate the tastes of individual readers and stimulate discussion and further research. To facilitate reading, all eighteenth-century documents have been edited according to the principles Bernard

A Lyme Miscellany

Bailyn established as editor for *Pamphlets of the American Revolution: 1750–1776* (Cambridge, Mass.: Belknap Press of Harvard University Press, 1965–). In general, spelling, punctuation, and capitalization have been modernized, but no words have been changed and care has been taken in every case to preserve the original meaning.

At a recent conference on local history Michael Kammen gave an address entitled "The American Revolution Bicentennial and the Writing of Local History." Kammen explained the importance of studying localities in order to learn more about the War of Independence, and he cited several new areas for further investigation. Collectively, the sundry parts of this *Miscellany* well exemplify his remarks.

Kammen first of all said that "the microscope will help us to verify (or correct) what we have been seeing, hitherto, primarily through the telescope."[1] Accordingly, Christopher Collier modifies the popular misconception that colonial towns began as Bible commonwealths in his study of the secular establishment and development of Saybrook and Lyme. Through statistical analysis Jackson Turner Main focuses on the economic and social structure of Lyme as a typical colonial community, and upon a study of probate court records Minor Myers, jr., reveals among other things that the leaders in Lyme were reading the political and philosophical works that inspired the Founding Fathers. Bernard Bailyn analyzes the tracts of a country parson in terms of the generalizations he makes in his book, *The Ideological Origins of the American Revolution*.

"Human interest" and "intrinsic charm," other uses of local history mentioned by Kammen, are particularly evident in John Ifkovic's biographical sketch of Matthew Griswold, the state's first governor.[2]

The "*interaction* of various levels of state and local history" is a new and challenging area of inquiry, according to Kammen, and it is one Bruce Stark and Harold Selesky have responded to in their respective studies of the Upper House and patterns of officeholding in the state legislature.[3]

I am indebted to many individuals who have helped me in numerous ways, and it is a pleasure to express my gratitude to them here. Mrs. John Crosby Brown comes to mind first because she initiated the project and has given immeasurable encouragement and support throughout. Over an extended period of time the counsel of Mr. Bernard Bailyn has been thoroughly appreciated. With good humor and promptness Miss Martha Anderson has used her editorial expertise to improve every portion of the book, and her good judgment and help have been invaluable. Mrs. Matthew Griswold, Mr. Bruce Stark, and Mr. Glenn Weaver have read portions of the text and made many helpful suggestions for improvement. For sharing his intimate knowledge of Lyme and his familiarity with primary sources I am especially grateful to Mr. Stark. Without him I could not have completed Part Two.

For generous aid of several kinds I am indebted also to Miss Helen Aitner, Mr. Christopher Collier, Miss Susan H. Ely, Miss Hazel Johnson, Mr. Randolph Klein, Mrs. Marion Mletschnig, Mr. Edmund Morgan, Mr. Harold Selesky, Mrs. Ernest Spitzer, Mrs. Frank Sisk, Mr. James Wheaton, and Mr. Ronald Wojcik. Members of the Old Lyme Bicentennial Commission have given their endorsement to the project, and I am most grateful for their faith in me.

Typing and retyping have been the responsibility of Mrs. Gene Minucci and Mrs. William Colopoulos, and I want to express my sincere gratitude to them for their cheerful cooperation and unstinting commitment to perfection. Finally, to my shadow editor, my wife, I give my heartfelt thanks for her help and support in uncountable ways.

G. J. W., Jr.

October 30, 1976

Notes

1. Michael Kammen, "The American Revolution Bicentennial and the Writing of Local History," *History News, XXX* (August 1975):183.
2. Ibid., p. 184.
3. Ibid., p. 185.

A
Lyme
Miscellany
1776-1976

Introduction:
A Note on Community Studies

JOHN DEMOS

RECENT SCHOLARSHIP in American history displays, as one of its distinguishing marks, a considerable preoccupation with local communities. This has been most fully evident in research on our colonial era, though urban neighborhoods of a later period and even some truly modern metropolitan settings have also received similar attention. From a plethora of monographs, articles, and academic colloquia has come the genus of the *community study* — a term which by now conveys a kind of historiographic imprimatur.

The community study is defined, in the first instance, by considerations of size and scope. The scholars most directly involved have been asking two strategic questions. First, what is the unit of study most appropriate to the themes which we — as historians — particularly wish to explore? Second, what is the average field of experience within which legions of men and women of the past — as historical actors — have largely organized their lives? There is a convergence of meaning here: the interests of the scholar and of his subject are jointly served. Local research provides a frame within which new questions can be raised, new data uncovered, new methods deployed. At the same time it serves to recreate the phenomenological world of past times. Both aspects deserve additional comment.

Community study has been a means, though not the only one, of infusing history with a substantial body of ideas and techniques borrowed from adjacent areas of the social sciences. The methodological arsenal of demography — family reconstitution, aggregate analysis, life tables, and the like — is a conspicuous case in point; and other forms of quantitative investigation have also played their part. In

3

addition, conceptual schemes borrowed from sociology, psychology, and anthropology have exerted much direct influence. In the latter discipline, most especially, historians have found models of the "little community," which throw strong light on some of their own materials.

Yet scientific system and precision comprise just a part of the motive for community study. Equally important, at least for some practitioners, are the aesthetic possibilities inherent in this approach. To unwind the taut threads of community is a challenge to art no less than to science. There is a wholeness here, a sense of life's texture, a chance to match individual human beings and the cultural web in their true relations one to another. Carefully pursued, local research yields an almost tangible result — the roadways, the houses, the people themselves, vividly recalled in the mind's eye.

To put it so is to claim for community studies a distinctive authenticity. But this claim is rooted in historical circumstance as well. The concerns of average people — so the argument goes — have not ordinarily extended beyond quite local bounds. Is it not true even today, in our technologically shrunken world, that most of us move in a rather narrow circle of preoccupation? How much more true, then, of our forebears in premodern times! Charters handed down by kings and bishops an ocean away, statutes enforced by governors and councilors, and even by popular assemblies: from all this they were largely separated. Such things might, on particular occasions, touch their lives directly; but for the most part the lines of influence were indirect, slow, and hard to perceive. What counted in the minds of ordinary folk was the routine activity of kin, neighbors, and local leaders. Weather, crops, cattle, fences, personal friendships (and quarrels), commissioners' courts, Sunday meetings, fast days and thanksgivings: such were the leading elements of their daily round. It made, if not quite a world unto itself, at least a world of limited scope and familiar shape. And it represents for us, in the title of one recent book, "the world we have lost."

The process of doing local research is, in some parts, difficult and tedious, but a fully executed community study has a special — one might well say, seductive — charm. Thus a scholar may come to feel a proprietary concern for "his" town or village, not unlike the feeling of anthropologists for particular field-work sites. There are, however, some dangers here.

Introduction

One danger is an exclusively local orientation. While the little community may largely circumscribe the interests of its individual members, it does not do so wholly. At the very least, neighboring communities interact and interfere with one another; moreover, the higher centers of power may profoundly influence local experience at certain times and under special conditions. The first generation of community studies mostly ignored these broader dimensions; it was necessary, so to say, to establish the importance of local boundaries. Perhaps in the future we may reasonably expect a second generation in which regional, or even national, connections are fully laid out. Without such progression there is real risk of a kind of scholarly involution — a retreat, indeed, into mere antiquarianism.

Another danger — which, in turn, suggests another avenue to explore — involves the themes brought forward in local research. There was an early and understandable tendency to narrow the focus and feature those themes intrinsic to community life. Internal governance, the arrangement of class and status-groups, local ceremony and custom, the transmission of power and influence across the generations: such were the leading items on most research agendas. In a sense, the community was studied for reasons sufficient to itself. But this work has, or should have, another aspect: it is a *method* as much as a topic, a *means* as well as an end. The strategies applied and developed here can be put to work in relation to a broad range of important and familiar historical problems. The process and meaning of economic growth, the impact of particular wars and political conflicts, religious movements, ideological enthusiasms — all this, and much more, can fruitfully be restudied in the context of particular communities. The results should constitute a considerable enrichment in historical understanding.

This brings us, finally, to the contents of the present volume. The trends and possibilities, the charm and even the pitfalls characteristic of community study are vividly epitomized in the pages that follow. *A Lyme Miscellany* includes, for example, some microscopic detection of tissues and structures inherent in the town itself; it also includes careful analysis of larger contexts — regional, imperial, and cultural in the broadest sense. There is a balance throughout between the concrete and the general, the unique and the typical, the personal and the collective. The essays are widely divergent in substance and in style, yet there are numerous points of intersection. And the docu-

5

ments invite the reader to participate actively in the quest for insight. There is no closure here: Lyme, like all communities, has history enough for many hands and minds.

There is one more point worth emphasizing. This project was planned and organized by individuals currently living in Lyme; and, one hopes, the published volume will interest other residents of the town. At the same time, professional scholars — generally unconnected with Lyme — have contributed the actual essays. This is an unusual, and extremely appealing, form of collaboration. Perhaps it suggests another virtue to be expected from community studies — a closer and more fruitful exchange between historians and the lay public, to which history ultimately belongs.

PART ONE

Saybrook and Lyme:
Secular Settlements in a Puritan
Commonwealth[1]

CHRISTOPHER COLLIER

IN THE early seventeenth century, from the European point of view, all America was wilderness. Only here and there along the eastern seaboard bits and pieces and patches of land constituted what would someday be a sweeping frontier of European settlement. In many ways this frontier was a cutting edge of innovation that ultimately made Europeans Americans. But in many other ways the frontier was a vestige of the expiring medieval economic and social system already wracked from its foundations in England and deeply undermined on the Continent. The economic and social structure of medieval society had been built solidly on land, the possession or control of which gave individuals social standing, economic independence, and political power. The opportunity for acquiring land had run out in England, however, for though much lay vacant — even primeval — engross-ment, enclosure, and royal prerogative shut out all but the very wealthy or the very powerful.[2]

America was land. As much as it represented a haven for collective social and religious experimentation, it was a place for gathering land. In New England economic sufficiency and independence would undergird communitarian religious ideology. Almost from the moment of settlement, however, the two would vie for dominance, and ideology would yield to economic and psychological imperatives. Vast tracts of field and forest were too strong a temptation to hold the children of the Puritan revolutionaries to their fathers' ideological commands. The Puritans' errand into the wilderness to establish their cities upon the hills of a new Canaan failed because there were so many hills and the new Canaan was so vast.

9

The original tripartite settlement of Connecticut illustrates the mixed motives that brought about the tension between the temptations of this world and the commands of the other. The river towns — Windsor, Hartford, and Wethersfield — had their secular Ludlows, as well as their godly Hookers, and at New Haven the merchant Theophilous Eaton was as influential as the Reverend John Davenport. At Saybrook, however, the dichotomy between the secular and the religious motives was not so evenly balanced for, though established by Puritans, the emphasis was clearly secular. To this settlement were sent "men and ammunition, and £2000 in money," but no ministers.[3]

The history of Connecticut in the seventeenth century is the story of the struggle between heaven and earth for the primary loyalty of her settlers. Saybrook is perhaps not so logical a place to begin because the ultimate victor in the conflict there was from the start paramount; the struggle was more apparent in the river towns and New Haven. Since the story of the foundation of Connecticut is customarily told from a religious perspective, however, a better overall balance can be achieved if attention is given to the economic impulse — especially land hunger — which so often secretly influenced the American Puritan migration.

Town Division

Connecticut comprises more than five thousand square miles and is divided into 169 towns and cities of various sizes. During the era of plantation and settlement, however, the present total area contained only 67 towns, which ranged up to ten times the present average size of about thirty square miles. Thus the typical Connecticut town is really a child of one of the original mothers, sometimes even a grandchild, for divisions begat divisions. Beacon Falls, for instance, is a fifth-generation descendant from New Haven, Milford, and Woodbury, while Farmington bore in whole or part nine other towns.

The process of town division usually resulted from a number of historical episodes with concurrent legislative actions. Typically, a group of inhabitants of an established town petitioned the General Court, as the General Assembly was called until 1698, for a grant of land at or about a particular place. If their request received favorable action, a number of them — called proprietors — were authorized to move there and organize a settlement.

By the middle of the seventeenth century a system of land distribution had developed which gave great authority to the resident grantees and imposed a series of rather rigorous conditions upon them. Once a tract of roughly described land had been granted, the initial sponsors were obligated to lay it out in shares according to some ratio, not necessarily equal, reserving lots for the support of the ministry and schools; to see that each grantee built a house of specified dimensions — usually twelve or sixteen feet square — and cleared five or six acres within three to seven years; to settle a family on every or nearly every house lot; to build a meetinghouse and settle a minister; and to post a bond against the execution of these duties. If these conditions were not met, and often they were not, the grant would revert to the colony, which it sometimes did, despite considerable leniency on the part of the General Court.[4] In Lyme, for instance, the proprietors required settlers to take up their lands and build on them within one year and then "possess" and pay rates on them for four more years before they had complete ownership.

Most settlements flourished, and the rise of new generations of inhabitants brought dispersal from the original center out to frontier areas, eight, twelve, and sixteen miles from the meetinghouse and schoolyard. As these second-generation communities gathered twenty to thirty families, they began to request and gain distinct and separate status. Customarily, an outliving group of inhabitants would first petition for winter ministerial privileges, then for relief from society taxes with authority to tax themselves for the establishment of the ministry and the construction of a meetinghouse. Then there would be requests for authority to establish a school district, to erect a pound, and to elect highway surveyors, fence viewers, and perhaps several other local officers. Finally, petitions requesting incorporation as a town would be filed with the General Assembly. When the petition was approved, a cattle brand and a name were assigned, boundaries were surveyed, authority was granted to elect selectmen, clerk, treasurer, and deputies, and the new town was listed separately and obliged to collect and pay colony-wide taxes. Town division provided an outlet for political ambitions, a mode for the reestablishment of community from geographically fragmented towns, and a means to bring churches, schools, and local civil government within easy walking distance.

In the preindustrial era, up to about 1830, an agricultural economy, with a small amount of commerce and artisanry, could support adequately about fifty people per square mile.[5] A town meeting of not more than five hundred yeomen — few of whom regularly attended — was certainly the maximum for efficiency. Thus a town of roughly six by six miles could accommodate a few thousand people, perhaps four hundred voters, who lived no farther than an hour and a half's walk from the center. This was precisely the pattern in Connecticut until the coming of industry created new needs in the agrarian society and brought forty or so town divisions after 1830. The municipal character of Connecticut, then, was established largely by the fragmentation of original towns: the break-up of both social and geographic unity and the effort to reestablish the sense and concrete manifestation of community.

Connecticut's earliest town division was carried out in Saybrook — a town that ultimately bore six municipal offspring and parts of three more. All but one of these divisions followed the customary pattern of evolution through parish organization. The one exception is Lyme, where the secular dominance of Saybrook permitted the colony's very first town division. The innovative nature of division is evident in the piecemeal way Lyme was granted town status. In 1663 the General Court allowed Saybrook an extension of its bounds with an explicit proviso for the commencement of a second plantation. The next year the part of Saybrook east of the Connecticut River was set off. Then in 1666 a committee was established to admit inhabitants there; the following year the area was named Lyme; and the year after that Lyme, along with all the other towns, received an allowance for its deputy's pay. However, no deputy seems to have attended the General Court from Lyme until 1670, and Lyme did not appear separately on the colony tax list until 1671.[6] Thus, the civil government took at least five years of gradual development to evolve, and except for providing a settlement with a name, the Court evidently made no explicit provision for incorporation with full town powers. It is significant, moreover, that the secular organization was completed long before ecclesiastical organization was commenced — the reverse of what became the traditional sequence.

Saybrook and Lyme: Secular Settlements

Saybrook was settled as a community built around a fort, potentially a garden spot for gentlemen farmers. It was not founded as a Bible commonwealth, as were, to some degree, New Haven and the river towns. Instead, the original intention was to establish a refuge for some of England's most prominent Puritans — political leaders who, throughout the 1630s, had to be prepared for flight at any moment. When conditions changed and their prospects at home improved, the plan was given up and the patent sold to Connecticut. This permitted settlement by anyone who could gather enough money or influence to obtain a "right" in the common proprietary. The General Court decided that government at Saybrook "shall be carried on according to such agreements, and in [the] way which is already followed there."[7] Consequently, ecclesiastical restrictions were much less strict than in the river towns or in New Haven.

A garrison of about twenty men was resident at Saybrook Fort in 1635, and John Winthrop and others joined them the next year. Unlike all the settlements on the river and along the sound, the community had no ecclesiastical society. When George Fenwick arrived also in 1636 he brought a twenty-year-old chaplain, but no church was established at that time.[8] It was not unusual in the eighteenth century for communities to remain without a settled minister for several years, but in the seventeenth century all persons were supposed to be under the scrutiny of an officially sanctioned church. In 1660, for instance, as Lyme settlers moved across the river and a good long boat row from the minister in Saybrook, twelve Derby families a dozen miles from Milford were ordered by the General Court either to gather enough people to support a minister or to "be removed and not suffered to live in such an unsatisfying way." When Greenwich applied for town privileges in 1665, the General Court declared "that Greenwich shall be a township entire of itself, provided they procure and maintain an orthodox minister; and in the mean time and until that be effected they are to attend the ministry at Stamford."[9]

For most of its first decade Saybrook was run like a manor with a nobleman's chaplain serving the resident soldiers, servants, and increasing numbers of inhabitant yeomen. In 1646 a church was established, and John Fitch was settled over the parish.[10] Hardly had this happened, however, when the town was divided into quarters (the term in no way reflected proportion, but was used merely to denote locality), and proprietors began to move to the outlands. This would not have been permitted in towns more completely under Connecticut's jurisdiction, but the purchase agreement of 1644 gave Saybrook the maintenance of local self-government.

Although there was continuous preaching at Lyme beginning in 1666 when Moses Noyes settled on the east side of the river, the inhabitants did not petition the General Court for permission to organize an ecclesiastical society until 1676 and did not in fact incorporate till 1693.[11] This was a matter of some significance. The town vote of 1676 stated, "In whereas the town hath been from the first settlement which is now ten or eleven years under the ministry of the word but yet without the administration of all the ordinances of Christ for want of being in a church way, the town, having considered of the requisitions of the same, are very unanimous that there may be a church gathered which may be for the glory of God and edification of each other according to the laws of the commonwealth."[12] The statement, perhaps, needs explanation.

In colonial Connecticut ministers held ordination only in relation to a particular parish. Laws of 1650 and 1658 established the authority of the General Court over parishes and forbade the erection of new ecclesiastical societies without its approval. The term "ecclesiastical society" refers to the areal jurisdiction of a parish and to the admitted inhabitants — qualified voters — resident therein.[13] These men could vote in society meetings where religious matters of concern to the entire community were arranged, such as levying rates for paying the minister and building the meetinghouse. The Church consisted of Church members only — those who had subscribed to the covenant and passed tests of proof of conversion. The Church meetings, very small in membership, decided matters of theology, liturgy, and admission and censure of members.[14]

In Lyme, with neither church nor ecclesiastical organization, the town conducted all religious affairs until 1693.[15] Religious matters were integrated with civil affairs in the town meeting book. Thus the secular dominance manifested in Lyme's history is intrinsic to its records. Without an approved church Moses Noyes was not ordained and was therefore officially unable to administer the sacraments of baptism and communion. It is hard to believe that the people of Lyme continued from 1666 to 1693 without these ordinances, but their petition of 1676 makes the point that this was the case for at least a decade. Subsequent events indicate that they continued without religious organization till 1693. This was certainly a most extraordinary lack of godly concern for seventeenth-century Connecticut. Indeed, this anomalous situation may have been unique.

Earthly Concerns

The concern of the yeomen of Lyme was with the earth, not the heavens, and an abundance of earth there was, too. In 1644 the General Court bought the Warwick Patent and the fort, and continued the town government of Saybrook. Five years later the Court bounded the new Connecticut town, the infant colony's eighth, "from the river eastward, five miles; and northward up the river, on the east side six miles; and on the west side the river, northward eight miles."[16] The boundary to the west was thought to be the Hammonasset River till the establishment of Killingworth in 1663, when the Court declared "that the land at Hammonasset doth not of right belong unto the Town of Saybrook." Then the dividing line was declared to be from the point "where the common passage over Manunketsuck River is, and so run north into the country and south into the sea." The actual survey was accomplished in 1675 — leisurely paced seventeenth-century administration allowed generations for such work — and it ran "from the river towards the west, three miles at their north bounds, and from thence to run a straight line till they meet with the line where the wading place is at Manunketsuck."[17] The area generally perceived as Saybrook, then, amounted to about thirty square miles east of the river and perhaps eighty square miles west of it.[18]

Saybrook proprietors considered all the land there their own. Whereas new plantations in and around the river towns had to be authorized by the General Court, Saybrook Town or Proprietor's Meeting — they were at first synonymous — could exercise the function. Thus in 1648 the proprietors divided their hundred or so square miles into three sections outside the compact village around the fort.[19]

There might have been justification for declaring themselves "straitened and disabled as to a comfortable subsistence one with another," if the forty families with house lots had been confined to the

"Neck," an area of hardly more than one square mile.[20] However, many homeowners had not only taken up lands outside the town plot but settled upon them. Dividends of land outside the Neck had been made prior to 1641, and there were settlers at Potapaug [Essex] perhaps as early as 1645. Matthew Griswold had cultivated land across the river at Black Hall five years earlier, and it is known that by 1649 there were dwellings, corn fields, and livestock at the future site of Lyme.[21] Thus the Saybrook families were not really crowded onto their acre-and-a-half home lots around the fort but were in fact spread over a very large area.

Nevertheless, their 1648 town meeting declared the families "straitened" and set up a committee to survey the outlands "extended to the utmost extent of our bounds . . . that thereby every person might have free choice to place himself and encouragement for some to go out upon those lands that thereby a more comfortable subsistence might be both to one and the other."[22] At the time of the sale of the fort and patent to Connecticut and the establishment of the Saybrook town bounds, there were thirty-seven proprietors, men who presumably had bought shares in the company from Fenwick. With confirmation of this arrangement in 1644, these men became the town proprietors and thus the joint owners of the whole tract which they thought to be in excess of 100 square miles. The committee to divide the area into quarters was instructed to appraise it to the value of £8,000 and assign a portion of that to each of the three sections. The size of a man's allotment of land would be determined by the size of his payment toward the appraised sum. The sections were valued at £2,800 for Oyster River, £1,700 for Eight Mile Meadow, and £3,500 for East Side, the future Lyme.[23]

The quarters were ultimately surveyed, bounded, and assigned to small groups of proprietors. Oyster River, mostly the present town of Westbrook, was given to twenty men, each of whom contributed a proportionate share of the assessed value of the area; Eight Mile Meadow, or Potapaug, was given to eight proprietors; and Lyme to twelve. There were three men who bought into more than one quarter, producing a total of thirty-seven proprietors — the same number, and in at least twenty-four cases the same men, who settled the original Saybrook site.[24]

These new proprietaries were established exclusively for the purpose of turning common lands over to private individuals. The proprietors were authorized by the town meeting to "measure, lay out & dispose each to the other as they see meet for corn, pasture, stone, timber & the like into parts and parcels according to each man's right." The proprietors are spoken of as having taken "possession" of the land, and some of them as later having "removed from Saybrook and sold their rights." It is clear, then, that the tracts were considered private property, a matter made explicit by the General Court in 1685 and reconfirmed in 1704.[25]

Land-Man Ratios

Some of the Saybrook area was, of course, unsuitable for pasture, salt hay, orchard, woodlot, or house site. Nevertheless, with fifty-three yeomen resident in 1654, a number that had swelled to seventy-two only three years later, a large number chose to move away in 1659 to found Norwich, taking the town's only minister and clerk with them as they went.[26] The move to Norwich may have been unrelated to problems of space; better harbor prospects there are a more compelling supposition. The mouth of the Connecticut River was marshy for more than a mile on each side, and good wharfage could be provided only for very small boats which could travel inland up such watercourses as the Lieutenant, Duck, or Black Hall rivers.

One might assume a population in 1659 of not more than three hundred at Saybrook, uncrowded under any conditions short of Saharan. But even as half the population departed for Norwich, including ten of Lyme's original proprietors, those who remained instructed their deputies in the General Court to present "their intentions to set up a plantation on the east side of the great river, and also maintain a plantation on the west side." They requested "some enlargement of their bounds," and were granted an additional "four miles on each side of the river northward, provided they do make two plantations, as aforesaid, within the space of three years."[27]

Extending the line north seemed to pose no problem, for Haddam was not established till the following year. To the south and west lay natural water boundaries, but the frontier to the east was a source of trouble for a decade or more. The new Saybrook bounds, however, would have included an area of about 126 square miles. A population of perhaps fifty-three families should have found plenty of room for sustenance at a time when 40 Connecticut acres was considered minimal but adequate, and yeomen in England could live on 10. But in Saybrook over 1,000 acres per family was not enough. For the twelve proprietors who chose lots on the east side in 1648 there was the prospect of dividing perhaps 30 square miles of land — some 1,600 acres each.

Lyme's northern line with Haddam was established in 1668 in a compromise which cost Lyme two of the four miles she once had. The boundary with New London was not settled until 1673, and a large piece of land was due to the sachem Uncas.[28] By 1669 there were more than thirty proprietors, because rights had been divided, sold, and granted by the town and by individuals. These settlers had the largest portion of about forty square miles for distribution.[29] There were over 850 acres for each family, yet this was not enough. Losses threatened in 1671 by the controversy with New London prompted Lyme's yeomen — wielding scythes, clubs, and other implements of mayhem — to wage war on its neighbor on the east. Lyme lost this battle, not on the field but in the General Court. The town's eastern boundary was extended only two miles rather than the four Lyme sought.[30] Thus at least thirty proprietors were willing to risk bodily harm to maintain their claim to about sixteen square miles of land when they already fully possessed forty square miles, certainly two-thirds of which, at least, was arable.

When Saybrook was divided into three quarters, the part east of the river was valued at £3,500, which the 12 original proprietors made up in varying individual amounts. The General Court required thirty families at least to make a town, however, so a number of men were admitted as inhabitants. In addition, several people were granted £50 rights in order to induce the settlement of a miller, tanner, smith, and weaver.[31] The £50 standard grant leads one to believe that the maximum population considered appropriate for the area would be seventy families. By 1676 the number of polls — white males between sixteen and sixty years old — had grown to 45, and there were at least 36 proprietors in 1677. Ten years later 59 heads of household appeared on "the Governor Andros Tax List."[32] Tax-payers are not all proprietors, of course, but they were all inhabitants or grown sons of inhabitants who would expect soon to come into lands of their own. The *Colony Records,* however, give 60 polls for 1678. There would have been no more proprietors than polls because proprietors who did not settle in town lost their land.[33] As late as 1702 the number of men eligible to draw lots for the fourth division was still 67, though there were 117 polls at that time, many of them sons or servants of proprietors.[34] Certainly there were not more than 400 people. At any event the maximum seventeenth-century population living in Lyme — at least fifty-six square miles — included 70 proprietors and perhaps half again as many nonproprietary white males between sixteen and sixty.

In seventeenth-century Connecticut the most important function delegated to proprietors by the General Court was the transfer of lands to private individuals. Although the eastern and northern town boundaries were disputed, Lyme proprietors nevertheless began to divide the tract among themselves. Throughout the colony grants were frequently made to nonproprietors to encourage settlement or to bring in artisans of specialized abilities such as millers and smiths. The presence of numerous landholders spread the tax burden more widely and provided a larger force for work on the highways and public fences and for civil and militia service. Incidentally, a larger, more diversified population also raised the value of lands in the towns, a matter of no small consequence to the proprietors.

For the most part, however, the authority to give away land was used to enlarge proprietors' holdings. In effect what resulted — and probably was intended — by the General Court's grant of authority to proprietors "to dispose of their own lands undisposed of, and all other commodities arising out of their own limits" was the accumulation of very large tracts by the proprietors themselves.[35] Across the colony there were exceptions of course. In Norwalk, for instance, the proprietors laid out only about 14,000 of 36,000 acres in the first fifty years of settlement. More typical was the practice in neighboring Fairfield, where virtually all of 52,000 acres was passed into private hands over only two generations of settlement, and where at least a third of the residents held over 400 acres each, with some in possession of 1,400 or 1,500 acres. In Norwalk even the wealthiest resident in 1704 owned only 300 acres.[36]

In Lyme the mode of proportioning the divisions was established in 1679 "according to the lists of each man's estate which have been ever since the beginning of the town." That is, a man who first put up £500 would always get twice as much land by value — upland, salt marsh, swamp, woodlot, all having different per acre values — as the man who had contributed only £250. In addition, every proprietor received credit of £18 for each male child and £9 for each female child for every year the child had lived in Lyme "since it was a town," presumably 1667.[37]

The allocation of land to children is of considerable interest. In some places deliberate efforts were made to withhold land from offspring, and in most places the granting of land to minors was unheard of.[38] Perhaps Lyme was unique, for grants were made to children individually and merely held in trust by their fathers. According to the *Record* of 1686, "the town doth declare that their intention was and is that although the said share be laid out together with or adjoining to the share of the heads of the families: yet they shall belong to those children & be possessed by them as soon as they came to age."

Traditionally, proprietors granted themselves small homesites clustered around a common on which they built a meetinghouse. In the first generation of Connecticut settlement after 1634, these homesites ranged from 1 to 7 acres, averaging about 3. In Saybrook, for instance, sites covered from ½ to 3½ acres. In Lyme, however, original homesites were 10 acres each.[39] The pattern initiated at Lyme caught on, and by 1697 Lebanon's homesites were 42 acres each, no longer clustered about a meetinghouse green but stretched out along a long central boulevard. By 1705 Voluntown was merely divided into 150 compact farms — thought to be about 150 acres each, with no common or green, nor any provision for town roads.[40] As early as 1669 an effort was made in Lyme to divide all the "arable and mowable land" that remained. This effort failed at the time, but before another generation had passed, the greatest part had been turned over to private ownership.[41]

It is impossible to know what proportion of the tract set out as Lyme was "arable and mowable," for much of the area too wet to farm today was considered in the seventeenth century valuable for its crop of salt marsh hay; and it is not known how much of the commons was permanently reserved under various agreements. Nevertheless, if the 35,840 acres were distributed equally to the sixty-seven proprietors of 1702, each family would have had about 535 acres. This was an immense tract for the time. Even if it were divided among two or three sons, it would last a few generations, assuming all the boys lived or stayed in town. Many, of course, moved on to vast unsettled areas of Connecticut and western Massachusetts. Actually, much more land was available. For by 1727 only thirty-seven families lived in the eight-by-eight-mile tract that constituted the First Society.[42]

With a population density of about three people per square mile, Lyme was far from the maximum of fifty that the colonial individually farmsteaded economy was able to support. Like those of most other seventeenth-century Connecticut towns, though to an uncommon degree, the settlers of Lyme were not content with two godly callings, but for the most part they exercised three. Heavenly obligations and secular vocations aside, the early settlers were also land speculators.

Maps of the Boundaries of Lyme, 1727[43]

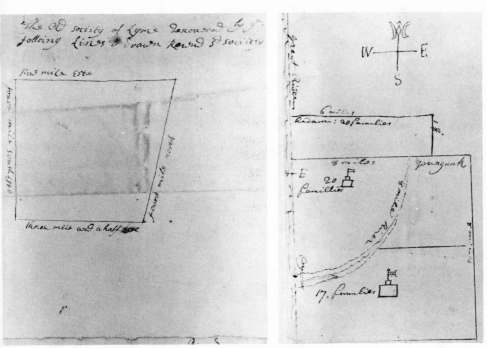

Proprietor-Inhabitant Conflict

The distribution of land inevitably produced jealousies, but during Connecticut's earliest years there was little conflict over proprietary rule because most heads of households were proprietors. An act of the General Court of 1640 permitting any man to take up 100 acres for the cultivation of grain assumed that the proprietors would inhabit their lands and called for the repossession of lands not cultivated within three years.[44] In those first days of settlement, proprietors were required to move onto their home lots within six months in New London, for instance, and usually within one year elsewhere. As newcomers arrived in larger and larger numbers, however, there were questions about the control of undivided lands.

The old Calvinist ideal of the Bible commonwealth with every citizen a church member and every church member a citizen had its secular parallel. In seventeenth-century New England communities every landowner was an inhabitant and every inhabitant a landowner. But the tension between the ideal of community and the opportunity for individual enrichment, manifested at the earliest stages of settlement in some places, was apparent virtually everywhere by the early eighteenth century. The first effort of the General Court to deal with this conflict encouraged the secular and individualist tendency. A schism developed between those who controlled the distribution of lands and those who did not, and legislation of 1723 sanctioned this fundamental fracture in the Puritan ideal.

Of course, the quarrel that rent so many Connecticut towns broke out in Lyme. In November 1676 all Lyme proprietors were ordered to present their claims, provide evidence for them, and pick their sites on penalty of forfeiture at failure to do so. At that time there were forty-seven landowners listed in the records, and three more registered in 1677. Other evidence indicates that only thirty-six of these were proprietors.[45] The sequence for fulfilling these claims was established by the proprietors who voted that "The eldest rights and grants shall be first supplied and satisfied — In order to which those grants from Saybrook came first to be considered."

There is evidence that the proprietors sometimes acted with very few in attendance. A September 1669 meeting was conducted with only six or seven proprietors present out of thirty. Thus it was necessary in 1677 for them to agree that "there shall be no further grants nor divisions made of the town lands without the full consent of two thirds parts of the accommodation men" — those who "personally inhabit in the town, and have a grant of fifty pound accommodations of upland at least." The meetings had to be properly warned, and at least two-thirds of those in attendance were required to make votes valid. There were thirty-six proprietors, so a minimum of sixteen could bind the rest. By this time between three and six of the original grantees were still in residence, and presumably theirs were the "eldest grants."[46]

Besides the thirty-six proprietors, there were in 1678 twenty-four additional polls — some of them residents who owned land but were not proprietors, others servants and minor sons.[47] The list of landowners of 1676–77 suggests there were twelve nonproprietor landowners, leaving twelve additional polls. A decade later there were thirty-eight proprietors among sixty-seven polls, and in 1702 sixty-five proprietors among 117 polls.[48] Obviously, a class of resident nonproprietors was developing. These men, if over twenty-one and landowners, could vote in town meetings but technically could not vote at proprietors' meetings, customarily held at the same time and place as the town meetings.

By 1694 the newcomers — at least those who had bought shares in the proprietary — had apparently attained a majority. In January the town meeting voted not to proceed to the fourth — and last — division that had been authorized as early as 1683 until all the grants already made had been surveyed and deeded. Further, the 1694 meeting voted that "afterward there shall not be any disposal of lands made to the three thousand five hundred pound estate so as to exclude the other inhabitants from sharing according to the proportion for which they are admitted."[49] At this time there were not more than six, and possibly as few as three, of the original twelve proprietors who had made up the £3,500 division in 1648.[50] Control over land was explicitly taken from the original proprietors and assumed by all those later comers who had bought shares subsequent to the 1648 quarter division. At the 1694 meeting those present voted not to "proceed unto any other division of land without the major vote of the present inhabitants who have interest in the commons." The document was signed, not by the proprietors of Lyme, but by "the inhabitants."[51]

The question of control over the town lands was still not settled, however. In 1698 the proprietors again asserted their authority by expanding the definition from merely those "who did derive their right from Saybrook" to include "also those who [were] received inhabitants to make up the numbers of thirty persons to make up the township according to the order of the several court [in 1667], also all those persons that are granted by the town a fifty pound accommodation." The meeting tried to substantiate its resolution by declaring that "these only are counted as proprietor and no person doth enter any thing against it but those and those only are proprietors." Two years later this liberalized but still exclusionary definition was sundered, and it "was voted that all the inhabitants of Lyme shall have liberty to vote in all town affairs as formerly except such only as are prohibited by law."[52] Since this coincided with the General Court's attempt to clarify proprietor versus town prerogatives, one may assume that the legal prohibitions referred to do not relate to land-granting authority.[53]

By the turn of century, however, the fourth division had been voted, though not completely apportioned to individuals. In March 1700 it was agreed that all land not laid out or to be laid out in the fourth division was to "lie for a perpetual commons for the whole town use, only some three acres for the minister." This was a victory for the nonproprietors, and the following December all inhabitants were reinvested with full suffrage.[54]

Virtually everywhere in Connecticut town lands were rapidly transferred from common to private ownership. Saybrook and Lyme are more or less typical of many other towns where large engrossments of land were frequent. Indeed, historians who have claimed that Connecticut Puritans became Yankees in the period from 1690 to 1765 have seen only half the settlement picture. The Puritan experiment with Bible commonwealths failed because of the temptation of an abundant landscape, but the experiment could not have been conceived or launched at all without the land to occupy. Connecticut's Puritans were Yankees from the start; the changes that began in the seventeenth century and continue to this day are ones not of quality but of degree.

What is unusual about Lyme is that secular affairs overbalanced godly concerns right from the start. The published records of town meetings — which include all ecclesiastical affairs, there being no separate church records before 1693 — reveal that about four out of five issues that came before them dealt with the distribution of lands to private individuals. The concern with the land that so dominated colony affairs by the mid-eighteenth century was apparent at Lyme a century earlier.[55] The great importance of land gathering coupled with a cavalier attitude toward ecclesiastical affairs made the settlement of Lyme unique.

Notes

1. This essay is based in part upon work in progress entitled "Towns, Lands and Yeomen: The Settlement of Connecticut Towns in the Seventeenth and Eighteenth Centuries."

2. Carl Bridenbaugh, *Vexed and Troubled Englishmen, 1590–1642* (New York: Oxford University Press, 1968), pp. 201–4.

3. John Winthrop, *Winthrop's Journal "History of New England, 1630–1649,"* ed. James Kendall Hosmer (New York: Charles Scriber's Sons, 1908), I:161; Robert C. Black, III, *The Younger John Winthrop* (New York: Columbia University Press, 1966), pp. 96–97.

4. Roy Hidemichi Akagi, *The Town Proprietors of the New England Colonies* (Philadelphia: University of Pennsylvania Press, 1924), pp. 207–8, 220, 228.

5. Samuel Blodget, *Economica: A Statistical Manual for the United States of America* (Washington: the author, 1806), p. 88.

6. J. H. Trumbull and C. J. Hoadly, eds., *The Public Records of the Colony of Connecticut,* 15 vols. (Hartford: Case, Lockwood, and Brainard Company, 1850–90), I:419, II:60, 130, 136, 160 (hereafter cited as *Colony Records*); Gilman C. Gates, *Saybrook at the Mouth of the Connecticut* (New Haven: Wilson H. Lee Company, 1935), pp. 221–22.

7. *Colony Records,* I:267.

8. See general accounts of the settlement of Saybrook in Gates, *Saybrook;* Benjamin Trumbull, *A Complete History of Connecticut Civil and Ecclesiastical,* 2 vols. (New London: H. D. Utley, 1898), I:*passim;* Black, *Winthrop,* ch. 8 and *passim;* Charles M. Andrews, *The Colonial Period of American History: The Settlements* (New Haven: Yale University Press, 1936), II:120–22.

9. *Colony Records,* II:328, 17.

10. Trumbull, *History of Connecticut,* I:85.

11. *Colony Records,* III:18; Trumbull, *History of Connecticut,* II:452.

12. Jean Chandler Burr, ed., *Lyme Records 1667–1730: A Literal Transcription* . . . (Stonington, Conn.: Pequot Press, 1968), p. 26.

13. *Colony Records,* I:112n, 311–12.

14. Williston Walker, *The Creeds and Platforms of Congregationalism* (New York: C. Scribner's Sons, 1893), pp. 220–22; Samuel Rankin, Jr., "Conservatism and the Problem of Change in the Congregational Churches of Connecticut, 1660–1760" (Ph.D. diss., Kent State University, 1971), ch. 1.

15. See Burr, *Lyme Records, passim,* for ecclesiastical affairs conducted at town meeting. Town histories are for one reason or another frequently written from civil records alone, and occasionally from church records alone. The former inevitably carry a strong secular bias, while the latter carry an even stronger religious bias. In the case of seventeenth-century Lyme, the fact that there was no church society, and all ecclesiastical matters were recorded in the town meeting book, provides an integrated religious-civil history in which the secular dominance is intrinsic.

16. *Colony Records,* I:267, 188; "Connecticut Archives" (hereafter "Arch."), Towns and Lands, second series, III:15–32.

17. *Colony Records,* I:418, II:256.

18. In 1649 the boundaries of Saybrook were established at an indefinite distance along the coast on the west, traditionally to the Manunketsuck River, about eight miles along the sound; and eight miles to the north along the Connecticut River. On the east side of the river the boundaries were five miles along the coast and six miles to the north. In 1663, both northern bounds were extended four miles but then were reduced by two miles in 1669. Lyme gained an additional two miles to the east in 1673.

Saybrook Bounds

	West of the River	East of the River
1649	10 × 8	5 × 6
1663	8 × 12	5 × 10
1669	8 × 10	5 × 8
1673		7 × 8
1675	3 × 8 × 8 × 12	

Colony Records, I:188, 418, 419, II:108, 213, 256; "Arch.," Towns and Lands, first series, I:98.

19. Gates, *Saybrook,* pp. 210–13.

20. Ibid., p. 210. As to the number of families, Gates (pp. 152–53) gives thirty-nine; Frances Manwaring Caulkins, *History of Norwich, Connecticut* (Hartford: the author, 1866), p. 54, says forty; and Daniel J. Connors, *Deep River: The Illustrated Story of a Connecticut River Town* (Stonington, Conn.: Pequot Press, 1966), p. 4, says forty-eight individuals owned land in Saybrook in 1648.

21. Gates, *Saybrook,* pp. 156, 134, 157; Barbara Deitrick, *The Ancient Town of Lyme* (n.p.: Lyme Tercentenary Committee, 1965), pp. 6–7; *Colony Records,* I:189.

22. Gates, *Saybrook,* p. 210.

23. Ibid., pp. 210–15.

24. Ibid., pp. 210–15.

25. Ibid., p. 211; *Colony Records,* IV:432–33. See Richard L. Bushman, *From Puritan to Yankee: Character and Social Order in Connecticut, 1690–1765* (Cambridge: Harvard University Press, 1969), pp. 44–47, for the reasons for General Court actions in 1664 and 1685.

26. *Colony Records,* I:265, 307. It is generally believed that a majority of the families left for Norwich in 1660. This is probably based on Benjamin Trumbull's statement that Fitch took with him "the principal part of his church or congregation." *History of Connecticut,* I:195. Caulkins follows Trumbull's estimate, but by her own account only twenty-seven heads of family left at a time when she estimates the population at nearly eighty families. *Norwich,* pp. 53, 54, 55.

27. *Colony Records,* I:419 (March 10, 1663).

28. Ibid., II:97, 108, 213.

29. Burr, *Lyme Records,* e.g., pp. 6, 8, 9; May Hall James, *The Educational*

History of Old Lyme, Connecticut, 1635–1935 (New Haven: Yale University Press for the New Haven Colony Historical Society, 1939), p. 80.

30. *Colony Records*, II:557–59; Frances Manwaring Caulkins, *History of New London, Connecticut* (New London: the author, 1852), pp. 165–69.

31. See for instance, *Colony Records*, I:408, II:148; Burr, *Lyme Records*, e.g., pp. 6, 8, 9.

32. *Colony Records*, II:290; Burr, *Lyme Records*, p. 30; *The New-England Historical and Genealogical Register* (Boston: New England Historic Genealogical Society, 1880), XXXIV:371–82.
The Governor Andros Tax List shows forty-eight men who owned real estate and paid a poll tax for themselves. There were eleven polls living with these men. Additionally, there were nine men who owned no land but paid the poll tax and taxes on livestock. There were seven men, some of whom may have been proprietors, who owned real estate but for one reason or another were excused from the poll tax. There were three widows who paid property taxes but no poll tax, and there was one dead property owner. Thus there were fifty-nine real estate owners, and twenty additional males between sixteen and sixty. There were sixty-eight polls plus seven able-bodied males. For our purposes the significant figure is the number of households, which is fifty-nine.

33. *Colony Records*, III:17.

34. James, *Educational History*, p. 38; *Colony Records*, IV:405. One estimate is that at least a quarter of the polls were minor sons of residents. Kenneth Lockridge, "Land, Population and the Evolution of New England Society, 1630–1790," *Past and Present* 39 (1969):62–80.

35. *Colony Records*, I:36. Originally applied only to Windsor, Hartford, and Wethersfield, this authority was delegated to all new towns as part of the general municipal grant.

36. Joan R. Ballen, "Fairfield, Connecticut, 1661–1691: A Demographic Study of the Economic, Political and Social Life of a New England Community" (M.A. thesis, University of Bridgeport, 1970), pp. 106–9; Erna F. Green, "The Public Land System of Norwalk, Connecticut, 1654–1704: A Structural Analysis of Economic and Political Relationships" (M.A. thesis, University of Bridgeport, 1972), pp. 50–63.

37. Burr, *Lyme Records*, p. 33.

38. Philip J. Greven, Jr., *Four Generations: Population, Land and Family in Colonial Andover, Massachusetts* (Ithaca: Cornell University Press, 1970), ch. 4.

39. Gates, *Saybrook*, pp. 152–53; James, *Educational History*, p. 19.

40. Anthony N. B. Garvan, *Architecture and Town Planning in Colonial Connecticut* (New Haven: Yale University Press, 1951), pp. 16, 63, 65.

41. Burr, *Lyme Records*, pp. 36, 45–102 *passim;* James, *Educational History*, p. 39.

42. Burr, *Lyme Records*, p. 90; "Arch.," Ecclesiastical Affairs, first series, III:52.

43. "Arch.," Ecclesiastical Affairs, first series, III:52.

44. *Colony Records*, I:58.

45. Burr, *Lyme Records,* p. 17; Lyme, Office of the Town Clerk, Lyme Town Records, pp. 23–26; Burr, *Lyme Records,* p. 80. These figures contain some inaccuracies. There were only forty-five polls listed in 1676 but forty-seven resident landowners. At another time there were sixty polls but fifty landowners. There could not have been more landowners than polls; indeed, the reverse was usually the case. *Colony Records,* II:290, III:17, 70.

46. Burr, *Lyme Records,* pp. 177, 36, 18.

47. Ibid., p. 30; *Colony Records,* III:17, 70.

48. Burr, *Lyme Records,* pp. 94–102; *Colony Records,* IV:297.

49. Burr, *Lyme Records,* p. 22.

50. Ibid.; Gates, *Saybrook,* p. 215.

51. Burr, *Lyme Records,* pp. 181, 22.

52. Ibid., pp. 86, 89.

53. See James, *Educational History,* pp. 66–67.

54. Burr, *Lyme Records,* p. 90.

55. Ibid., *passim.* The extraordinary freedom from restraint by the General Court enjoyed by Saybrook and Lyme is clearer when contrasted with events at Milford in the same year Lyme became a separate plantation. Settlers moving out from Milford in 1667 were required to settle a minister in order to "enjoy the ordinances of God," that is, to establish an ecclesiastical society and a church; and they were further ordered not to "impropriate any more land to themselves than at present they do possess." *Colony Records,* II:64.

The Economic and Social Structure
of Early Lyme

JACKSON TURNER MAIN

THE earliest record we have of the people of Lyme is an "assessment" list drawn for tax purposes in 1688.[1] The town dates officially to 1667, but until after King Philip's War few settlers ventured
east of the Connecticut River, and Lyme did not have 50 taxable
persons — a few hundred people — until danger from Indians diminished in 1677. The population then stabilized for a decade at
approximately 60 taxable persons, growing to 70 in 1688, and to 100
at the end of the century.

Different frontiers attract different kinds of people. New areas
that seem to promise a high rate of return for dangerous effort attract
venturesome young men, as do areas where a labor shortage creates
high wages. Connecticut offered neither quick riches nor good pay,
and from the start the population consisted primarily of grown men
with families. Such a community supplied its own labor force and a
decent living. Each new town repeated the same pattern, and so did
Lyme. In 1688 it contained relatively few young men, and few over
fifty, but mostly married men in their thirties and forties with growing
children, an ideal society for an agricultural frontier.

The 1688 list names three women and sixty-eight men, of whom
six were nonresidents and one was dead. To obtain a total of adult
men we must add some of the extra "persons" for whom taxpayers
were assessed: males aged sixteen and older who did not pay their
own tax, sometimes servants, but usually sons; for example, Wolstone
Brockaway's twenty-two-year-old son, William. Thirty families
formed the town's core, while a dozen individuals were temporary
residents. The following chart shows the probable age structure:

Age	Number	Percent
21–29	19	30
30–39	23	35
40–49	13	20
50–59	6	9
60 plus	4	6
Total	65	100

The primary occupation in Lyme was farming. Three farmers shared in a sawmill; the family that owned the sawmill served also as carpenters and joiners while another man was, or became, a cooper. John Wade ran a grain mill. The community also included a minister, the owner of a very small shop, and a tanner. The elder Matthew Griswold presumably advised his neighbors on legal and political matters, and William Ely either then or later engaged in trade. As neither stock-in-trade nor money at interest was subject to taxation, we cannot spot entrepreneurs; probably none existed.

Itemizing improved land, some livestock, and the supposed value of an individual's income from a nonagricultural pursuit, called a "faculty," the assessment list reveals economic and social differences within the town. Total taxable wealth other than polls came to about £2,650.[2] The Beckwiths (Matthew and John), the Elys (William and Richard), the Griswolds (Matthew Sr. and Jr.), Thomas Lee, and Joseph Sill accounted for three-eighths, and another half-dozen names also familiar in the town's history contributed one-fourth. Thirteen men, three percent of the total, possessed almost no taxable property. This inequality may strike the reader as excessive. However, in societies characterized by a serious maldistribution of wealth, the top ten percent of taxpayers would own considerably over half of the assessed property, whereas in Lyme they held only a little more than one-third; and most of Lyme's poor were young and their position at the bottom was often temporary. What we need to know is the relative situation of mature men who had accumulated some wealth. Among them, the degree of inequality diminishes markedly — the "richest" ten percent owned only one-fourth of the total. Even allowing for the regressive nature of the tax system, Lyme's society at this time tended more toward a level than toward a maldistribution.

The list distinguishes also certain men by title: four misters, a major, a captain, a lieutenant, and an ensign. The major we may disregard, for he was really a New Londoner. The others, however, deserve our attention, for titles in the seventeenth century really did identify a local elite. These men were, in order of their appearance, Mr. Matthew Griswold, Sr., the town's richest man; Mr. Moses Noyes, the minister; Ensign Joseph Peck, the tenth-largest taxpayer; Capt. Joseph Sill, owner of the fourth-largest estate; Mr. Matthew Griswold, Jr., the eighth-largest taxpayer; Mr. Richard Ely, who probably derived his status from his recently deceased father; and Lt. Abram Brunson, the ninth-largest taxpayer.

The elder Griswold had the unusual honor of being chosen moderator of the town meeting "until the town shall choose another," which did not happen for eighteen years. He also represented the town in the legislature, as had William Measure, who had just died. Brunson and Peck would soon become deputies, as would Ely's brother William and the younger Matthew Griswold. The town had been electing its selectmen from the same group — Sill, Brunson, Peck, and Measure.

Like the colony in general, Lyme grew slowly after 1688 until the end of the century, when its population leaped by half in a few years, steadied, then reached 2,500 by midcentury and over 4,000 by 1776. Economic growth, however, did not keep pace with population. Taxable property declined from £63 per taxpayer in 1676 to £61 in 1688, £50 in 1700, £36 in 1756, and £33 in 1774. As no detailed tax records for the period between 1688 and 1781 have survived, we must rely upon estate inventories. These show a decline in the value of taxable property until the end of the colonial era.[3]

Estate inventories cannot be taken at face value because they itemize the property of older men more often than that of younger — death being selective — and they may exclude too many of the poor. Despite their deficiencies, however, they do permit some generalizations and even some accurate statements.

Let us first consider personal wealth. The earliest records up to 1709 indicate a low average level, similar to that of other agricultural villages throughout the colony, and much below that of older, more diversified towns.[4] No really wealthy men lived in Lyme. About a third were poor, and most people owned small properties. The richest ten percent owned thirty-five percent of all personal property.[5]

During the next twenty years most Lyme residents held their own. A few left sizeable estates, notably John Wait, the miller, Matthew and Samuel Griswold, and Richard Lord, but these were large only for Lyme. During the 1730s the economy declined sharply. A revival, probably because of "King George's War," improved the position of a few families, but another decline after 1750 lasted until the Revolution. All the indices, including both means and medians and all adjustments, record all-time lows at the end of the colonial period.

Real estate — property in land and buildings — declined less. The mean, in fact, remained constant at £175–180, fluctuating of course from year to year but without a long-term trend. The median holding, however, decreased from almost £100 before 1740 to £50 thereafter.[6] Throughout the colonial period ownership of land was much more concentrated than personal property, ten percent of the men owning half of the total land (the reverse is usual in agricultural villages). Contrary to a commonly held hypothesis that population pressure in late colonial society raised prices of land, the shift reflects an increase in the proportion of those owning very small properties.[7] Prices for land, except meadowland, remained relatively low until the last few years of the colonial period.

As the decrease in personal wealth suggests, agriculture became less profitable. The small amount of productive soil meant that most people could not support themselves by farming, though they generally owned a house and lot. They therefore tended to enter nonfarming occupations. Before 1740 probably at least two-thirds of the men had been primarily farmers, but during the later decades only half were farmers, the rest craftsmen. In addition, demand for land may have been alleviated by Lyme's extension northward into the Hadlyme and eastward into the Chesterfield societies. Had trade or manufacturing flourished, the switch might have brought an improvement, but that was not the case. Few inhabitants found opportunity for advancement, and upward mobility probably diminished during the last years before the Revolution.

Let us now consider the town in terms of age, occupation, and social position. At any given time about one-third of the men were in their twenties. They rarely owned much property — as often as not, no land — and seldom more than £50 in personal wealth. Most stayed with their parents until they married, during which time they received a subsistence for their labor but little more. Marriage brought a significant rise in economic status — indeed a spouse's property tripled, reflecting a gradual increase in earning capacity, essential for family responsibilities, but primarily an inheritance, above all a share of the parental farm, transferred by the father. After marriage a man's property increased slowly, reaching a peak at mid-age when his sons were old enough to help efficiently. When he had to give away marriage portions to both sons and daughters, his estate diminished until, as might be expected, most men over seventy owned less than did those in their thirties. During the whole century before 1776, the sequence in probated estates was

Age	21–29	30–39	40–49	50–59	60–69	70 plus
Mean £	72	224	442	517	335	347

If we subtract the single large estate of John Griswold from the final figure, the mean for those over 70 becomes £262.[8] Clearly middle age and wealth went together in Lyme.

The most significant feature of this series is the first, for it suggests that Lyme's poor — its laboring class — consisted primarily of young men. The 1688 tax list, as remarked earlier, shows some small estates, and probably one-third of the adult men worked for wages or their keep. Of these all except a handful were young and single. Estate inventories show much the same situation. Of men who left properties worth less than £100 prior to 1750, all except half-a-dozen were either young or old, so that fewer than five percent of mature men in Lyme can be classified simply as laborers. During the final quarter-century the town's economy was declining, as we have seen, and the proportion of men with small estates increased greatly, from under twenty percent of probated estates to over forty percent, but again these consisted primarily of men in their twenties (one-third) or over sixty (one-fifth). Probably among the living population, as opposed to the probate, one-fourth of those between thirty and sixty were wage laborers; many of these laborers were still in their thirties, with some hope of future success. Not good, not bad, but typical of rural Connecticut.[9]

In some Connecticut towns manufacturing offered a profitable outlet for surplus farm boys. Probate records confirm that Lyme never developed beyond the average for its type. About one in five men worked primarily as an artisan, to which group we might add farmers who also worked at a trade, another seven percent of the men. The town supported a smith; a cooper (to make barrels for flour, cider, salted meats, and the like); a miller; a weaver; a shoemaker; and a few skilled woodworkers — housewrights, joiners, turners; a tanner; a hatter; a shipwright; a tailor; a clothier; a wheelwright; a mason; and a fuller. Among these a few accumulated large estates: Thomas Wait, a miller and substantial farmer with fifty-nine cattle; Elisha and John Lee, a tanner and a miller; Capt. Samuel Selden, a hatter with a handsome landed property; Joseph Starlin, a smith; Daniel Ayer, a miller; and Deacon Reynold Marvin, who probably acquired his valuable real estate from his father, not from the profits of barrelmaking. Not a long list! Indeed, only one-third of the artisans held over £100 in personal property, the median being £66, and for real estate just over £100. Both medians are thus close to the general norm.

Farming was Lyme's chief occupation. As a group farm owners acquired over half again as much wealth as artisans.[10] The usual Lyme farm consisted of about one hundred acres, though fewer could support a family. It supplied pasturage for a yoke of oxen, nine other cattle, two horses, five pigs, and often some sheep — a farmer either had a flock or didn't bother with sheep. The number of livestock actually declined as did their value, for prices changed little (horses up, sheep down).[11] From the beginning some men tried raising grain for sale, but never with much success, and most produced only enough for home consumption. Of the farmer's entire personal property livestock constituted about half until 1740, when it began to drop to a third by 1776. Few families had many servants or slaves (four percent of all personal property). Few estates list money or silver articles. Capital and production goods, including tools, amounted to £92 before 1740, consumption goods to £32 (twenty-six percent). Subsequently, capital and production goods remained constant, but consumption wealth rose to £54 (thirty-seven percent). Thus the town's economic decline during these last years reflected not a worsening condition for the established farmers and artisans but a growing number of laborers: the farmers of 1776 lived a bit more comfortably than their forebears.

Averages may conceal great differences within a group. Lyme's farmers ranged from poor to well-to-do — no one was rich. At one extreme was Matthew Griswold, who died in 1716, leaving £540 in personal and £3,763 in real wealth.[12] He owned at least 200 acres of good land and probably 1,000 more; 6 oxen and 50 other cattle, 139 sheep, 16 pigs, and 23 horses, worth in all £341. Almost half a century later, Thomas Lord (1694–1762) left over 560 acres in addition to his son Abner's inheritance. Thomas worked 3 oxen and pastured 27 other cattle, 4 horses, 20 sheep, and 8 pigs. He did not own slaves or keep servants but relied on his three sons and doubtlessly on seasonal help.

At the other extreme was Joseph Emerson (c. 1705–37), who had no land at all, but since he owned two oxen, five other cattle, a horse, and four pigs, he was clearly a farmer and presumably rented land. Similarly, although Job Gidding (c. 1709–48) had only three acres around his house and barn, his yoke of oxen, four other cattle, a horse, six sheep, and three pigs, together with a few farming tools, suggest he was a farmer. Both were young married men in their thirties when they died. We may therefore suppose that they would have become in ten or twelve years "average" farmers. One example of such a farmer might be Richard Parson (1717–73), who left to his wife, two sons, and six daughters, sixty-six acres, eleven cattle, three horses, three pigs, three and a half acres of rye growing on the ground (£2.12.6), plus £26 in corn, hay, flax, flax seed, oats, wheat, and meslin, with £13 in lumber, but few household goods. He recommended that his elder son learn the cooper's trade and that his younger son become a house-joiner.

Most of the men in colonial Lyme were laborers, artisans, or farmers, but there were exceptions. The minister, as was usual in the early years, ranked high on the economic as well as the social scale. The first in Lyme, Moses Noyes (1643–1726), paid a tax in 1688 above the average though not really high. New England was lenient with its ministers, and he may have been quite well off. His two sons left substantial estates. The first inventory we have, that of Rev. David Deming (1685–1746), is modest, but George Griswold (1694–1761) left £252 in personal and £1,486 in real property, the total being nearly five times the general mean. George was a son of Matthew and the first minister of the Second Ecclesiastical Society; his inheritance may well account in part for his prosperity. The equal prosperity of Stephen Johnson (1720–86), the third minister of the First Society and successor to Jonathan Parsons, may be attributed in part to three marriages to wealthy women. The only doctor, Capt. Thomas Anderson (1710–61), had a slave to help him with his 110-acre farm and cooper's shop. In his library was a volume of Homer. Full-time lawyers did not appear until rather late in the colonial period, especially in farming communities, and the only Lyme lawyers with inventories we can be certain about were John Griswold (1690–1764), brother of the minister, and Col. Samuel Selden. Griswold left the second-largest estate on record during the prerevolutionary period, including some 1,300 acres and a Negro girl to help his wife. Selden, who died in 1777, also possessed an exceptional property. From such few cases we cannot generalize, but Lyme's professional men seem to conform to a pattern common in Connecticut of owning a relatively large amount of property and being connected with the "best families."

Limited data discourage generalizations also about Lyme's traders. Important local business activity centered in New London. Lyme, with one exception to be discussed below, did not possess sufficient wealth to attract many ambitious entrepreneurs. The exceptions, like traders elsewhere, prospered above the norm. John Lay, Jr. (1692–1723), the innkeeper, owned a fine farm. John Mack (1682–1734) doubled his father's estate, and Nathan Beckwith earned a good income. Two colonial inventories belonged to ship captains, each of whom, incidentally, had a slave. As a group these traders possessed only average amounts of land but large amounts of personal wealth.

If we combine such data crudely expressed by arithmetic means and view the entire colonial period, the relation between occupation and wealth is clear:[13]

	Personal	*Real*	*Total*
Laborers	24	13	37
Artisans	111	234	345
Farmers	137	369	506
Business and professional men	325	685	1,010

Obviously, future success lay in trade or a profession, not in farming.

Lyme's social structure was a hierarchy of occupation and wealth combined with status or prestige. The nuances of social hierarchy are too fine for a historian to capture, but we can examine its manifestations and symbols. In particular we can identify in Lyme, as elsewhere, an elite identifiable by its political and judicial offices, military rank, and position in the church, as well as property. From these data we can derive a list of the town's eminent families. Below the elite we might distinguish at least two more categories, based upon church membership, freeman oaths (carrying the right to vote), and local officeholding, as well as the ownership of property already examined.

Probably the one-third who made up the laboring class correspond to those who did not participate in politics, who seldom joined a church, and whom the town sent off to war. Most residents (fifty-five to sixty percent) belonged to a middle group of voters and church members with modest properties.

At the top of the religious status order were the ministers and deacons. The estates of the clergy included, as one might expect, exceptional libraries, averaging £12 at a time when laborers boarding with a family cleared little more for a year's work. The same applies to the deacons, among whom there were four Marvins, two Colts, an Ely, and a Lord. The position was held by older men, and although property was not a requisite, most deacons left estates well above the median, £529, averaging nearly £1,500. All owned books, generally above £1 in value.

Military leaders also belonged, as a rule, to prominent families. Col. Samuel Selden, who achieved the highest rank during the colonial period, descended from an early settler of Hadley, Massachusetts. His father, Capt. Samuel, left a property of £2,520 which Col. Samuel, a lawyer, increased. Maj. Daniel Ely's inventory amounted to only £467 when he died in 1776, but he was over eighty and had formerly possessed a much larger property. Capt. William Ely, his father, and other captains averaged £1,000 at their deaths, almost never leaving below-average estates except when they were old. Among those with military titles were two Colts, four Elys in addition to Maj. Daniel, two Lees, and four Marvins. The Griswolds and Noyeses did not ordinarily aspire to military leadership, though the prominent lawyer John Griswold was a lieutenant in the militia. As Griswold's position suggests, lieutenants had a status comparable to that of captains, at least until mid-century; for example, Richard Lord's father, Lt. William, was one of the town's largest landowners, and Lt. Richard himself served as a deputy while his son became an esquire and acquired an exceptional property. Lt. Timothy Mather also held the office of justice of the peace; his brother Lt. Joseph attained the same rank, and Lt. William Minor the first (1670–1725) left nearly £1,200 at his death.

The most important political officers in colonial Connecticut were the assistants in the Assembly. The first Lyme resident sufficiently prominent to win election to a colony-wide post was Matthew

Griswold in 1759. Griswold's great-grandfather, also named Matthew, was the brother of Edward, a Windsor lawyer, deputy, and founder of another influential family. Matthew's father John, a lawyer, justice of the peace, and deputy, inherited one of Lyme's largest estates. Matthew himself was rich, and like Griswolds elsewhere who had become ministers, army officers, deputies, and large property owners, belonged to the colony-wide elite.

Every May the legislature selected for each county justices of the peace who thereby acquired the prestigious title of "Esquire." Relatively few Lyme men attained this status. Two Griswolds, two Lees, two Noyeses, and no less than four Elys comprised over half of the total before 1780, while other families contributed one each, including a Lay, a Lord, a Mather, a Parsons, and a Selden. With one exception, these men belonged to the economic upper class. Most had begun their political careers as deputies, elected at town meetings twice each year, in the lower house of the legislature. Excluding the few who served just one or two years, only twenty-five men became deputies during the colonial era. Among these the Ely family contributed three, the Griswolds four, the Lees three, the Lords two, and the Seldens two — over half of the total. In addition Lt. Abram Brunson had married a Griswold; Capt. John Colt and Capt. Nathan Jewett married Lords.

Often these men did not depend solely upon farming for their living. The Griswolds and Seldens practiced law, Captains William Ely and Stephen Lee engaged in trade, Capt. John Lee was a miller, and Capt. Nathan Jewett had considerable outstanding credits, as did Richard Lord (1690–1776). Deputies were often military as well as political leaders: sixteen of the twenty-five held militia offices. The following table suggests the deputies' economic position:

Distribution of Deputies' Wealth

Value of Inventory	Number
£ 1–99	0
100–199	2
200–299	0
300–499	2
500–999	4
1,000 plus	11
unknown	6

Deputies leaving estates under £500 died at an old age: one was over ninety and another was eighty-three. On the 1688 assessment list, six of the seven men who became deputies before 1710 (the exception had died before 1688) were assessed for at least £90, which placed them among the upper twenty-five percent of taxpayers.

Another segment of the political elite consisted of the principal town officials, especially the moderator of the town meeting and the "townsmen," now called selectmen. These can be identified until 1727.[14] After Matthew Griswold's long tenure as moderator, no individual monopolized the post but it was still passed among the same group: Lt. Abram Brunson, Capt. William Ely, and Capt. Thomas Lee. A larger number served as townsmen, but the deputies supplied leadership in both the local and colony governments.

Lyme contained, then, a political-military-religious elite. Did this elite constitute the economic upper class as the assessment list suggests? Ten men, whom we may properly call well-to-do, left property worth £2,000, and fourteen more £1,000. The first group comprised only three percent of the total population, and the two combined about eight percent. Collectively they owned forty percent of the inventoried wealth.

Who were these men? Only a third were farmers, the rest were professionals, relatively large-scale craftsmen, or entrepreneurs. Among the £2,000 plus group, all except two — Thomas Griswold, son of John, Esq., and Moses Noyes, the minister's son — belonged to the political, military, or religious elite. This included, with some overlapping, seven deputies, one assistant, four justices, one colonel, two captains, one lieutenant, and two deacons. Far fewer leaders emerged from the group assessed at £1,000: a minister, a deacon, and two captains, one of whom was also a deputy. Some of the ten who did not so contribute came from elite families, notably Thomas Lord, Samuel Griswold, Elisha Lee, and John Lay, Jr. This second group, however, did not possess enough property to qualify as part of an economic elite even in Lyme.

Clearly many men who rose to the top in political, military, or religious fields did not acquire large properties for the obvious reason that there were too few wealthy men in Lyme to fill these positions. If we add to the above ten, two well-to-do residents whose inventories appeared after 1776, we obtain the left-hand columns of the table below. If we eliminate inventories of old men, which so often were misleadingly small, and incorporate other information supplementing that derived from tax lists and probate records, we obtain the right-hand columns:

Total Wealth
Inventories of the Political-Military-Religious Elite

	Number	Percent of Known	Number (Adjusted)	Percent of Known (Adjusted)
Poor (under £100)	1	2.7	1	2.3
Below average (£100–349)	8	20.5	2	4.6
Above average (£350–999)	9	23.1	11	25.0
Substantial (£1,000–1,999)	10	25.6	17	38.6
Economic elite (£2,000 plus)	11	28.2	13	29.5
Uncertain	26		21	
Total	65	100.1	65	100.0

To those in the elite group we should add two very rich men (£2,000 plus) who held no political, military, or religious office, making a total of sixty-seven. Obviously, the economic and noneconomic rank orders overlap, with two-thirds of the latter belonging to the former, but they certainly are not identical.

If we focus on family units instead of on individuals, we find that ten families provided more than two leaders each, collectively over half of the total. These same families included all except one of the wealthiest men. In other words, families with a large property-holder contributed half of the leaders. Moreover, as previously remarked, others had married into this social elite, which therefore furnished over two-thirds of all leaders. In a small agricultural town this proportion is certainly not unusual, and for as many as ten families to belong to such a group, and for more than that number to join them occasionally, suggests a relatively open society.

What happened after 1776? For 1781 and subsequent years we have tax lists although they give only the total assessed upon each person.[15] Listed are some five hundred men who probably paid taxes for another fifty. These figures reveal a considerable decline in population after 1774, and we may postulate an exodus of both civilians and military men. The ages of the taxable persons furnish clues to the nature and extent of the loss. The following table shows the relation between the expected percentage of individuals within an age group and the actual percentage.[16]

Age group	21–29	30–39	40–49	50–59	60 plus
Expected percentage	35	28	15	12	10
Actual percentage	32	23	20	13	12

Evidently, wartime circumstances and better opportunities elsewhere had taken about ten percent of the town's young men. Most had left from the longest-settled parts of the town. In addition Lyme probably contained about fifty poor men who were not taxed because of their poverty.

The average assessment per taxpayer had recovered from the prewar low of £33, though it did not quite reach the 1700 level and by 1784 had declined sharply. As the share of the top ten percent had not risen, Lyme's population had probably not altered drastically. Instead, the economic deterioration affected almost everyone. Even though we assume that many young men were absent, far more poor appear in the 1781 record than a century before. Thirty-six percent were assessed for under £30 in 1781 versus twenty-seven percent a century before. Moreover, the median had fallen. Fewer well-to-do residents are listed, with only half as many, proportionately, assessed for £100. This decline may simply reflect a shift in the nature of property held from taxable wealth (mostly land and livestock) into nontaxable forms. We must await analysis of estate inventories for a full explanation, but meanwhile the tax lists reveal certain other attributes of revolutionary society.

The town, greatly expanded, had separated into five districts, or "societies": the First, Second, North, Hadlyme, and Chesterfield. Of these the First and North contained most of the old families and large estates. The names of those paying a large tax indicate strong continuity. The list shows Matthew Griswold, Esq., with the highest assessment, followed by John Griswold, George Griswold, and Andrew Griswold, Esq. Also on the list is William Noyes, Esq., the grandson of the first minister, and three descendants of the original William Peck. Beckwiths, Lees, Elys, and Lords were still among the economic elite.

Lyme continued to draw its political leadership primarily from these families and from others among the economic elite. Of deputies and justices about a third were in the top ten percent of taxpayers, and the rest ranked not far behind, the principal exception being George Dorr, Esq., who died bankrupt. The war produced a relatively large number of army officers, and although military ability may not necessarily correlate highly with financial or social success, there was some connection in Lyme: forty-four percent of captains and above paid taxes of £60–99; thirty percent taxes of £100 plus.

Percentage Distribution of Taxable Wealth

	All Lyme	Deputies and Justices of the Peace	Captains and Above
Under £30	37	6	11
£30–59	35	18	15
£60–99	20	41	44
£100 plus	8	35	30

The fact that some leaders came from lower economic ranks again suggests that Lyme's society was not closed to newcomers. Indeed men who did not belong to elite families paid some of the highest assessments, notably John Mumford in Chesterfield Society and John McCurdy in the First Society. Nevertheless, the general impression conveyed by these records indicates a lack of opportunity. Although most of the poor were young, a much larger proportion of the middle-aged, probably twenty-five percent, had failed to acquire enough property to support their families. A century earlier such a situation was almost unknown.

Turning again to probate records, we find at first glance a paradoxical situation. During the three five-year periods beginning in 1775, we have thirty-two, twenty-seven, and thirty-nine inventories. Mean personal wealth had declined from a general level of slightly over £100 before 1750 to £90 during the final prerevolutionary years. It rose dramatically to £140 in 1775–79, £160 for the next five years, and over £1,000 during 1785–90! For the last figure, John McCurdy is primarily responsible. In 1785 he left an extraordinary personal estate of £33,751.

Let us begin a series of adjustments by removing McCurdy. We still have a mean of £160, far above any prewar figure and unbelievable in a depression. Perhaps an adjustment for age bias in the probate records will resolve the difficulty. Moving as best we can from the estate inventories to the probate wealth of the living population, we obtain a new set of figures, inexact but suggestive:

to 1739	£ 92	1775–79	£ 96
1740–59	92	1780–84	112
1760–74	70	1785–89	161 (exclusive of McCurdy)

These remain puzzlingly high. The trimmed mean, without the top tenth of the estates, and the medians indicate the same sharp increase beginning in 1775. We still cannot reconcile the high value of inventoried wealth with the low level of taxable property. Is the disparity due to diversification in forms of wealth not subject to taxation? Let us study the composition of wealth in three periods: the years before 1730, the prewar period 1760–74, and 1775–89:

Mean Value Per Person, Inventoried Personal Property

	N	Money	Live-stock	Grains	Tools	Serv-ants	Trading Stock	Debts	Con-sumption
to 1730	65	3	52	4	3	3	1	10	38
1760–74	106	4	26	4½	3½	5	3	14	34
1775–89	96	14	33	7	5	3	1	22	40

As "money" after 1775 consisted primarily of state and federal certificates of indebtedness, the dramatic jump in inventory values reflected almost entirely the rise in public and private debts.

In the probated inventories we can compare net personal wealth, exclusive of public and private debt, before and after 1775. Our table displays five types of data: a distribution, medians, means, the mean of all estates except the richest ten percent, and the share of wealth of that richest decile.

	to 1740	1740–74	1775–89
£ 1–49	46%	56%	48%
50–99	27%	26%	21%
100–199	20%	10%	20%
200–499	5%	6%	7%
500 plus	2%	2%	4%
Median	£60	£40	£55
Mean	£92	£80	£112
Trimmed mean	£84	£63	£51
Share of top 10%	37%	43%	59%

These data show a wartime prosperity which was confined primarily to the top group of wealth-holders, as the rise in the mean demonstrates, and a decline in the fortunes of small property-holders. The difficulties of the latter are emphasized by private debts, which during the last years of our survey, 1785–89, equaled the value of all inventories combined. McCurdy and Nathaniel Matson, both large creditors, owned almost ninety percent of inventoried personal wealth! Had this kind of property been subject to taxation, the tax records would have reflected this spectacular development.

Inventoried real estate confirms these conclusions. The proportion of landless men and those with small properties remained about the same because land prices rose slowly, and as men shifted into nonagricultural pursuits they continued to own houses, lots, and barns. After 1775, however, the number of large estates and the mean value of real property rose, bringing the share of the top ten percent of wealth-holders to fifty-two percent. A few men, notably Col. Samuel Selden, Nathaniel Matson, and John McCurdy, acquired large tracts of land.

At the bottom of Lyme's revolutionary society were laborers and poor artisans, mostly young, nearly half of the population, a proportion which would have been higher except for emigration. The rising concentration of real, and even more of personal wealth, sharpened the contrast between them and the well-to-do. The Revolution, at least before 1789, made matters worse, in part because the young poor became soldiers and were in no position to cope with the postwar depression. An almost equal number were farmers and artisans. Skilled craftsmen scarcely held their own. Farmers benefited at first from the high prices of livestock and grain, but these profits vanished after the war.

A few Lyme families at the top did prosper. Estates inventoried for over £1,000 had gradually increased from five percent of the total before 1740 to seven percent before 1775, and to sixteen percent by 1789. At first their owners held only twenty-nine percent of inventoried wealth, then forty-one percent, still a relatively equal distribution, but by the 1780s their owners held seventy-five percent or, without McCurdy, fifty-seven percent. This economic elite, as the tax lists show, included Lyme's long-established leaders: Deacon Joseph Colt, Samuel Ely, Esq., Deacon Richard Lord, Esq., Capt. Dan Marvin, Capt. John Peck, Capt. Ezra Selden, Jr., and Col. Samuel Selden, Esq. To these we add two: Nathaniel Matson (1725–87), a businessman whose wealth consisted primarily of money and credits, and John McCurdy.

Integrating McCurdy is difficult. If we consider him a maverick and exclude him on the ground that he distorts our picture of Lyme, we would be right up to a point. If we regard him as symbolic, representing the end of the "old" Lyme and the beginning of nineteenth-century America, we would also be right.[17]

McCurdy (1725–86) immigrated from Ireland, apparently with a good education and capital. One might have expected him to settle in an important trading town, perhaps New London, rather than agricultural Lyme. He engaged in trade and must have prospered before 1775. He then gambled successfully on privateering and invested his profits primarily in loan office certificates. In 1787 his administrators presented a summary of his property totaling £37,118, of which £24,645 was in liquidated state and federal notes, properly certified and adjusted for depreciation. His private debts receivable totaled £6,249, and he owned £3,367 in real estate, including at least 526 acres besides a valuable home farm. This was an extraordinary property, large even for Boston, Newport, or New York, one of the largest if not the largest in all Connecticut and possibly unique for a town such as Lyme.

Yet McCurdy played a relatively minor role in the community. He served on local committees in 1774–75, but the town never sent him to the legislature. Indeed as far as public records go, he was notable primarily for successfully protesting his taxation. He paid less than some neighbors whose combined estates he could have easily bought. Men like McCurdy account for the widespread resentment against profiteers prevalent throughout the war years and after.

Colonial Lyme possessed a certain unity. Relatively few people failed to acquire large estates, and the wealthier men did not monopolize property or power. The Griswolds, Noyeses, Elys, Lees, and Lords and their peers were the core of an integrated society, married within it, and were trusted by their fellow citizens. McCurdy, for all his long residence, remained an outsider, without a religious, military, or political role, yet he amassed a fortune which changed the distribution of wealth in the town from moderate to extreme inequality. He anticipated and in part accomplished the transition from the old cooperative, consensual society to one beset by conflict, as individuals struggled for property and power. The Revolution in Lyme, instead of preserving the old social order, introduced the nineteenth-century businessman.

Notes

1. "Taxes under Andros," *New England Historical and Genealogical Register* (Boston: New England Historic Genealogical Society, 1880), XXXIV: 371–82.

2. For tax purposes, a yoke of oxen was valued at £10, a horse at £5, a cow at £3, a pig at £1, and a sheep at 10s. local money (about one-third higher than the currency of 1776 which, in turn, exceeded sterling by one-third). In contrast to these realistic values, land was undervalued for tax purposes and the disparity increased over time.

3. Lyme probate court records can be consulted most conveniently at the Connecticut State Library in Hartford, which contains also excellent indexes of personal names, family histories, and other basic sources, presided over by an exceptionally helpful and efficient staff.

4. These inventories do not include the estate of Matthew Griswold, who died in 1699, presumably the town's richest resident. If we may judge from his son's property, adding his inventory would raise the mean personal wealth from £105 to £137, still in the same range.

5. If we include our estimate of Griswold's estate, the figure becomes thirty-seven percent, precisely the average for the colony as a whole about 1700.

6. The median for the living population. The median of estate inventories is £123 for the early years, £96 for the later.

7. A change in the coverage of inventories may disguise a growing number of landless men, but we do not have any evidence of this. For one thing, the proportion of young single men in the probate records did not decline. For another, study of a 1781 tax list, discussed in the text below, shows little or no wealth bias.

8. The N here is, respectively, 44, 53, 50, 47, 52, and 42.

9. The table shows on the left the distribution of total probated wealth by age groups, and on the right the distribution of wealth among the living population by percentages, on the assumption that Lyme's age-structure conformed with that of Hartford County (the ages of the men whose estates entered probate correspond very closely). The small N and methodological difficulties limit the accuracy of the figures to ten percent at best.

Distribution of Wealth by Age Groups 1750–74

	Estate Inventories							Living Population					
	20s	*30s*	*40s*	*50s*	*60 plus*	*?*	*Total*	*20s*	*30s*	*40s*	*50s*	*60 plus*	*Total*
£ 1–49	17	8	2	6	8	3	44	19	8	1	2	2	32
50–99	9	9	0	4	7	2	31	11	10	0	2	1	24
100–199	3	5	2	5	12	3	30	3	5	1	2	2	13
200–299	1	3	4	2	5	1	16	1	3	3	1	1	9
300–399	1	1	4	2	3	0	11	1	1	3	1	0	6
400–499	0	0	2	4	5	1	12	0	0	1	1	1	3
500–999	0	1	6	7	8	0	22	0	1	4	2	2	9
1,000 plus	0	0	3	2	5	0	10	0	0	2	1	1	4
Total	31	27	23	32	53	10	176	35	28	15	12	10	100
Mean £	66	130	492	432	370	137	294						220

10. The medians are £97 and £260, the means £137 and £369.

11. Average number of livestock, Lyme farmers' inventories:

	Cattle	*Horses*	*Sheep*	*Pigs*	*Total*
to 1739	17	3	17	6 plus	43 plus
1740s	13	2	16	4	35
1750–75	12	2	20	6½	40½

12. These inventory figures must be reduced twenty percent to allow for price inflation.

13. Omitted are two major groups: the old whom we would today call "retired" and the unknown. Some of the former were prosperous, but usually they had given away much of their property, leaving a comparatively low mean of about £70 in personal and £150 in real wealth. The latter are a mixed bag and might, if identified, augment the proportion of laborers, artisans, and tenant farmers. Their approximate mean properties were £40 in personal and £100 in real wealth.

14. The volume of town records covering the revolutionary period is missing.

15. These lists are preserved in the Connecticut State Library.

16. Expected, if Lyme resembled other similar agricultural communities in New England and elsewhere.

17. The "Connecticut Archives" contain a petition from McCurdy claiming losses in privateering in order to contest a high tax assessment. He had almost nothing to do with the major business firms of revolutionary Connecticut: among the Jeremiah Wadsworth papers, for example, only one letter is from him, and among Governor Trumbull's apparently none.

Letters, Learning, and Politics in Lyme: 1760–1800

MINOR MYERS, JR.

WHAT were the residents of Lyme reading in the years before the Revolution? Historians often write that the political philosophies of John Locke, Charles, Baron de Montesquieu, Jean Jacques Burlamaqui, Algernon Sidney, and Thomas Paine inspired the colonists.[1] *Cato's Letters* by John Trenchard and Thomas Gordon have also been advanced as highly influential.[2] A modern reader almost imagines the colonists burning candles late into the night studying these stirring defenses of liberty and awaking the next morning ready to fight the British. Did Lyme's citizens read these books? For the most part they did not, but they were influenced by the philosophies contained within them.

What historical figures may have read inevitably remains conjectural to a degree. Quotations and citations, such as those by the Reverend Stephen Johnson to Sidney and Locke, are sure evidence that a writer was acquainted with the source or at least had read a book by someone who presumably was. Private libraries also offer clues to reading, and the inventories of many eighteenth-century Lyme libraries survive in probate records. To answer the questions posed in this essay, I have examined virtually all of Lyme's estate inventories recorded between 1760 and 1800,[3] as well as later inventories of political activists including those who represented Lyme in the Connecticut General Assembly between 1760 and 1800 and those who served on the Committee of Correspondence just before the Revolution. Special attention went to the inventories of all college graduates and to revolutionary officers who died before 1800. In the case of each inventory I noted the title of every book listed.

Connecticut probate law required a detailed inventory of estates, and until about 1830 appraisers were meticulous in their records. For example, the appraisers of one estate noted that the deceased had owned, among other things, a teapot with a cracked spout worth seventeen cents. Some appraisers even recorded the monograms on silver or linens. Fortunately, books were often inventoried with the same care given to furniture, tools, and clothes; and thus it is possible to form a good idea of the books present in revolutionary Lyme. Sometimes, however, the appraisers lumped books together, as in the inventory of Daniel Ayer (1764) in which twenty-four pamphlets are appraised at 5*s.* 8*d.* In two disappointing inventories whole libraries are evaluated and entered without details: the Reverend George Griswold (1761) had a "Library of Books" worth £12, and John Sill's estate (1796) had 540 "old and damaged books," making it the largest and most enigmatic library in Lyme.[4] Most estates were inventoried carefully, but unfortunately not all; for example, there is no inventory for Lyme's first native governor, Matthew Griswold (1714–99).[5]

Many activists died several decades after the Revolution, and the character and size of their libraries may have changed greatly during those subsequent years. Books could be bought, lent, lost, or given away, but probably were seldom discarded. Nevertheless it is useful to see what appears in the inventories.

Lyme inventories reveal one copy of Locke's *Of Civil Government,* two copies of John Dickinson's *Letters of a Pennsylvania Farmer,* and one copy of Montesquieu's *Spirit of the Laws,* first translated into English in 1750. There are no copies of Sidney, Paine, or *Cato's Letters.* One entry in John Griswold's estate (1813), "Appeal to Common Sense," suggests Paine's title, but probably refers to James Oswald's *An Appeal to Common Sense in Behalf of Religion,* published in London in 1766.[6] Inadvertently appraisers may have buried influential titles in groupings of "old books" or "miscellaneous pamphlets," but if the classics of political philosophy were as directly influential as sometimes stated, one would expect them to appear at least once in the Lyme probate records.

Should one then conclude that these authors were not as influential as initially expected? Before answering this question, it is useful to look at what Lyme residents *did* have in their libraries, then to consider who might have been familiar with the teachings of those texts.

The Appendix lists all of the titles found, together with the number of times each title appears in Lyme inventories.

Comparatively few people had libraries of any size. Of the 308 inventories studied only 80 had any books except a Bible or Psalter. If a household had only one book (as many did), it was likely to be the Bible, and undoubtedly well read. Religious books predominated in most smaller libraries. Sermons, explications of the Bible, books on religious life, and ecclesiastical biographies appear frequently. For example, Isaac Watts was especially popular, and Jonathan Edwards's *Account of the Life of the Late Rev. David Brainerd,* published in Boston in 1749, appears in five inventories. Brainerd (1718–47) was of local interest, for he was born in Haddam and served as a missionary to the Delaware Indians.

Although religious books are common in the inventories of both those who were and those who were not active in politics, many politicians had books not owned by others — on law and history. To a degree Lyme inventories bear out one of the earliest generalizations about the reading habits of American revolutionaries. In 1775 Edmund Burke delivered his *Speech on Conciliation with America* in the British Parliament and discussed the origins of the American spirit of resistance.

> Permit me . . . to add another circumstance in our colonies, which contributes no mean part toward the growth and effect of this untractable spirit. I mean their education. In no country perhaps in the world is the law so general a study. The profession is numerous and powerful; and in most provinces it takes the lead. The greater number of deputies sent to the congress were lawyers. But all who read, and most do read, endeavour to obtain some smattering in that science. I have been told by an eminent bookseller, that in no branch of his business, after tracts of popular devotion, were so many books as those on the law exported to the plantations. The colonists have now fallen into the way of printing them for their own use. I hear that they have sold nearly as many of Blackstone's Commentaries in America as in England. . . . This study renders men acute, inquisitive, dextrous, prompt in attack, ready in defence, full of resources.[7]

Lyme inventories reflect Burke's remarks. Works of "popular devotion" are the most common in all households, while books on law turn up in the houses of those politically active. Blackstone's *Commentaries* appear in the estates of Samuel Selden (1777) and John Griswold (1813), both members of the General Assembly. Capt. Ezra Selden (1815), another legislator, owned Priestley's *Appendix to Sir W. Blackstone's Commentaries.* The largest identifiable collections of law-books in the years before the Revolution belonged to Samuel Selden, Marshfield Parsons (another legislator and the brother of Samuel Holden Parsons), and John McCurdy. After the Revolution John Griswold acquired a large collection of texts or perhaps inherited them from his father, Gov. Matthew Griswold. Clearly these promi-nent and active men had readily at hand fundamental books on British constitutional law.

The inventories include also a modest number of books on his-tory, which, like the lawbooks, were concentrated in only a few households. George Dorr and John Griswold owned Bishop Burnet's *History of the Reformation,* and John McCurdy owned the bishop's *History of His Own Time,* Rapin's *History of England,* and a *History of Queen Ann* (one of several works, all with a similar title). Samuel Selden owned Gov. Thomas Hutchinson's *History of the Colony of Massachusetts Bay,* and Nathaniel Shaw Woodbridge (1797) owned Smollett's *History of England,* Dodd's *Beauties of History, The Life of Franklin,* and Washington's *Letters.* Samuel Mather (1809) also owned Smollett's his-tory as well as later histories of America and France. Ezra Selden (1784) too had a copy of Rapin as well as Goldsmith's *History of Eng-land* and the *British Register.* Of these men only McCurdy, Wood-bridge, and the Ezra Selden who died in 1784 were not members of the legislature. Comparatively few historical works appear in other estates. Josephus' *History of the Jews* appears in four inventories, but not one belonged to a member of the legislature.

Even rarer than books on law or history are those on political philosophy. Only three important titles can be identified. John McCurdy and John Griswold both owned copies of John Dickinson's highly influential *Letters from a Farmer in Pennsylvania to the Inhabitants of the British Colonies* (1768), and the Reverend Stephen Johnson pos-sessed a work inventoried as "Lock Vol," almost certainly Locke's treatise *Of Civil Government* since Johnson quotes from the latter in his *Some Important Observations Occassioned by, and Adapted to, the Public Fast* (1765).[8] "Dickinson's Works," listed in Johnson's inventory, are more likely a small collection of volumes by Jonathan Dickinson, the first president of Princeton, than any writings by John Dickinson, the pa-triot. Marshfield Parsons had the only copy in Lyme of Montesquieu's *Spirit of the Laws.* Among Judge John Griswold's collection of fifty-six pamphlets, "consisting partly of election sermons," one might expect other political works, but there is no certain evidence to this effect.

Novels were rare both before and after the Revolution, and in eighteenth-century Lyme the only large collection of such "polite literature" was on the shelves of the fashionable Nathaniel Shaw Woodbridge, who died in 1797 at the age of twenty-five. Woodbridge was a Yale nongraduate in the class of 1789 of whom President Stiles had written in his diary on June 6, 1786:

> Mr. Shaw of New London applied for dismissal of Woodbridge his nephew, because of his puerile profuseness & dissipation and that he may study in retirement at Long Island. I gave leave absolutely to pursue studies elsewhere, as Mr. Shaw pleases; and after settlement of tumults etc. — dismissal.[9]

Woodbridge in many ways mirrors the development of American life after the Revolution. The luxurious decor of his house, described in great detail in his inventory, his interest in the amenities and polite literature, and his seeming disregard for theology are a far cry from the typical Lyme inventory of even twenty-five years before.

In addition to Lord Chesterfield's *Principles of Politeness* (quite probably the New London edition of 1793) and his *Advice to His Son,* Woodbridge owned novels by Fielding, Sterne, and John Moore, among others, as well as the complete works of Shakespeare. American literature also was on his shelves: Enos Hitchcock's *Memoirs of the Bloomsgrove Family* (1790), Susanna Rowson's *Charlotte, or a Tale of Truth* (1791), and *American Poems, Selected and Original,* edited by Elihu Hubbard Smith and published in Litchfield, Connecticut, in 1793.

The libraries of Lyme's delegates to the Connecticut General Assembly between 1760 and 1800 little suggest their owners' political activities (Table 1). Inventories are lacking for some, but four — James Huntley, Daniel Ely, Samuel Ely, and Richard Mather — apparently died owning no books at all. Elisha Way had only a Bible. Moses Warren, Andrew Griswold, Elisha Marvin, and Richard Wait owned small theological collections but no books on politics, history, or law. It is unclear from probate records or genealogies which John Lay represented Lyme in the General Assembly between 1761 and 1767. If it were the one who died at age 92 in 1788, he did not own any books. The John Lay who died in 1792 owned Salmon's *Gazetteer.* David F. Sill owned a Bible and "sundry books" valued at $12. George

Dorr had a copy of Burnet's *History of the Reformation* and of a work on reason by John Locke. Ezra Selden had Morse's *Geography,* a gazetteer, and the *Appendix* to Blackstone by Priestley and others. Nathaniel Matson owned some books on theology, Salmon's *Geography,* a state law book, and two volumes on the "Manners of the Ancients." John Griffing owned Franklin's works, "Church History," a dictionary, and twenty pamphlets, which may or may not have been political in character. David M. Jewett, a Yale graduate of 1787, owned two lawbooks and a collection of "school books."

Four of Lyme's revolutionary officers died before 1800. Three evidently did not own any books, but Joseph Jewett had two dictionaries, Watts's *Psalms,* and a "Military Book." From the inventories alone, one would not expect these representatives and officers to have been political leaders of the community.

Some libraries, however, do suggest the political activism of their owners. The comparatively large law library of Samuel Selden with its 7 volumes, including Blackstone, has already been mentioned. Marshfield Parsons, who represented Lyme during the Revolution, had 97 volumes. In addition to a great deal of theology, he owned many lawbooks, bound pamphlets, and the town's only identified copy of Montesquieu. John Griswold, who served in the legislature after the Revolution, had more than the 117 titles in his inventory, including a large collection of theology and philosophy, many lawbooks, a few histories, and Dickinson's *Letters of a Pennsylvania Farmer.* Among Samuel Mather, Jr.,'s 38 volumes was a good collection of English and American history, several novels and works of theology, but no tracts on political philosophy.

Probate records of the members of the Lyme Committee of Correspondence are sparse, but of the five members as it stood in September 1774, only John McCurdy is known to have had a large and political library.[10] Samuel Mather, Jr., did not own any political tracts, and most of the histories he had were published after the Revolution. Inventories for Eleazar Mather (Yale, 1738) and William Noyes are not available, and John Lay had either one book or none.

Though few Lyme citizens read the classics of Whig political philosophy, a small but important segment — its college graduates — was familiar with the ideas and doubtless disseminated them. During the eighteenth century no fewer than thirty-four college graduates either came from or lived in Lyme (Table 2) and virtually all would have learned something about political philosophy from their college studies in moral philosophy.

Most Lyme men attended Yale because of its proximity. Only three graduated from Harvard, one each from the classes of 1659, 1700, and 1756. The flow to Yale was not steady but rather clustered as local teachers or ministers took the time to prepare students for college. Such a group graduated from Yale in the mid-1740s, a few more in the 1750s, and seven between 1764 and 1766. After one more Lyme graduate in 1768 and another in 1769, there was a hiatus until 1773 when three took degrees. Three more followed in 1775 and one more in 1777. Many of these graduates chose to move elsewhere. Only occasionally was the movement reversed as graduates who were natives of other towns, for example the Reverend Stephen Johnson from Newark, New Jersey, settled in Lyme.

When the Revolution began in 1775, seven Yale graduates were living in Lyme. Samuel Holden Parsons, who became a major general in the war, had moved to New London the preceding year, shortly after being appointed king's attorney. Ezra Selden was a lawyer, Eleazar Mather and John Noyes were physicians, and Elisha Hall was an increasingly eccentric farmer.[11] Stephen Johnson and George Beckwith were ministers, and Beckwith's short-lived son, Baruch, was possibly a farmer.[12]

A Yale education in the 1760s and 1770s helped to pave the way for revolution.[13] Colonial college curricula treated politics as an adjunct to the study of ethics, but President Stiles's *Literary Diary* notes that Yale used four basic textbooks on ethics before the Revolution, none of which dealt extensively with politics: Henry More's *Enchiridion Ethicum* (1668), William Walloston's *Religion of Nature Delineated* (1724), and Jonathan Edwards's *Careful and Strict Enquiry into the Modern Prevailing Notions of the Freedom of the Will* (1754) said little more about politics than affirming the notion that citizens ought to obey rulers and positive laws.[14] President Thomas Clap's *Essay on the Nature and Foundation of Moral Virtue* (1765) was likewise an investigation of moral epistemology. Clap did not mention principles of politics in his *Essay*, yet he recorded that he regularly lectured upon political subjects. Very likely his successors, including Napthali Daggett and Ezra Stiles, did likewise.

In describing the college in 1766 Clap noted that while many

Yale men went into the ministry, some inevitably chose other professions.

> Yet inasmuch as more have been educated than are necessary for the immediate services of the churches, and are designed for various other public and important stations in civil life, the president therefore frequently makes public dissertations upon every subject necessary to be understood, to qualify young gentlemen for those various stations and employments; such as the nature of civil government, the civil constitution of *Great-Britain,* the various kinds of courts, and officers superior and inferior, the several kinds of laws by which the kingdom is governed; as the statute, common, civil, canon, military, and maritime law; together with their several various origins and extents.[15]

Such presidential lectures contributed to basic training in political and legal ideas.

Geography was a subject laden with political ideas. President Stiles recorded that when he took office in 1777 the sophomores regularly "recited" William Guthrie's *New Geographical, Historical, and Commercial Grammar,* first published in 1770. Earlier generations of Yale men had probably studied one of Thomas Salmon's geographies published initially in the 1740s. Guthrie's text taught not only basic geography but what the modern social scientist would call comparative politics. Guthrie praised England's free government for its constitutional structure.

> Herein consists the true excellence of the English government, that all the parts form a mutual check upon each other. In the legislature, the people are a check upon the nobility, and the nobility a check upon the people; by the mutual privilege of rejecting what the other has resolved: while the king is a check upon both, which preserves the executive power from encroachments.[16]

Guthrie's accounts of the governments of France, Russia, and Turkey gave students glimpses of despotic and arbitrary constitutions. Despite the difficulties of the revolutionary era, many Americans remained convinced of the excellence of the British constitution, perhaps because of analyses like those by Guthrie and Salmon.[17]

Yale students heard lectures, read about governments, and discussed political questions. In regular disputations one student was assigned to defend one side of a question against another arguing the opposite view. The notebook of Joseph Camp illustrates this point. In July 1766 Camp criticized slavery, in April 1765 he defended monarchy as opposed to aristocracy or democracy, in July he argued against toleration, and in April 1766 he held that a prince has no right to pardon a criminal justly condemned. The notebook makes clear that the positions argued were often those of assignment, not conviction.[18] Although Camp was from Newington, Connecticut, three of his thirty-six classmates of 1766 were from Lyme, and Camp probably knew the five Lyme men in the classes of 1764 and 1768. No doubt all these students engaged in similar political discussions.

Further evidence of political studies at Yale comes from the surviving lists of questions and theses for debate at the annual commencements. From the late 1740s on, political topics were regularly included in the *Theses Ethicae*. In 1743, the year Stephen Johnson was graduated, candidates for the bachelor's degree debated whether all laws not contrary to superior law, i.e., natural law, were to be obeyed. Three years later, when Johnson returned to take his A.M., he defended a theological thesis and heard his classmate Samuel Fisk argue that the people could not limit the supreme power of government by laws established at the time governors were chosen. That same year, however, another classmate, David Burr, argued that Parliament could limit the succession to the crown of England. As the 1770s approached, the political theses increased in number and in Whig orientation. The tone of the questions suggests that students were taught that political power originates with the people and is entrusted conditionally to rulers only for the public good. As early as 1751 a Lyme student dealt with the question of resistance. Reynold Marvin took the master's degree defending the thesis that a prince's inability to preserve the republic constituted grounds for resistance.

In the 1760s and 1770s social pressure on the students reinforced Whiggish tendencies of the faculty. After the Sugar Act in 1764 and the announcement of the forthcoming Stamp Act of 1765, Yale's students undertook the first of several political protests that preceded the Revolution. They began a boycott of foreign liquors. Roswell Grant of Windsor, Connecticut, a member of the class of 1765, wrote to his father:

> Shall not want that cherry you reserved for me before vacancy, as all the scholars have unanimously agreed not to drink any foreign spiritous

liquors any more, a scheme proposed by Mr. Woodhull [a tutor, 1756–61, 1763–65] & seconded by the other tutors & the scholars in succession; there was no compulsion, but all a voluntary act.[19]

During the Stamp Act crisis of late 1765 Joseph Lyman of Lebanon, Connecticut, and the class of 1767 delivered a fiery oration in the chapel, where presumably he was heard by all five students from Lyme then in residence. Several months later the Yale Corporation disciplined him for "unjustifiable reflections on that august body the British Parliament, and as appears by plain implication on the laws and authority of this college."[20]

The strong expression of revolutionary sentiments at Yale was only beginning, but rumors spread about political activity at the college. In 1765 Gen. Thomas Gage wrote to Sir William Johnson referring obliquely to some graduates of Yale as "pretended patriots, educated in a seminary of democracy."[21] In 1769 Yale students, together with those at other colleges, supported the nonimportation agreements by resolving to appear at commencement "wholly dressed in the manufactures of our own country." David McClure of the class of 1769, a classmate of David Ely of Lyme, recorded further in his diary the resistance of three or four of his classmates to the scheme, but their protests failed. With effort, the students found appropriate American clothing, and McClure recalled that "inspired with the patriotic spirit we took pride in our plain coarse republican dress, & were applauded by the friends of liberty."[22]

Protests and political orations continued. In December 1774 some classes voted to discontinue drinking tea until its taxation ceased, and in February 1775 the students organized their own military company. Obviously, Tories had a difficult time. In June 1775 the sophomore class voted to advertise their Tory classmate Abiathar Camp of New Haven as an enemy of his country, and in August the *Connecticut Journal* carried the allegation beyond the grounds of the college.[23]

A Yale education thus gave the men from Lyme and elsewhere a reservoir of developed political thought and analysis that could be readily tapped in the years preceding the Revolution. One Yale graduate, Stephen Johnson, stands above all others as a significant force in shaping public opinion in Lyme. After being graduated in 1743 he studied theology, probably in New Haven, and refused a call to New Milford before accepting one to Lyme in 1746, where he served until his death in 1786.

In autumn 1765 Johnson reacted sharply to the Stamp Act. His series of six articles in the *New London Gazette* preceded his sermon of December 18, 1765.[24] In all seven essays he opposed, explicitly or implicitly, what he believed were British attempts to enslave America. In 1770 he entitled an election sermon *Integrity and Piety the Best Principles of a Good Administration of Government.*[25] In it and in the fast sermon of 1765 the influence of his copy of John Locke is evident: in the latter he even gives footnotes with page references. Johnson's political analysis presented in his writing and forceful preaching undoubtedly spurred revolutionary sentiment in Lyme, and in 1765 when a crowd of angry citizens converged in Wethersfield to force Jared Ingersoll to resign his commission as royal stamp agent for Connecticut, a good number of that crowd were Johnson's parishioners from Lyme. Those who did not own Locke's treatise learned of its substance through such men as Johnson.

The other great political leader in revolutionary Lyme, John McCurdy, had one of the largest libraries, which he began assembling as early as 1756 and seems to have read with care. Born in Ireland of Scottish ancestry, he immigrated in 1745 and within two years had established himself as a merchant in New York City. In 1750 he opened a store in Lyme and by his death in 1785 had amassed easily the largest estate in the town. Early histories speak of him as a "gentleman of education."[26] I cannot find any evidence revealing what that education was, and McCurdy family historians, who had access to the McCurdy papers, do not mention collegiate training. Presumably McCurdy, like Roger Sherman, was self-educated. Although a merchant, he collected more lawbooks than many lawyers. His copy of Fitzgibbons's *Reports* is inscribed "Bought in Boston, 1758," and he purchased Holt's *Reports* in Boston in 1760.[27]

McCurdy and Johnson were close friends, working together to promote the cause of liberty. Johnson's publications offer tacit evidence of the many hours he had spent with McCurdy's books. Johnson's references to Magna Carta and the laws of England are very likely attributable to books in his friend's library, for McCurdy owned a book on Magna Carta, a *History of the Common Law of England,* and a *Compendious System of the Laws of England* as well as other law texts.

William Gordon's history of the Revolution, published in 1788, confirms the political collaboration of Johnson and McCurdy. Although Gordon writes that Johnson produced only "three or four" essays, the historian seems to have been in correspondence with the Lyme parson himself.[28] In 1765 he wrote about Johnson's activities:

> The Rev. Mr. *Stephen Johnson* of *Lyme,* vexed and grieved with the temper and inconsiderateness of all orders of people, determined if possible to rouse them to a better way of thinking. He consulted a neighboring gentleman, an Irishman by birth [John McCurdy], who undertook to convey the pieces he might pen to the *New London* printer, so secretly as to prevent the author's being discovered. Three or four essays were published upon the occasion. The eyes of the public began to open, and fears were excited. Other writers engaged in the business, while the first withdrew, having fully answered his intention. The congregational ministers saw further into the designs of the British administration than the bulk of the colony; and by their publications and conversation increased and strengthened the opposition.[29]

Gordon in the eighteenth century thus reached the conclusion Alice Mary Baldwin presented in the twentieth: an educated clergy was especially important in the formation of a community's political thinking before and during the Revolution.[30]

On the eve of the Revolution, libraries in Lyme were overwhelmingly theological, and few of its political activists were reading the classics of Whig political thought. Yet the people of the town knew the substance of those works through Stephen Johnson, John McCurdy, and those trained at Yale or Harvard, who owned the few of these texts to be found in the town and whose writings, sermons, orations, and activities moved Lyme toward resistance and revolution. In one rural Connecticut community the influence of Locke, Sidney, and Burlamaqui, though indirect, was evident.

TABLE 1

Representatives from Lyme to the Connecticut
General Assembly, 1760–1800

Name	Service	College	Died	Number of Titles in Inventory
Dorr, George	1760		1787	5
Ely, Daniel	1761		1776	0
Ely, Samuel	1760		1784	0
Ely, Seth	1777, 1781–83, 1786, 1788		1821	no inventory
Griffin, John	1785, 1787–88		1790	25
Griswold, Andrew	1786		1813	3 + "diverse books"
Griswold, John	1785, 1787–88		1813	117 + "sundry old books and pamphlets" and "old statutes and law books"
Griswold, Gov. Matthew	1748, 1751, 1754–56, 1758–59		1799	no inventory
Griswold, Matthew, Jr.	1789–90, 1794–1804	Yale 1780	1842	no inventory
Huntley, James	1793		1815	0
Jewett, David M.	1799–1804	Yale 1787	1821	9
Jewett, Nathan	1760		1761	9 + "number of old books"
Lay, John	1761–64, 1766–67, 1769–70, 1772, 1774, 1776–77		1788 or 1792?	0 or 1
Leach, M.	1791–92		?	no inventory
Lee, Lemuel	1791–93, 1797		?	no inventory
Marvin, Elisha	1766		1801	5
Mather, Eleazar	1751, 1759, 1760	Yale 1738	1798	no inventory
Mather, Joseph	1766, 1770		?	no inventory
Mather, Richard	1761		1796	0
Mather, Samuel, Jr.	1781, 1790, 1792–94		1809	38
Matson, Nathaniel	1782–83		1788	12 + "sundry pamphlets"
Noyes, John	1797, 1800	Yale 1775	1808	no inventory

TABLE 1 *(continued)*

Name	Service	College	Died	Number of Titles in Inventory
Noyes, William	1761, 1765, 1767, 1771, 1773–74, 1777		1807?	no inventory
Noyes, William	1788, 1791	Yale 1781	1834	no inventory
Parsons, Marshfield	1775–76, 1778, 1780, 1785, 1787, 1789		1813	97
Parsons, Samuel H.	1762–64, 1767–73	Harvard 1756	1789	not found
Perkins, Samuel	1792		?	no inventory
Reece, Isreal	1793, 1795–96		?	no inventory
Richard, Capt. ———	1760		?	?
Selden, Ezra	1768, 1774–75, 1778–79, 1782–85, 1787, 1789–90, 1796		1815	6
Selden, R.	1800		?	no inventory
Selden, Samuel	1762–63, 1765–66, 1768, 1771–73, 1776		1777	25 + "col-tion of pam-phlets"
Sill, David F.	1786, 1788, 1794–96, 1798–99		1813	2 + $12 worth of "sundry books"
Wait, Ezra	1795		?	no inventory
Wait, Richard, Jr.	1779, 1781, 1783, 1787		1810	1
Warren, Moses	1780, 1799		1805	22
Way, Elisha	1794		1802	1

TABLE 2

College Graduates in or from Eighteenth-Century Lyme

Name	Born	College	B.A.	Career spent	Died
Beckwith, Baruch	?	Yale	1773	Lyme	1778
Beckwith, George	1703	Yale	1728	Lyme	1794
Beckwith, George	1747	Yale	1766	New York, Connecticut	1824
Beckwith, Nathaniel	?	Yale	1766	Lyme	1769?
Brockway, Thomas	1745	Yale	1768	Lebanon	1807
Colt, Peter	1744	Yale	1764	New Hampshire	1824
Denning, David	?	Harvard	1700	Lyme	1745
DeWolf, Daniel	1726	Yale	1747	Lyme	1752
DeWolf, Nathan	?	Yale	1743	Nova Scotia	c. 1799
Ely, David	1749	Yale	1769	Stratford	1816
Ely, Richard	1733	Yale	1754	Guilford, Saybrook	1814
Ely, Samuel	1740	Yale	1764	Connecticut, Massachusetts	1795
Ely, Simon	1723	Yale	1745	New York, New Jersey, Connecticut	1765
Griswold, Matthew, Jr.	1760	Yale	1780	Lyme	1842
Griswold, Sylvanus	1733	Yale	1757	Massachusetts	1819
Hall, Elisha	1740	Yale	1764	Lyme	1812
Jewett, David M.	1767	Yale	1787	Lyme	1821
Johnson, Diodate	1745	Yale	1764	East Haddam	1773
Johnson, Stephen	1724	Yale	1743	Lyme	1786
Lee, Andrew	1745	Yale	1766	Lisbon	1832
Marvin, Elihu	1752	Yale	1773	Norwich	1798
Marvin, Reynold	1726	Yale	1748	Litchfield	1802
Mather, Eleazar	1716	Yale	1738	Lyme	1798
Noyes, John	1757	Yale	1775	Lyme	1808
Noyes, Moses	?	Harvard	1659	Lyme	1729
Noyes, William	1760	Yale	1781	Lyme	1808
Parsons, Samuel H.	1737	Harvard	1756	Lyme–New London (1774)	1789
Peck, William	1755	Yale	1775	Rhode Island	1832
Selden, Charles	1755	Yale	1777	New York	1820
Selden, Ezra	1752	Yale	1773	Lyme	1784
Sheldon, Elisha	1709	Yale	1730	Lyme–Litchfield (1763)	1779
Sill, Elijah	1724	Yale	1748	Connecticut, Vermont, New York	1792
Sill, Elisha	1730	Yale	1754	Goshen	?
Sill, Richard	1755	Yale	1775	Albany, N.Y.	?

Appendix: Books in Lyme

The following lists, grouped by subject alphabetically, include all legible titles found in the Lyme probate records of the estates mentioned in the essay. Single quotation marks indicate the title or notation of a work as it appears in the probate record when not further identifiable. Italicized titles are those for which identification is fairly certain. Parentheses indicate dates of first edition of a title; crosses before some titles indicate that an edition of the work was printed in nearby New London. The years in which a title appears in the probate inventories are given as follows. Where one or two copies of a book appear, the appropriate dates are given. Where three or more copies are found, the earliest and latest dates are cited.

Author and Title	*Number of times title appears in inventories*	*Date of inventory*
HISTORY, POLITICS, AND GEOGRAPHY		
Anson, George, Baron. *A Voyage Round the World* (1748)	2	1797, 1813
'Argal' =? Argal, Sir Samuel. *The Voyage of Capt. S. Argal from James Towne in Virginia* (1625)	1	1797
Blainville, de. *Travels through Holland, Germany, Switzerland, and Other Parts of Europe* (1743)	1	1790
Brissot de Warville, Jacques Pierre. *The Commerce of America with Europe* (1795)	1	1797
Burnet, Gilbert. *Bishop Burnet's History of His Own Time* (1724)	1	1786
———. *The History of the Reformation of the Church of England* (1679)	2	1787, 1813
Dickinson, John. *Letters from a Farmer in Pennsylvania* (1768)	2	1786, 1813
Dilworth, W. H. *The History of the Conquest of Mexico* (1759)	1	1797
Dodd, William. *The Beauties of History* (1787)	1	1797
Douglass, William. 'History of America'	1	1813
Drage, Theodore S. *An Account of a Voyage for the Discovery of a North-West Passage* (1748–49)	1	1786
Eachard, Laurence. *The Gazetteer's: or Newsman's Interpreter; Being a Geographical Index* (1695)	2	1765, 1777
Franklin, Benjamin. *The Life of Doctor Benjamin Franklin* (1791)	2	1797
———. *Works of the Late Benjamin Franklin* (1794)	2	1790, 1797
'French Revolution, 2 vols.' (This title is *not* Edmund Burke's *Reflections on the Revolution in France,* which was not issued in two volumes,	3	1797–1809

Author and Title	Number of times title appears in inventories	Date of inventory
nor is it John Adolphus's *Biographical Anecdotes of the Founders of the French Republic,* a two-volume work not issued until 1799.)		
Goldsmith, Oliver. *The History of England* (1771)	1	1784
Gordon, Patrick. *Geography Anatomized: or, A Compleat Geographical Grammar* (1693)	3	1765–84
Gordon, William. *History of the Rise, Progress and Establishment of the Independence of the United States* (1788)	1	1809
Guthrie, William. *A New Geographical, Historical, and Commercial Grammar* (1770)	1	1797
'History of the Four Quarters of the World'	1	1765
'History of the World'	1	1813
'History of Queen Ann.' (Identification is impossible because of several similar titles: Abel Boyer, *The History of Reign of Queen Anne* [1703]; Paul Chamberlen, *An Impartial History of the Life and Reign of Queen Anne* [1738]; Conyers Harrison, *An Impartial History of the Life and Reign of . . . Queen Anne* [1744].)	1	1786
Hutchinson, Thomas. *History of the Colony* (or *Province*) *of Massachusetts Bay* (1764)	1	1777
Josephus, Flavius. *The Wonderful . . . History of the . . . Jews*	4	1765–81
Langworthy, Edward. *Memoirs of the Life of the late Charles Lee* (1792)	1	1809
Le Page du Pratz, ———. *History of Louisiana* (1758)	1	1790
'Life of Howard'	1	1797
Locke, John. 'Vol' = *Of Civil Government* (Locke's second treatise of the *Two Treatises on Government*) (1690)	1	1787
'Manners of the Antients, 2 vols.' =? Fleury, Claude. *The Manners of the Ancient Christians*	1	1788
A Memorial of the Present Deplorable State of New England (1707)	1	1813
The Mirror, a Periodical Paper Published at Edinburgh (1779)	1	1809
Montesquieu, Charles Secondat Baron de. *Spirit of the Laws* (1748)	1	1813
Morse, Jedidiah. *The American Gazetteer* (1797)	1	1819
———. *The American Geography* (1789)	5	1790–1815

Author and Title	Number of times title appears in inventories	Date of inventory
Neal, Daniel. 'History' — either *The History of New England* (1720) or *The History of the Puritans or Protestant Non-Conformists* (1732)	1	1813
Oldmixon, John. *Bellisarius* (1713)	1	1787
Putnam. 'Life'	1	1813
Ramsay, David. *History of South Carolina* (1809)	1	1809
Rapin-Thoyras, Paul de. *History of England* (1728–32)	3	1784–91
Salmon, Thomas. *The Geography and History of England* (1765)	4	1777–97
————. *The Modern Gazetteer* (1746)	2	1788, 1819
————. *A New Geographical and Historical Grammar* (1749)	4	1777–88
'Secret History of the Court of St. Cloud'	1	1813
Smollett, Tobias. *The History of England* (1757)	2	1797, 1809
Washington, George, pseud. *Letters from George Washington to Several of His Friends in the Year 1776* (1778)	2	1797
Wells. 'Geography'	1	1813

LANGUAGE

Bayle? 'French Dictionary'	1	1797
Buxtorf, John. *Lexicon hebraicum et chaldaicum* (1615)	1	1784
'Hebrew Grammar'	1	1784
'Introduction to the Latin Tongue'	1	1777
'French book'	3	1784–97
'Greek Testament'	1	1784
'Latin Bible'	1	1784

LAW

'Abridgement of the Statutes'	1	1786
The Attorney's Compleat Pocket Books (1767)	1	1777
Bacon, Matthew. *A New Abridgment of Law* (1736)	1	1813
Blackstone, Sir William. *Commentaries on the Laws of England* (1765–69)	2	1777, 1813
'British Register'	1	1784
Brown. 'Reports'	1	1813
Brownlow, Richard. 'Pleadings'	1	1786
Burn, Richard. *The Justice of the Peace and Parish Officer* (1755)	1	1777
Carter, Samuel. *The Law of Executions* (1706)	1	1777

Author and Title	Number of times title appears in inventories	Date of inventory
'Cases in Chancery'	1	1813
'Civil Officer'	1	1809
Coke, Sir Edward. *Reports* (1658)	1	1813
Cooke, Sir George. *Practical Register of the Common Pleas* (1743)	1	1786
'Compendious System of the Laws of England'	1	1787
†Connecticut. *Acts and Laws Passed by the General Court or Assembly* (editions uncertain)	4	1781–1813
English Pleader: Being a Collection of Various Precedents (1734)	1	1786
Fitzgibbon, John. *Reports of Several Cases Argued and Adjudged* (1732)	2	1786, 1813
Fitzherbert, Anthony. *New Natura Brevium* (1534)	1	1786
Francis, Richard. *Maxims of Equity* (1727)	1	1786
Hawkins, William. *A Treatise of the Pleas of the Crown* (1716)	1	1786
'History of the Common Law of England'	1	1786
Holt, Sir John. *A Report of all the Cases Determined by Sir John Holt from 1688 to 1710* (1738)	2	1786, 1813
Jacob, Giles. *A Law Grammar, or Rudiments of the Law* (1749)	1	1794
———. *Lex Mercatoria, or the Merchant's Companion* (1718)	1	1786
———. *A New Law Dictionary* (1729)	5	1777–1819
Jenkins, David. *Eight Centuries of Reports* (1734)	1	1786
'Law of Bills of Exchange'	1	1813
'Law of Evidence'	3	1777–1813
'Lawyers Magazine'	1	1813
Lucas, Robert. *Cases in Law and Equity* (1700)	1	1786
'Magna Carta' =? Blackstone, Sir William, *The Great Charter and the Charter of the Forest* (1759), or Daines Barrington, *Observations on the More Ancient Statutes from Magna Charta to the Twenty-first of James I* (1766), or Samuel Johnson, *A History and Defense of Magna Charta* (1769)	2	1777, 1786
Modern Convenancer or Conveyancing Improved (1704)	1	1786
Nelson. 'Justice'	1	1809
New York. 'Laws of New York'	1	1813
Priestley, Joseph, Philip Freneau, et al. *An Interesting Appendix to Sir W. Blackstone's Commentaries on the Laws of England* (1773)	1	1815

Author and Title	Number of times title appears in inventories	Date of inventory
Raymond, Sir Thomas. *Reports of Divers Special Cases* (1743)	1	1813
'Reports in Chancery'	1	1813
Saint Germain, Christopher. *Dialogues in English between a Doctor of Divinitie and a Student in the Laws of England* (1580)	1	1786
Salmon, Thomas. *A New Abridgement and Critical Review of the State Trials* (1738)	1	1786
Shaw, Joseph. *The Practical Justice of the Peace and Parish and Ward Officer* (1728)	1	1813
Sheppard, William. *Precedent of Precedents* (1655)	2	1786, 1813
Shower, Sir Bartholomew. *Reports of Cases Adjudged in the Court of Kings Bench* (1708–20)	1	1813
'Statutes of England'	1	1813
United States. 'Laws of Congress'	1	1813
Wood, Thomas. 'Institutes'	1	1786

LITERATURE

Author and Title	Number of times title appears in inventories	Date of inventory
Addison, Joseph and Sir Richard Steele. *The Guardian* (1713)	2	1761, 1813
———. *The Spectator* (1711)	4	1784–97
———. *The Tatler.* (1709)	2	1790–1809
American Poems, Selected and Original (1793)	1	1797
'Art of Courting'	1	1813
Austen, James. *The Loiterer* (1790)	1	1797
Blackmore, Sir Richard. Title unspecified	1	1773
Brooke, Henry. *The Fool of Quality, or the History of Henry, Earl of Moreland* (1770)	2	1797, 1809
Burney, Frances. *Camilla or a Picture of Youth*	1	1809
Cervantes Saavedra, Miguel de. *Don Quixote* (1605)	1	1761
'Characters & Manners of the Present Age'	1	1813
'Charles Grandison'	1	1809
Chesterfield, Philip Dormer Stanhope, Fourth Earl of. *Lord Chesterfield's Advice to His Son* (1774)	2	1797, 1813
†———. *Principles of Politeness and of Knowing the World* (1793)	1	1797
?'Childreth Abbey'	1	1809
The Complete Letter Writer (1761 or 1790)	1	1809
'Count Roderick Castle'	1	1797
'Enfield Speaker'	1	1809
'Entertainer'	1	1761
Fielding, Henry. *Tom Jones* (1749)	1	1797

Author and Title	Number of times title appears in inventories	Date of inventory
Fontenelle, Bernard, Le Bovier de. *Dialogues of the Dead* (1683)	1	1777
Freneau, Philip. 'Poems'	1	1809
Goldsmith, Oliver. *The Citizen of the World, or Letters from a Chinese Philosopher* (1762)	2	1797, 1809
———. *Vicar of Wakefield* (1766)	1	1809
Gordon, Thomas. *A Cordial for Low Spirits* (1750)	1	1797
?'Grenville'	1	1809
Haywood, Eliza. *The Female Spectator* (1746)	3	1790–1813
Hitchcock, Enos. *Memoirs of the Bloomsgrove Family* (1790)	1	1797
Holmes, John. *The Art of Rhetorick Made Easy* (1738)	1	1784
Inchbald, Elizabeth. *Simple Story* (1791)	1	1797
Johnstone, Charles. *Chrysal, or the Adventures of a Guinea* (1765)	1	1797
Kilner, Dorothy. *Moral and Instructive Tales* (1797)	1	1797
'Ladies Library'	1	1787
Lesage, Alain. *Gil Blas* (1715)	1	1809
'Life of Mr. Cleveland' = John Cleveland, the poet?	1	1761
'Londoners Works'	1	1791
'Lyrick Poems'	1	1771
'Management of the Tongue'	1	1813
Milton, John. *Paradise Lost* (1667)	3	1777–86
———. *Paradise Regained* (1671)	1	1784
'Modest Critics'	1	1813
Moore, John. *Zeluco* (1789)	1	1797
'Moral Essays'	1	1797
'The Museum'	1	1781
Pigott, Charles. *The Jockey Club* (1793)	1	1797
Pope, Alexander. 'Works'	1	1797
Pratt, Samuel Jackson. *Emma Corbett* (1780)	1	1797
'Puttings Out'	1	1771
Ramsay, Andrew Michael. *Travels of Cyrus* (1727)	1	1771
Richardson, Samuel. *Clarissa Harlow* (1748)	1	1784
Rowson, Susanna. *Charlotte, or a Tale of Truth* (1791)	1	1797
Shakespeare, William. 'Works' — 8 vols., edition unknown	1	1797
Smollett, Tobias. *Roderick Random* (1748)	1	1797
Sterne, Laurence. *A Sentimental Journey through France and Italy* (1768)	1	1809
———. 'Works'	2	1797, 1809
'Unfortunate Mistress'	1	1761

Author and Title	Number of times title appears in inventories	Date of inventory
'Widows in Miniature'	1	1797
Webster, Samuel. *A Winter Evening's Conversation* (1757)	1	1757
Wolcot, John. *The Poetical Works of Peter Pindar* (1789)	1	1797
†Wolcott, Roger. 'Leisure Hours' = *Poetical Meditations; Being the Improvement of Some Vacant Hours* (1725)	1	1770
Yearsley, Ann. *Royal Captives* (1795)	1	1797

MEDICINE

Buchan, William. *Buchan's Family Physician* (1769)	3	1777–1809
Carven. 'On Typhus'	1	1781
Huxham, John. *Essay on Fevers* (1739)	1	1777
Lewis, William. *The Edinburgh New Dispensatory* (1753)	2	1777, 1799
Pringle, John. *Diseases of the Army*	1	1777
Quincy, John. *Lexicon Physico-Medicum: or, a New Physical Dictionary* (1719)	1	1777
Smellie, William. *The Practice of Midwifery* (1752–64)	1	1777
'System of Anatomy'	1	1799
'System of Surgery'	1	1799
Tissot, Samuel Auguste. *Advice to the People . . . in Regard to their Health* (1766)	1	1777

MISCELLANEOUS

'Barclay's Life'	1	1813
'Baron French'	1	1809
'The Companion'	1	1813
Dillon, Humphery. 'Works'	1	1791
'Freemasonry'	1	1809
Gerald. 'Trial'	1	1797
'Gilbert'	1	1790
Horne. 'Life'	1	1813
'?Lentour[?] Not Fabulous'	1	1777
'Life of Signor de Guadentio'	1	1813
'Marier'	1	1809
'Newen' or 'Newell'	1	1771
'Pike, Marshal and Girish'	1	1787
'Webster's, Cole's, and Durham's' ('Sermons'?)	1	1786
Webstir.	1	1800
West.	1	1787
Willson. 'Works'	1	1786

Author and Title	Number of times title appears in inventories	Date of inventory

REFERENCE

Bailey, Nathan. *The Universal Etymological English Dictionary* (1721)	8	1761–1813
Brady and Tate. *Dictionary*	1	1787
Coles, Elisha. *English Dictionary* (1676)	1	1776
Dyche, Thomas. 'Dictionary'	2	1781, 1790
Enclycopaedia Britannica; or a Dictionary of the Arts and Sciences Compiled upon a New Plan (1771)	1	1797
Entick, John. *Entick's New Spelling Dictionary* (1784)	3	1790–97
Johnson, Samuel. *Dictionary of the English Language* (1755)	2	1777, 1809

SCIENCE, MATHEMATICS, AND APPLIED SCIENCE

Atkinson, James. *An Epitome of the Art of Navigation* (1706)	1	1784
Crocker. 'Arithmetic'	1	1761
'Daily Assistant'	1	1797
Gordon, John? 'Accountant'	1	1786
Gouch, John. *A Treatise of Arithmetic* (1788)	1	1797
Love, John. *Geodaesia, or the Art of Surveying*	1	1809
Mortimer, Thomas. *Every Man His Own Broker* (1761)	1	1786
'Nature Displayed' =? Goldsmith, Oliver. *A History of the Earth and Animated Nature* (1774). Goldsmith's work was issued in 8 volumes: Daniel Calkins owned volumes 5 and 6 of 'Nature Displayed'; possibly also Samuel Ward's *System of Natural History* (below).	1	1790
'Plan of Commerce'	1	1786
'Poor Man's Pocket Book'	1	1770
'Practical Navigator'	1	1797
The Shipmaster's Assistant and Owner's Manual (1797)	1	1797
'Traders Sure Guide'	1	1777
'Treatise on Foods'	1	1786
Ward, John. *The Young Mathematician's Guide* (1707)	2	1784, 1788
Ward, Samuel. *System of Natural History*, 12 vols. (1775)	1	1790
Whiston, William. *Astronomical Lectures* (1715)	1	1794
———. *A New Theory of the Earth* (1696)	1	1786
Wigglesworth. 'Spelling book'	1	1800

Author and Title	Number of times title appears in inventories	Date of inventory

THEOLOGY, PHILOSOPHY, AND RELIGIOUS BIOGRAPHY

Author and Title		
Alleine, Joseph. *An Alarm to Unconverted Sinners* (1703)	1	1760
Allen, William. *The Works of Mr. William Allen, Consisting of Thirteen Distinct Tracts on Several Subjects* (1707)	1	1769
'Articles of Faith'	1	1813
†Baldwin, Moses. 'Sermons'	1	1781
Bates. 'Works'	1	1813
Baxter, Richard. *A Call to the Unconverted* (1658)	1	1797
———. *The Saints' Everlasting Rest* (1650)	1	1813
Beattie, James. *Essay on the Nature and Immutability of Truth* (1770)	2	1787, 1813
Bellamy, Joseph. *An Essay on the Nature and Glory* (1762)	1	1813
———. *Four Dialogues on the Half-Way Covenant* (1769)	1	1777
———. *True Religion Delineated* (1750)	1	1813
———. *Sermons upon the Following Subjects* (1758)	1	1813
———. 'Works, 2 vols'	1	1787
Bennet, Thomas. *An Answer to the Dissenters' Pleas* (1700)	1	1813
Benson, George. *The History of the First Planting of the Christian Religion* (1735)	1	1813
Berriman, William. 'Works on law and grace'	1	1781
'Berry Street Sermons'	1	1813
Blackall, Offspring. 'Sermons'	1	1813
Blackwell, Thomas. *Forma Sacra, or a Sacred Platform*	1	1813
†Bolles, John. *To Worship God in Spirit, & in Truth is to Worship Him in the True Liberty of Conscience* (1756)	1	1767
Boston, Thomas. *A View of the Covenant of Grace* (1742)	2	1786, 1813
———. *The Whole Works of the late . . . Mr. Thomas Boston* (1767)	3	1787–1813
'Branty's History'?	1	1809
Bruden. 'Compendium'	1	1794
†Bulkley, John. *An Impartial Account of a Late Debate at Lyme in the Colony of Connecticut* [on the subject of baptism] (1729)	1	1764
†Bragge, Robert. *Church Discipline* (1768)	1	1781

Author and Title	Number of times title appears in inventories	Date of inventory
Brown, Moses. *Observations on Samuel Shepard's Three Letters* (1793)	1	1813
Buchanan, Claudius. *Christian Researches in Asia* (1811)	1	1813
Bunyan, John. 'Works' (edition uncertain)	1	1769
Butler, Joseph. *Fifteen Sermons*	1	1813
'Cain's Lamentation'	1	1809
Calamy, Edmund. *An Abridgement of Mr Baxter's History of His Life* (1702)	1	1813
Chadwick. 'Exposition'	1	1777
———. 'On the Creed'	1	1777
Chauncey, Charles. *A Compleat View of Episcopacy* (1771)	2	1794, 1813
———. *Seasonable Thoughts* (1743)	1	1813
Chauncey, either Nathaniel or Charles. No title given.	1	1773
? *The Christian Faith of the Quakers* (1692)	1	1813
Christian Prudence (1766)	1	1813
'Church Constitution'	1	1791
'Church History'	3	1790–1813
'Church & Morton History'	1	1773
'Clamor of Wisdom'	1	1813
Clap, Thomas. *A Brief Vindication of the Doctrines Received and Established in the Churches of New England* (1755)	1	1755
Clarke, Samuel. *The Scripture Doctrine of the Trinity* (1712)	1	1813
Clarke. 'Sermons'	1	1813
Colman. 'Sermons'	1	1813
'Commentaries on the Book of Exodus'	1	1766
†*A Confession of Faith Owned and Consented to by the Elders and Messengers of the Churches in the Colony of Connecticut* (the Saybrook Platform) (1710)	3	1787–1813
Coryles. 'Exposition on the Book of Job'	1	1794
Darling, Thomas. *Remarks on Clap's History of the Churches* (1757)	1	1794
Darrell, William. *A Gentleman Instructed in the Conduct of a Virtuous and Happy Life* (1704)	1	1765
Defoe, Daniel. *The Family Instructor* (1715)	2	1777, 1783
———. *Religious Courtship; Being Historical Discourses on the Necessity of Marrying Religious Husbands and Wives Only* (1722)	1	1765
Derham, William. *Physico-Theology; or, a Demon-*	1	1786

Author and Title	Number of times title appears in inventories	Date of inventory
stration of the Being of God, from his Works of Creation (1713)		
Dickinson, Jonathan. *A Display of God's Special Grace* (1742)	1	1799
———. *The True Scripture-Doctrine Concerning Some Important Points of Christian Faith* (1741)	1	1783
———? 'Works'	1	1787
'The Disciple Warming Himself by the Fire'	1	1777
'Divine Analogy'	1	1809
Dodd, William. *Thoughts in Prison* (1777)	1	1797
Doddridge, Philip. 'Family Exposition'	1	1813
———. 'Lectures'	1	1813
———. 'Life'	1	1813
———. *The Rise and Progress of Religion in the Soul* (1745)	2	1789, 1813
———. *Practical Discourses on Regeneration . . . in Ten Sermons* (1742)	1	1813
———. 'Tracts, 3 vols'	1	1813
———. Unspecified works	2	1787, 1791
Dyer, William. 'Discourse'	1	1781
'Dying Man's Testament'	1	1813
Edwards, Jonathan. *An Account of the Life of . . . David Brainerd* (1749)	6	1761–1813
———. *The Great Christian Doctrine of Original Sin* (1758)	2	1789, 1813
———. *An Enquiry into the Modern Prevailing Notions Respecting Freedom of the Will* (1754)	1	1786
———. *Eighteen Sermons on Various Important Subjects* (1765)	2	1787, 1797
———. *History of the Work of Redemption* (1774)	1	1813
———. *Some Thoughts Concerning the Present Revival of Religion in New-England* (1742)	2	1765, 1777
———. *A Treatise Concerning Religious Affections* (1746)	3	1777–1813
———. 'Works' '3 vols'	1	1787
Eliot, Andrew. 'Sermon'	2	1781, 1787
Erasmus. *Twenty Select Colloquies,* tr. Sir Roger L'Estrange (1680)	1	1813
Erskine, Ebenezer. *A Collection of Sermons* (1744)	6	1761–1813
———. 'Gospel Sonnets'	1	1813
'Essays on Redeemer'	1	1791
'Explanation of ye Catticise'	1	1761

73

Author and Title	Number of times title appears in inventories	Date of inventory
'Evidences of Religion'	1	1797
Fisher. 'Works'	1	1787
Fisk, Joseph? *Anti Christ Discovered?*	1	1787
Flavel, John. *The Whole Works of . . . J. Flavel* (1701)	4	1761–94
Fleming, Robert. *The Fulfilling of the Scripture*	3	1777–86
Fleming, Robert or William? 'Works'	1	1791
Fordyce, David. *Dialogues Concerning Education* (1745)	2	1761–65
Fordyce, James. *Addresses to Young Men* (1782)	2	1797, 1813
Frothingham, Ebenezer. Title uncertain	1	1770
'? Legal[?] Gallatians'	1	1813
Gardiner, John. 'Redemption Redeemed'	1	1794
'Gerard[?] on Leviticus, 13 vols.'	1	1777
Gerard. 'Sermons'	1	1813
Gessner, Salomon. *The Death of Abel* (1761)	1	1790
Gilbert. 'Preface'	1	1813
'Godly Life'	1	1813
'Gospel Mysteries'	1	1777
'Gospel-Times, or Oaths Forbidden'?	1	1777
Greenhill, William. *An Exposition of . . . Ezekiel . . . Delivered in Several Lectures* (1662)	1	1794
Guthrie, William? 'Works' = *The Works of Mr. W. Guthrie* (1771)?	1	1791
Guyse. 'Sermons'	1	1813
Hall, Joseph. *Contemplations on the History of the New Testament* (1759)	2	1813
Harris, Henry or Matthias. 'Sermons'	4	1777–1813
Hayward, Samuel. 'Works'	1	1781
Henry, Matthew. *The Communicant's Companion*	1	1813
———. Uncertain works	2	1776, 1787
Hervey, James. *Dialogues between Theron and Aspasio*	1	1813
———. *A Collection of the Letters of James Hervey*	1	1813
———. *Meditations among the Tombs* (1746)	3	1776–1813
'History of the Martyrs'	1	1765
Hooker, Thomas. *The Application of Redemption by the Effectual Work of the Work and Spirit of Christ* (1656)	1	1764
'Hours' or 'Hornes Blessed'	1	1813
†Huntington, Joseph. *Calvinism Improved*	3	1797–1809
Jencks? 'Meditations'	1	1777
Jenyns, Soame. *A View of the Internal Evidence of the Christian Religion* (1776)	1	1790
†Johnson, Stephen. *The Everlasting Punishment of*	3	1791–1815

Author and Title	Number of times title appears in inventories	Date of inventory
the Ungodly (1786). (Johnson's son and namesake possessed 70 copies when he died in 1791.)		
Johnson, Stephen? Titles uncertain	2	1769, 1790
Kenrich, William. *The Whole Duty of Woman* (1761)	1	1769
Klopstock, Friedrich Gottlieb. *The Messiah* (1788)	1	1797
Knox, Vicesimus. *Essays Moral and Literary* (1792)	1	1813
Leslie, Charles. *The Snake in the Grass* (1696)	1	1791
The Light of the World in a Most True Relation of a Pilgrimess (1696)	1	1765
'Bishop Lin. Sermons in Fol.' =? Sanderson, Robert, Bishop of Lincoln. *XXXV Sermons* (1681)	1	1794
Locke, John. 'On the Right Use of Reason' =? J. Wynne's abridgment of the *Essay Concerning Human Understanding* (1696) or *Locke's Conduct of the Understanding* (1762)	1	1787
'Looking Glass' =? Rogers, John, 3rd, *A Looking Glass for the Presbyterians at New-London* (1767), or Hunt, Issac, *A Looking Glass for Presbyterians* (1744), or Berquin, Arnaud, *The Looking Glass for the Mind* (1794)	1	1797
Bishop Man? Title uncertain	1	1787
McEwen, William. *The Most Remarkable Types, Figures, and Allegories of the Old Testament* (1763)	1	1797
'Martyrs Book and Bible'	2	1800, 1813
Mason, John. *Penetential Cries* (1704)	1	1771
'Master Key to Popery'	1	1813
Mather, Cotton. 'Life'	1	1813
Mather, Increase. *Several Sermons* (1715)	1	1781
Mather, Samuel. 'Works'	1	1791
Mather, Increase or Samuel. 'On the scriptures'	1	1794
Mead. 'Work'	1	1791
Mercier? 'Church History'	1	1813
Morse. 'Sermons'	1	1813
Murray, James. *Sermons to Asses* (1768)	1	1813
Newman, Samuel. *A Large . . . Concordance to the Bible* (1693)	1	1813
Newton, Thomas. *Dissertations on the Prophecies* (1754)	1	1791
†Occum, Samson. 'Sermons'	1	1773
Owen. 'On Justification'	1	1813
Owen. 'Sermons'	1	1787
Parsons. 'Good News from a Far Country'	1	1813
Parsons. 'Sermons'	1	1813

Author and Title	Number of times title appears in inventories	Date of inventory
Pearson, John. *Exposition of the Creed* (1659)	1	1794
Pemberton, Ebenezer. *Practical Discourses* (1741)	1	1741
———. *Sermons on Several Subjects* (1738)	1	1738
Perkins, William. 'Divinity'	1	1786
Perry. 'Sermons'	1	1813
Pike, Samuel. 'Sermons'	1	1781
Pool. 'Annotations'	1	1813
Prideaux, Humphrey. *Bibliotheca Cornubiensis*	1	1813
Puttings. 'Discourses'	1	1813
Reid, Thomas. *Inquiry into the Human Mind* (1763)	1	1787
'Remarks on Higdon by an Englishman'	1	1813
†Rogers, John. *A Mid-Night Cry from the Temple of God to the Ten Virgins Slumbering and Sleeping* (1705)	2	1789, 1791
Rogers, John, Sr. or Jr.? 'Works'	1	1789
Romains. 'Covenant'	1	1813
Romney. 'Servants'	1	1813
Roston. 'On the Covenant'	1	1790
———. 'On the Fourfold State'	1	1790
Sault, J. *The Second Spira, Being a Fearful Example of an Atheist . . . Who Dyed in Despair* (1693)	1	1781
Saurin, Jacques. *Sermons* (1800)	1	1809
Scott, Job. *Journal of the Life . . . of Job Scott* (1797)	1	1813
'The Scripture Bishop[?] Examined'	1	1794
Seabury, Samuel. 'Sermons'	1	1813
Searl, John? 'Last [word uncertain]'	1	1770
'Self Knowledge'	1	1813
Sheppard, Thomas. Work uncertain	2	1770, 1791
Sherlock. 'On the Future State'	1	1813
Sherlock, Thomas or William. Title uncertain	1	1787
Steele, Richard. *Christian Hero* (1701)	1	1813
Stiles, Isaac. *A Prospect of the City of Jerusalem* (1742)	1	1809
Stoddard, Solomon. *The Safety of Appearing in Righteousness in Christ* (1687)	2	1783, 1813
———. 'Works'	1	1776
Strong, Nathan. *Sermons on Various Subjects* (1798–1800)	1	1815
'Sum of the Christian Religion'	1	1813
Taylor. 'Essays'	1	1813
Tennent, Gilbert? 'Works'	1	1787
'Thoughts on Life and Death'	1	1777

Author and Title	Number of times title appears in inventories	Date of inventory
'Time and the End of Time'	1	1765
'Time of Danger'	1	1777
'Treatise on Scandal'	2	1787
'Vision [of the?] New Testament'	1	1787
Walker. 'Sermons'	1	1786
Walker, Obadiah? 'Sermons'	1	1786
Waterland, Daniel. *A Vindication of Christ's Divinity* (1719)	1	1813
Watts, Isaac. 'Christian Church'	1	1813
———. *Discourses on the Love of God and Its Influence on All the Passions* (1729)	2	1787, 1813
———. 'Essays'	1	1813
———. *The Glory of Christ as God-Man*	1	1813
———. *Hymns* (1707)	5	1761–86
———. *Logick, or the Right Use of Reason in the Enquiry after Truth* (1725)	2	1777, 1813
———. 'Lyre and Poems'	1	1777
———. 'Lyrick Poems'	1	1813
———. 'Miscellaneous Thoughts'	1	1813
———. *The Psalms of David* (1719)	7	1775–97
———. *Rational Foundation of the Christian Church*	1	1813
———. 'Repentence'	1	1813
———. *Sermons on Various Subjects* (1721)	5	1765–88
———. 'Works' (edition uncertain)	1	1787
Westminster Assembly. *The Larger Catechism* (1745)	1	1813
———. *The Shorter Catechism* (1665)	2	1813
Weston. 'Revelation'	1	1813
†Wetmore, Izarhiah. *A Sermon Preached before the Honorable General Assembly* (Connecticut Election Sermon, 1773)	1	1781
Whitefield, George. *The Two First Parts of His Life* (1765)	1	1777
———. Title uncertain	1	1787
Whiston, William. 'Sermons, 2 vols' = *Memoirs of the Life and Writings of Mr. Whiston, 2 vols.* (1749–50)	1	1787
Wilby. 'Discourses'	1	1813
Wilkins, John. *A Discourse Concerning the Beauty of Providence* (1718)	1	1813
'The Will of the Lord Be Done'	1	1777
Willard, Samuel. *A Compleat Body of Divinity* (1726)	2	1765, 1813

Author and Title	Number of times title appears in inventories	Date of inventory
Willison, John. *The Balm of Gilead* (1786)	1	1787
Wise. 'Works'	1	1813
Wollaston, William. *The Religion of Nature Delineated* (1724)	2	1787, 1790
Wyeth, J. *Anguis Flagellatus, or a Switch for the Snake in the Grass* (1702)	1	1813
Young, Edward. *The Love of Fame, the Universal Passion, in Seven Characteristical Satires* (1728)	2	1784, 1797
———. *The Complaint or Night Thoughts on Life, Death, and Immortality* (1743)	2	1777, 1784
———. *The Poetical Works of the Rev. Edward Young* (1778)	1	1797
'The Young Man's Companion' (1710)	3	1777–97
'Vademecum' — several possible works	1	1781

Notes

1. Alpheus Thomas Mason, *Free Government in the Making,* 3rd ed. (New York: Oxford University Press, 1965), pp. 80–86; Bernard Bailyn, *Ideological Origins of the American Revolution* (Cambridge: Harvard University Press, 1967); Louis Hartz, *The Liberal Tradition in America* (New York: Harcourt Brace, 1955); Ray Forrest Harvey, *Jean Jacques Burlamaqui: A Liberal Tradition in American Constitutionalism* (Chapel Hill: University of North Carolina Press, 1937).

2. David L. Jacobson, ed., *The English Libertarian Heritage* (Indianapolis: Bobbs Merrill, 1965), pp. xlviii–lx.

3. About four years, 1777–81, are missing from the chronological records of inventories in the New London collection. Also, because of faulty preservation methods, the middle pages of one volume are impossible to read without destroying the pages. The probate records are in the Probate Court, Municipal Building, New London.

4. Inventories are lacking for several prominent figures in Connecticut politics; e.g., the following Connecticut delegates to the Continental Congress: Oliver Ellsworth, Stephen Mix Mitchell, Jeremiah Wadsworth, William Williams, and Oliver Wolcott. Probate papers for all Connecticut towns, including the originals of Lyme probate inventories, are in the Connecticut State Library in Hartford.

5. As George Griswold's library undoubtedly appears again in his heir's, John Griswold's, inventory of 1813, many of its titles are known.

6. A less likely possibility is Thomas Burnet's *An Appeal to Common Sense, or a Sober Vindication of Dr Woodward's State of Physick* (London, 1719).

7. Edmund Burke, "Mr. Burke's Speech on Moving his Resolutions for Conciliation with the Colonies, March 22, 1775," *The Works of the Right Honourable Edmund Burke* (Boston: West and Greenleaf, 1807), II:37.

8. One should note, however, that in his letters to the *New London Gazette* in 1765 Johnson included a reference to Algernon Sydney's *Discourses upon Government,* yet there is no reference to this large book in the minister's inventory.

9. Quoted in Mary E. Perkins, *Chronicles of a Connecticut Farm, 1769–1905* (Boston: privately printed, 1905), p. 128.

10. Its membership is given in Ezra Stiles, *The Literary Diary of Ezra Stiles,* ed. Franklin Bowditch Dexter (New York: Scribner, 1901), I:510.

11. Elisha Hall is discussed in Franklin Bowditch Dexter, *Biographical Sketches of the Graduates of Yale College* (New York: Holt, 1903).

12. Apparently Dexter did not discover anything about Baruch Beckwith's occupation, and unless another occupation is listed in the records it is usual to assume a man was a farmer. Ibid., III:472.

13. Louis Leonard Tucker, *Puritan Protagonist: President Thomas Clap of Yale College* (Chapel Hill: University of North Carolina Press, 1962); Richard Warch, *School of the Prophets: Yale College, 1701–1740* (New Haven: Yale University Press, 1973); and Louis Leonard Tucker, *Connecticut's Seminary of Sedition: Yale College* (Chester, Conn.: Pequot Press, 1974).

14. Stiles, *Literary Diary,* II:349, 387–88.

15. Thomas Clap, *The Annals or History of Yale College in New Haven* (New Haven: Hotchkiss and Mecom, 1766), p. 84.

16. William Guthrie, *A New Geographical, Historical, and Commercial Grammar and Present State of the Several Kingdoms of the World* (London: Knox, 1770), p. 156.

17. Nathaniel Shaw Woodbridge, who left Yale in 1786, owned a copy of Guthrie, and nine Lyme citizens owned at least one of Thomas Salmon's works on geography published between 1746 and 1782. Other estates contained Patrick Gordon, *Geography Anatomized* (1693) and Laurence Eachard, *Gazetteer,* also published in the seventeenth century. Sterling Library at Yale has a copy of the 1787 edition of Guthrie, underlined extensively, which suggests careful study.

18. Joseph Camp, "Notebook of Disputations," 1764–66, Manuscript Collections, Sterling Library, Yale University.

19. Roswell Grant to Ebenezer Grant, November 28, 1764, quoted in Dexter, *Biographical Sketches,* III:94.

20. Ibid., p. 170.

21. Thomas Gage to Sir William Johnson, September 20, 1765, *The Papers of Sir William Johnson,* ed. Alexander C. Flick (Albany: University of the State of New York, 1933), IV:851–52.

22. David McClure, *Diary of David McClure, Doctor of Divinity,* ed. Franklin Bowditch Dexter (New York: Knickerbocker, 1899), entry for September 13, 1769.

23. Dexter, *Biographical Sketches,* III:545–46. Originally the class limited its

announcement to a notice posted on the door of the dining hall. The story appeared in the *Connecticut Journal* for August 30, 1775.

24. Stephen Johnson, *Some Important Observations Occasioned by, and Adapted to the Publick Fast, Order by Authority, December 18, 1765* (Newport: Hall, 1766).

25. (New London: Green, 1770).

26. See, e.g., D. Hamilton Hurd, comp., *History of New London County* (Philadelphia: Lewis, 1882), p. 548.

27. Edward Elbridge Salisbury and Evelyn McCurdy Salisbury, *Family Histories and Genealogies* (privately printed, 1892), I:63n. Thomas Burnet's *Theory of the Earth* is inscribed "John McCurdy's book, in which he often likes to look, and study the wonder works of creation."

28. See Johnson to Gordon, May 8, 1776, in Salisbury and Salisbury, *Family Histories,* II:320. In another letter of the same date, Johnson again refers to Gordon. II:319.

29. William Gordon, *The History of the Rise, Progress, and Establishment of the Independence of the United States of America* (London: Dilly and Buckland, 1786), I:168.

30. Alice Mary Baldwin, *The New England Clergy and the American Revolution* (Durham: Duke University Press, 1928).

The Reverend Stephen Johnson
and the Stamp Act in Lyme:
Religious and Political Thought in
the Origins of the Revolution

BERNARD BAILYN

R ELIGION *was no singular entity in eighteenth-century American culture and it had no singular influence on the revolutionary movement: it was in itself both a stimulus and a deterrent to revolution, brought to different focuses in different ways by different men. The whole of American culture was "religious" in the sense that common modes of discourse in both ordinary life and high culture were derived from Protestant Christiantiy, and it is a gross simplification to believe that religion as such, or any of its doctrinaire elements, had a unique political role in the revolutionary movement. The effective determinants of revolution were political, and though religious ideas in general and the views of specific denominational groups in particular provided significant reinforcement to the revolutionary movement, that movement was shared equally by the Catholic Charles Carroll of Carrollton, the humanist philosophe Jefferson, the theologically liberal preacher Jonathan Mayhew, and the New Divinity Calvinist Stephen Johnson.*

Johnson was a wonderfully obscure Connecticut parson, but his writing is extremely revealing. I have sought to show, through a juxtaposition of two works written by him over the same period of weeks – the one a formal sermon, the other a series of anonymous newspaper articles – the precise role of biblical imagery and mythology in the political thought of the time. The central documents are newspaper articles, three of which, since they are important in themselves, are reprinted in Part Two.

I N A short period of weeks late in 1765 Stephen Johnson, then in his twentieth year as pastor of the First Congregational Church of Lyme, Connecticut, broke his accustomed silence on public affairs and dashed off a total of some 31,000 words directed to the problems of political liberty in general and the threat of the Stamp Act in particular.[1] The importance of this outburst, aside from the quality of the writing, flows from the fact that it took two different forms, the first a series of six anonymous newspaper articles, published in the *New London Gazette* from September 6 to November 1, 1765, three of which are republished in Part Two; the second a pamphlet, *Some Important Observations . . .*, originally a fast day sermon delivered on December 18 and published in Newport the following March.[2] The two publications are impressive; written in colorful prose, they anticipate almost the entire range of arguments that would be debated in the coming decade, and they anticipate too the fear of civil war between England and America. But their significance exceeds that. The six newspaper articles are not identified as the work of a Congregational minister; they take no singularly "Christian" point of view, and they develop purely secular arguments that rest for their effect on the evidence they mobilize, on their cogency, and on the rhetoric of their presentation. The pamphlet, on the other hand, ostensibly celebrates a religious ritual and repeats a variety of specific Protestant formulas in explaining the meaning of the public controversy. The two publications seen as products of the same clerical mind at almost the same moment in time illustrate with rare precision the relationship of religious and secular thought in the ideological history of the Revolution.

The structural relationship is perhaps most obvious. If one draws the six newspaper pieces together and views them as a unit they merge into the familiar form of a Puritan sermon.[3] There is no stated text, it is true, but the general theme is announced in the short opening article (September 6) attacking the Stamp Act and the arguments that had been set forth in the *Connecticut Gazette* by "Civis" (Jared Ingersoll) to defend it.[4] Three major "heads" of discussion are then announced (September 20), followed in the remaining issues by an elaborately subdivided discussion in the stated order of topics. The conclusion at the end of the last number (November 1) is in effect an "Application" characteristic of the sermon form: an exhortation to the audience, applying the principles of the discussion to the immediate situation; it is written in intensely emotive prose, and printed entirely in italics with heavy punctuation. The very last passage is a paean, ending with a prayerful "Amen."

It is doubtful that Johnson deliberately intended the newspaper essays to fit into the pattern of a sermon: for two decades he had cast his weekly or semi-weekly compositions in this form, and in all probability his thought simply arranged itself automatically in that way. More important than the similarity in form is the relationship in substance between the articles taken as a group and the sermon-pamphlet. Though the sermon invokes familiar religious formulas, the autonomous, self-justifying categories of thought in both the sermon and the articles are secular; they are the presuppositions, the framing notions, shared in some degree by the entire British political community, and most fully by the opposition groups; and while it is true that the Puritan tradition, like the American situation, lent particular emphasis to this widely shared body of belief and presumptions, the political ideas themselves, the attitudes, motivations, and goals expressed, are independent of a specifically Puritan, or Congregational, or even Protestant tradition.[5] Yet the religious formulas in the sermon made a great difference in the presentation and the effect of these ideas — a difference that emerges unmistakably from a close comparison of the substance of the two works.

Almost all of the contents of the five main articles fall under the first of Johnson's headings, "evils apprehended from the late measures of the British ministry." These evils as they are discussed prove to be secular evils — evils, that is, not so much in the sight of God as in the experience of men, and they are demonstrated to be such, first, rationalistically, in terms of tendencies, probabilities, and logic, and second, empirically, in terms of the record of history. In his preliminary attack (September 6) on the Stamp Act and on the ministry's claim that America was "virtually" represented in Parliament, Johnson states his case primarily by running out the logical implications of the administration's position to the point of absurdity. *Why* are we virtually represented, he asks, and *how?*

> Whether . . . because the British Parliament are an assembly of men and of the same species with us, or because they are Englishmen, as we are, or because they represent the nation from whence we descended, or because we are under the same king, or in what other view, is uncertain. In any of those (views) the boroughs and towns in England are as

virtually represented in our General Assemblies as the colonies are in Parliament. And all the Jews scattered throughout the world would be as virtually represented by a meeting of the rabbis of Hungary.

Not one member of Parliament had the consent or vote of one American, and "five hundred noughts can never make an unit." And since America could in no way be represented in England, and in addition since the colonies "have by royal grant and compact certain privileges," the colonies could not be governed in the same way that England itself was governed. To assume the opposite, Johnson declares, would lead directly to "self-repugnancy" — a concept profoundly involved in the most fundamental and subtle questions of British constitutionalism that had first been formulated by the great Chief Justice Coke in *Bonham's Case* (1610) and had recently been revived by James Otis — which served in these essays by the obscure Lyme pastor as the ultimate form of refutation.[6] For while in the context of English institutions, Parliament's power was a balancing element, contributing to the limitation of the undue use of executive power and to the protection of individual liberties, in America its rule as now asserted would be a limitless, authoritarian power, unrestrained by countervailing forces, and hence by definition anti-constitutional and illegal. If Parliament were free to impose a stamp tax on America, it could also impose

> a poll tax, a land tax, a malt tax, a cider tax, a window tax, a smoke tax, and why not tax us for the light of the sun, the air we breathe, and the ground we are buried in? If they have a right to deny us any trials by juries, they have as good a right to deny us any trials at all, and to vote away our estates and lives at pleasure.

The claim that such a power was in any way constitutional refuted itself, Johnson wrote.

The concept of "self-repugnancy" was drawn on in a variety of forms in the *Gazette* articles as Johnson worked through the details of his arguments against the new regulations. If the aim of these measures was to raise a revenue, they would defeat themselves, for the colonists "cannot have money enough but for a short time to pay these taxes. . . . And what must be the consequence but [that] their lands, the dear patrimony of their fathers . . . must pass to taskmasters here, or to men of ease and wealth in Britain who have schemed them away for nought" — an eventuality Americans would never endure "till they have lost the British spirit, are scandals to the English name, and deserve to wear an eternal chain." The result would be not only severe opposition in America but powerful resistance in England itself when trade, as it would inevitably, came to a stop, and "the merchant, the husbandmen, and the manufacturer of every sort" realized the cost to themselves. The concession that "Civis" had been obliged to make, that Americans did have "certain rights, powers, and privileges circumscribed within their respective limits," Johnson showed by a carefully drawn argument to be either precisely the rights vacated by the Stamp Act or no rights at all: "if we have not these, we have none"; if they could be rightfully taken from the colonists they would become "both rights and no rights, or ours and not ours at the same time . . . our rights only in name, but theirs in reality, which is contrary to the supposition and concession allowed us." The "grand argument" of "Civis" was therefore logically so weak "that it can by no means support itself."[7]

But the argument whose internal contradiction Johnson demonstrated with the greatest zest and originality was the claim, here directly challenged for the first time in the revolutionary literature, that Parliament's power rested on the unitary and exclusive character of sovereignty. As the sovereign power, it was claimed, Parliament had by definition "that supreme jurisdiction which . . . every supreme legislature in every state always must have over every part of the domain . . . and to suppose the contrary would be at once to destroy the very foundation and principles of all government." It was inevitable, Johnson wrote, in attempting for the first time to reply to this assertion of the meaning of sovereignty — an assertion which the British government would never withdraw, though, as Edmund Burke foresaw, it would cost England an empire — it was inevitable, Johnson said, that some such claim would be forthcoming. Whenever in history there had been "extraordinary exertions of power unsupported by reason and the constitution to be palmed upon the people" use had been made of "some favorite court maxim of a specious sound and appearance the fallacy of which few will be at pains to search out and detect." The concept of Parliamentary sovereignty when applied to the American colonies, he said, contradicted the initial premise of the argument advanced for it: that the colonies had rights subordinate to Parliament's — rights of specific validity even if "circumscribed within their respective limits." Since the purpose of all government was to secure the people in whatever rights they had,

85

what Parliament in its sovereign power was attempting to do was to secure America's rights by destroying them, an action that "savors of contradiction and is plainly self-repugnant." To preserve something by destroying it, Johnson believed, was patently absurd.

His mind instinctively sought circularities, anomalies, and contradictions. Were the new regulations and taxes justifiable as *quid pro quos* for the protection England gave the colonies? *What* protection, Johnson asked, "past — or future — or present?" *Past?* "When our forefathers were few and poor and encompassed with innumerable enemies, they greatly needed help and protection, yet then . . . they were left unassisted to their own efforts and the protection of their God." Now that the colonies were numerous and strong, and "scarce an enemy dare lift up his head in all the land" — *now* there was "concern and bustle about it," for now there was wealth "to go into the pockets of placemen and stamp officers." As for England's expenses in the recent wars, they had long since been repaid — by the capture of Cape Breton by New Englanders, by direct colonial contributions, and by the vast acquisitions (Canada, Louisiana, Florida) that had accrued to England — to *England,* "and not a farthing to these colonies." *Protection in the future?* If the colonists' limited money supply is drained off by taxes, "is our protection and security against an invasion better in this situation than with our monies and all the profits of them in our own hands?" It would in fact "expose us to be an easy prey to any enslaving power that may invade us." *For present needs?* What needs? Salaries of governors and common-law judges? "Gross stupidity and superlative nonsense." Conceding that the crown had a legal right to collect "duties upon navigation," the only visible "need" for the internal taxation of the colonies, he said, was "to support arbitrary courts of admiralty and vice-admiralty and a numerous tribe of stamp officers and taskmasters, all . . . a dead weight upon an honest, industrious community. But is this our better protection?" Or perhaps it was to support the 15,000 regular troops said to have been assigned to the colonies "to awe and keep them in order and make them to submit to these taxes, etc." But even the most craven sycophants of a power-hungry ministry should know that a standing army in time of peace was in flat contradiction to the principles of the British constitution — that it had led to the destruction of the liberties of Rome, France, "and many others" — that it had had catastrophic effects in England in the reigns of Charles I and James II — that it

86

might well give rise to "a Caesar to break off our connection with Great Britain and set up as a protector of the liberties of the colonies" — and finally that it might "plunge us here and at home into a bloody civil war, the damage of which to the nation an hundred thousand hireling scribblers could not countervail."[8]

The evidence of history, Johnson pointed out, was compelling. Assuming, as almost every writer of the time did, that "human nature [was] the same as in foregoing ages, and that like causes will have like effects,"[9] what, he asked, were the likely consequences of the new measures? Throughout history such grievances had caused "the most terrible civil wars and rivers of blood in England." The threat to immemorial rights had caused the Barons' War under King John; the raising of taxes without consent and the creation of "arbitrary courts . . . corruption of trials . . . trampling upon the privileges of royal charters . . . the refusing to hear petitions . . . arbitrary suspense of laws" had resulted in the Glorious Revolution.[10]

The pattern of these crises was only too clear. A ruthless gang of corrupt power-seekers panics a weak but liberty-loving nation with cries, first of nonexistent dangers, then of the immediate need for "better security and protection"; deliberately misinforms and deludes an essentially right-minded sovereign into building up instruments of power (new offices to buy the allegiance of public people; standing armies to intimidate the private) which it and not the sovereign would know how to use in a crisis; and finally begins its assault on the most vulnerable member of the body politic, gradually working inward to the heart.[11]

So in the present circumstances, Johnson writes, the ministry attempts to panic the nation with unreal dangers, among them the fear that the colonies were secretly plotting to throw off their dependence on England; then undertakes new programs — of trade regulation, of tax collection — to multiply the "places" at its disposal and to weaken the capacity to resist; finds excuses to station troops in America; deliberately misinforms the Crown about conditions in the colonies; and step by step moves closer to its ultimate goal, the destruction of liberty everywhere in the British world. For if the liberties of Americans are most immediately affected by the Stamp Act,

> in the conclusion it may equally affect the subjects in Britain and Ireland. If the colonies are enslaved, no doubt Ireland will soon be stamped and enslaved also . . . nothing but expediency now restrains

from taxing Ireland . . . , and if this succeeds it will be so great an accession to the number of placemen and to the power of the m——y that the inexpediency will soon be got over as to Ireland also; and then I conceive the liberty of Great Britain will be worth very little and cannot long survive.[12]

Parliament, moving gradually at the will of an imperious ministry, "first on the colonies — then upon Ireland — then upon Great Britain itself,"[13] could destroy the liberties of England. But in the end, the effort, Johnson concluded, was not likely to succeed. For America would rise to its dangers and fight for its freedom — with two possible consequences. If the English people and their government responded wisely to the colonists' resistance, these early efforts of the ministry would be reversed, the chief manipulators cast out, and the country and its empire put back on their former course. If the proper responses were not forthcoming, the result would be, not ministerial success but "a very fatal civil war": "such a revolt and wide breach" between England and America "as could never be healed"; "a bloody civil war in which, by sending away their men of war and forces against America [the English people] would have everything to fear — from the sword in their own bowels from the power of France and Spain and the invasion of the Pretender, who would not fail to improve such an opportunity"; a "most unnatural war with the colonies," resulting not only in "the loss of two million of the best affected subjects" but also "one third, some say one half, of the profits of the national trade." He hoped, however, "in the mercy of God, things may never be pushed to this bloody! this dreadful issue! which must be attended with infinite ill consequences to the mother country and colonies, and, considering the advantage France and Spain would certainly make of such a crisis, could scarce fail of ending in the ruin of England and America." Americans must prevent it from happening not only by being generally vigilant at this early stage but by launching a specific program of action, which Johnson crisply outlined: investigation of the truth; petition for redress; propaganda to counter the misinformation ("printing and dispensing many thousands of tracts . . . it can't fail of a great and good effect"); and the organization of resistance on a continental scale.[14]

Johnson's six newspaper articles, written and published in a short period of time in the fall of 1765, encapsulate almost the entire range of arguments and issues that would be discussed in the decade that followed. They bring to bear on the Stamp Act crisis the everyday inheritance of British political thought, and while occasional phrases and references — "taskmasters," "counsellors of Rehoboam's stamp" — reveal a mind attuned to the language of the Bible, they can in no significant way be described as derivatives or applications of essentially religious ideas. There is scarcely a notion in the series that is not squarely compatible with, if not essentially repetitive of, ideas that had been familiar in opposition writing, including that of the most un-Puritan Bolingbroke, for half a century, or that would not be advocated in the coming years by Americans of every denomination and persuasion and by Englishmen as different as Burke and Priestley. How does Johnson's fast day sermon, *Some Important Observations*, preached from the pulpit of Lyme's First Congregational Church and written at almost the same time as the *New London Gazette* articles, relate to the six essays?

Johnson's fast day sermon translates the political arguments of the six essays into a universal and categorical language of the highest moral sanction. Setting out "to arouse and animate" his listeners by laying before them an ultimate extrapolation of their problems, he associates the colonists' situation with that of the Jews oppressed in Egypt, not by explicitly analogizing the two but by conflating themes and episodes; and he then probes in this cosmically dilated example "the general nature and consequences" of the category of evil the colonists were faced with. The four main headings he lists at the start and follows in the body of the sermon are topics that allow him to examine in the magnification of the Bible story implications too subtle or too extravagant for the crude and still unresolved politics of the Stamp Act crisis, and to do this in a mode of discourse so deeply familiar to his audience and so much a part of their moral universe as to command their immediate assent.[15]

The conflation of the biblical and secular historical worlds — a process familiar to every eighteenth-century preacher and for which there existed an authoritative model in Samuel Shuckford's famous *"Connection" : The Sacred and Prophane History of the World Connected* (1728)[16] — is continuous throughout the sermon, and it results not in a single sustained identification of images but in a shifting series of overlays — of individuals, events, and statements — the net impact of which is an unspecified yet comprehensive portrayal of seventeenth-

and eighteenth-century problems in biblical terms. So, in this costume drama, the Old Testament Jews descended into Egypt in the condition of the Puritans escaping from Archbishop Laud: they were a "free people . . . they had a right to freedom afterwards, as they had done nothing to forfeit it, and no man nor nation had a right to take it from them." Then the image blurs in the confusing identification of Indians and Egyptians, but quickly refocuses on Pharaoh and the Stuarts. The Mosaic confrontation becomes the Exclusion Crisis, with Pharaoh exercizing the Stuarts' dispensing power, to his own inevitable doom, as once again "cruel oppressions prove the means of [a free people's] deliverance." The focus shifts ("so it happened in the case of Rehoboam's oppression of the ten tribes"), shifts again ("so also in the oppression of Holland, which brought on the revolution and independency of those high and mighty states"), and shifts again ("and it is possible that sooner or later it may happen to the British colonies"), and yet again (for "Rome fell by corruption"), and settles into one of the great flights of rhetoric on the theme of corruption (the purest milk of eighteenth-century opposition thought) in the literature of the Revolution:

> If the British empire should have filled up the measure of its iniquity and become ripe for ruin; if a proud, arbitrary, selfish, and venal spirit of corruption should ever reign in the British court and diffuse itself through all ranks in the nation; if lucrative posts be multiplied without necessity and pensioners multiplied without bounds; if the policy of governing be by bribery and corruption, and the trade and manufactures of the nation be disregarded and trampled under foot; if all offices be bought and sold at a high and extravagant price, which in the end must come out of the subject in exorbitant fees of office or lawless exactions; and if, to support these shocking enormities and corruptions, the subjects in all quarters must be hard squeezed with the iron arms of oppression — thence we may prognosticate the fall of the British empire — its glory is departing — the grand pillars of the state tremble, and are ready to fail.[17]

The king is Pharaoh — the king is James II — Charles I — *Ahasuerus*, "when Esther must go in to petition the king (in the time of great calamity, great like ours, yea greater than ours)." The conflation is continuous and infinitely flexible. So "there arose a new king over Egypt, which knew not Joseph" — that is to say, who was "willfully ignorant, or very ungratefully forgetful, of the eminent services done to the nation by the Jews" — which is to say, ungrateful and forgetful "of the good services the colonists have done for Great

Britain . . . services in which the colonists, at a vast expense of blood, toil, and treasure, have greatly contributed to the wealth, power, and glory of the British empire" — though Britain "knew not Joseph."[18]

This fusion, abstraction, and magnification of the immediate, parochial world into a mythic, dilated universe allow Johnson to probe freely the hidden impulses and the ultimate dangers of the problems the colonists faced. Slipping easily from the biblical *ur*-world to present-day realities, he expounds at length the innocence not only of "our gracious King (whom God forever bless)," but of Parliament and the British people in general, and fixes the blame for the present calamities on those latter-day Hamans, "the late British ministry" and their tools and hangers-on in England and America. Their ambitions are nothing new; such lusts as theirs are immemorial, elemental, racial; and their techniques of corruption are as patterned as the movements of the tides. Inevitably they promote falsehoods calculated to panic the innocent; inevitably they raise the cry that a peaceful subordinate people plans to rise in rebellion. Thus Exodus i, 9, 10, 11: "Come on, let us deal wisely with them, least . . . when there falleth out any war, they join also unto our enemies . . . and so get them up out of the land." Here, Johnson writes, "here you have the grand, the whole strength of the enslaving cause; nothing can be added to it of any avail." For designers of "enslaving measures" needed then what they need now and always will need: a "colorable show of necessary, deep, refined policy," and they therefore devised the "plausible pretext of danger of Israel's independency." Some such "popular turns" must always be given to efforts of this sort "otherwise they are so abominable to nature they cannot go down with a people of common sense and honesty." And so, educated by this "specimen of what has been commonly practiced by arbitrary enslavers in all ages," the colonists must be quick to respond to false accusations of seeking independence from England. They must be quick to point out (as Johnson does at great length) that such dark and false prophecies of colonial independence, if acted upon, will inevitably become self-fulfilling, as they did in the case of the ten tribes, in the oppression of Holland, in the deliverance from Egypt — " 'violent arbitrary oppressions has drove the oppressed into that state of independency which the oppressors feared and the oppressed by no means desired.' " Given a "wise, kind, and gentle administration of the colonies: they have no temptation to independency," but if "there be left to the colonies but this single, this dreadful alternative — slavery or independency — they will not want time to deliberate which to choose." Take warning in time, therefore; forestall the choice of such alternatives, and put to use the ample securities that are part of the "transcendent excellencies of the British constitution," the greatest instrument for the protection of freedom ever devised by the wit of man.[19]

The sermon probes motives, explains tendencies, counsels action, on the basis not simply of reason and ordinary historical evidence but of what are seen as the profoundest experiences of the human race. It translates political arguments into cosmic imperatives, and freed thereby from the restraints of ordinary debate, presents a magnified version of present problems that is at once clearer, less tractable, and politically more dangerous than what had appeared in the *Gazette* essays. In this way, and not because of its putative Calvinist derivation or the ritual "jeremiad" that Johnson includes toward the end, the fast day sermon — a brilliant performance of its kind — reveals the force of religious ideas in the process by which political arguments became a revolutionary creed.

Johnson's publications in the fall of 1765, together with the Lyme Resolves against the Stamp Act, which he either wrote or inspired,[20] are the highlights of his public career. Little otherwise is known about him. A graduate in 1743 of Yale College, of which he became a fellow thirty years later, he married three times, fathered eight children, was appointed pastor of the Lyme church in 1746 at the age of twenty-two, and served there successfully and contentedly until his death forty years later. In theology he was conservative, an adherent of the severely predestinarian New Divinity, publishing in the year of his death a 400-page treatise attacking Universalist heresies and the notion "that the end of the creation of the moral world was the happiness of the creature."[21] His only other publication is his election sermon of 1770, an ordinary performance that follows the formulas of the genre closely and without flair.[22] Legend has it that his remarkable outburst of 1765 was inspired by a neighbor of his, one John McCurdy.[23] It may be more reasonable to suppose that Johnson's mind and imagination simply took fire in the explosive atmosphere of the Stamp Act crisis and burned briefly with a hard and brilliant flame.

Notes

1. The only biographical account of Stephen Johnson (1724–86) is that of Franklin B. Dexter, in *Biographical Sketches of the Graduates of Yale College* (New York: H. Holt, 1885–1912), I:738–40, but it is little more than a rudimentary summary of his career. Edward E. Sill's *A Forgotten Connecticut Patriot*, in *Publications of the Connecticut Society of the Order of the Founders and Patriots of America*, no. 4 (New Haven: Tuttle, Morehouse, and Taylor, 1901), intended as a biographical essay on Johnson, is in fact a dismal antiquarian discourse and contains nothing substantive on Johnson. The only serious attention that has hitherto been given to Johnson's writing is that by Alice M. Baldwin in her still exceedingly valuable book, *The New England Clergy and the American Revolution* (Durham, N.C.: Duke University Press, 1928), especially pp. 99–102, 130, 64.

2. The attribution of authorship of the articles to Johnson was made explicitly by Ezra Stiles, who wrote at the bottom of the first page of his personal copy of the last of the articles, "This is part of a publication in five New London papers, by the Reverend Stephen Johnson," and added at the end of the piece, "By Stephen Johnson, AM and Pastor of the First Church in Lyme." Stiles Papers, Yale University. There can be little doubt of the accuracy of Stiles's information. He knew Johnson well. It was Johnson, in 1777, then a member of the Yale Corporation, who conveyed to Stiles the offer of the Yale presidency and who negotiated the appointment with him. Johnson preached in Stiles's pulpit that year, and Stiles stayed at Johnson's house when his travels took him to Lyme. Their official relationship kept them in close contact in the final decade of Johnson's life. Edmund S. Morgan, *The Gentle Puritan* (New Haven: Yale University Press, 1962), pp. 292, 295; *The Literary Diary of Ezra Stiles*, ed. Franklin B. Dexter (New York: C. Scribner, 1901), II:215, III:95. It was probably through Stiles that in 1788 Johnson's authorship of the articles first became public knowledge since it was in all likelihood Stiles who supplied the information to William Gordon for publication in his *History of the Rise, Progress, and Establishment of the Independence of the United States of America* ... (London: the author, 1788), where it appears in vol. I:168; cf. Morgan, *Gentle Puritan*, p. 405. There is in addition a variety of stylistic idioms that occur both in Johnson's *Important Observations* and in the articles (repetitions for rhetorical effect, for example: "all, all is gone" [*Observations*, p. 7]; "liberty once lost, how hardly, hardly regained" [*New London Gazette*, September 6, 1765]; "as a great family, who perished in Holland for far, far less provocation" [ibid., November 1]). On the recurrence of the concept of "self-repugnancy" in the two publications, see below, note 6.

3. On the structure of the Puritan sermons, see A. W. Plumstead, ed., *The Wall and the Garden* (Minneapolis: University of Minnesota Press, 1968), pp. 31–37, and the works cited there, especially Babette M. Levy, *Preaching in the First Half Century of New England History* (Hartford: American Society of Church History, 1945), ch. 5.

4. "Civis" 's essays, digested in Johnson's replies, appeared in the *Connecticut Gazette*, August 16 and 23, 1765. For a discussion of Ingersoll's role in the controversy, see Lawrence H. Gipson, *Jared Ingersoll* (New Haven: Yale University Press, 1920), pp. 161–64.

5. They were, for example, fully shared by American Catholics such as Charles Carroll of Carrollton; see Bernard Bailyn, ed., *Pamphlets of the American Revolution* (Cambridge: Belknap Press of Harvard University Press, 1965), I:57–58, 606, and the references cited there and on pp. 741 and 743. There is no support whatever in Johnson's writings for the belief that there is a fundamental difference between "rationalist ministers" like Jonathan Mayhew and Calvinist New Divinity men like Johnson in their reliance on reason in discussing civil government and politics. Cf. Alan Heimert, *Religion and the American Mind, from the Great Awakening to the Revolution* (Cambridge: Harvard University Press, 1966), passim, especially pp. 240–41.

6. On the background of the use of the concept of "self-repugnancy" as the basis for and meaning of judicial "voidance" of legislative enactments and on the importance of the idea in Otis's thought, see Bailyn, *Pamphlets,* I:412–17. The idea serves the same purpose and is used in almost identical phraseology in Johnson's sermon, *Some Important Observations:* "No obedience is required by civil constitutions to edicts unconstitutional and subversive of its fundamental privileges. They cannot bind; it is a flagrant absurdity to suppose a free constitution empowers any to decree or execute its own destruction. For such a militating self-repugnancy in a constitution necessarily carries its own destruction in it." P. 21.

7. The quotations in the paragraph are taken from the *New London Gazette* articles, issues of October 4, November 1, and October 11.

8. The quotations in the two preceding paragraphs are all taken from the *Gazette* article of October 11.

9. For illustrations, see Bailyn, *Pamphlets,* I:55, n. 28, and the expansion of the point in Bailyn, *The Ideological Origins of the American Revolution* (Cambridge: Belknap Press of Harvard University Press, 1967), p. 85, n. 31.

10. *New London Gazette,* October 4.

11. Ibid., November 1.

12. Ibid., November 1.

13. Ibid., October 11.

14. Ibid., October 4 and November 1.

15. *Observations,* pp. 4, 5.

16. Shuckford's *"Connection,"* which, to judge from a footnote reference on page 16 of the pamphlet, Johnson had at his side as he wrote the sermon, was an effort to complete the earlier work of the orientalist Humphrey Prideaux, who in his *Old and New Testament Connected . . .,* 2 vols. (London: n.p., 1716–18), had combined scriptural and secular sources to write the history of the world from the point the Old Testament leaves off to where the New Testament begins. Shuckford's aim was to write a similarly composite history of the world, conflating biblical and secular sources, from the creation of the world to the point Prideaux picked the story up. The task remained unfinished at

his death (1754), but the volumes he did complete were often reprinted in the mid-eighteenth century and became a standard reference work, especially for the clergy. The task that Shuckford originally undertook was completed a century later by Michael Russell, the prolific bishop of Glasgow and Galloway, in his *Connection . . . To Complete the Works of Shuckford and Prideaux . . .*, 3 vols. (London: n.p., 1827). Though Shuckford himself had no political goal in writing the book, the information he assembled and even more the method he used proved invaluable for writers like Johnson who did. For other references to Shuckford in the pamphlets of the Revolution, see Bailyn, *Pamphlets,* I:28 and n. 15.

17. Quotations are from *Observations,* pp. 6, 15, 19, 20.

18. Ibid., pp. 39, 16, 17.

19. Ibid., pp. 14, 13, 19, 19–20, 29.

20. Excerpts from the Lyme Resolves are printed in Baldwin, *New England Clergy,* pp. 177–78. For full text see Part Two. pp. 224–26.

21. Morgan, *Gentle Puritan,* pp. 416, 172ff.; Stephen Johnson, *The Everlasting Punishment of the Ungodly* . . . (New London: T. Green, 1786), p. v.

22. Stephen Johnson, *Integrity and Piety the Best Principles of a Good Administration of Government* . . . (New London: T. Green, 1770).

23. Martha J. Lamb, "Judge Charles Johnson McCurdy, 1797–1891," *Magazine of American History* 26 (1891):331; Gordon, *History,* I:168.

Matthew Griswold: Lyme's Revolutionary Magistrate

JOHN W. IFKOVIC

THE long and distinguished public career of Gov. Matthew Griswold of Lyme was most directly the product of the assiduous employment of his own considerable and varied natural abilities. It also had the advantage of a respected name, well established by three previous generations of Griswolds. Two Griswold brothers, Edward and the first colonial Matthew, came from England to Connecticut about 1639 and settled at Windsor. Either just before or just after marrying Anna Wolcott, Matthew left for Saybrook, then encompassing land on both sides of the mouth of the Connecticut River, where he served as business agent for George Fenwick, head of the settlement. In 1645 Fenwick granted Griswold a large tract of land on the east side of the river.[1] This estate was first called Black's Hall, presumably because Griswold built on it a log hut for a Negro, and from this came Black Hall, the name of the Griswold property up to the present time.[2]

Not long after his arrival Matthew Griswold actively participated in the public affairs of Saybrook. In 1654 he was a deputy to the General Court. He also belonged to several committees concerned with boundary disputes between New London and Saybrook, and to another one appointed to survey the outlands of the town for the purpose of dividing it into several quarters. When "the Loving Parting" took place and the land on the eastern side of the Connecticut River was set apart in 1665 as the town of East Saybrook, called Lyme after 1667, Matthew Griswold signed the articles of separation as a committeeman for the east side. His continuous rise to prominence in the new town is evident in the fact that he thrice represented Lyme in the General Court and served in several other public offices.[3] When Griswold became one of Lyme's proprietors with the right to control the town's undivided lands in 1685, he assured himself and his descendants a secure place in the upper levels of Lyme's social and economic structure.[4]

The second Matthew Griswold, oldest son of Matthew and Anna Wolcott Griswold and grandfather of Gov. Matthew Griswold, was born in 1653.[5] He increased his legacy through a career similar to his father's. For several terms he served as deputy for Lyme to the colonial legislature.[6] The second Matthew Griswold was also one of three school committee members chosen in September 1695 "to agree and covenant with a schoolmaster."[7] Upon his father's death in 1698, he received the title to the old gentleman's estate, to which he added by purchase. In May 1683 he married Phoebe Hyde, and they had eleven children.[8] Because the third Matthew Griswold, the couple's first son, spent five adventurous years at sea and died unmarried at the age of twenty-four, John, the eldest surviving son, inherited a double portion of his father's estate, to which he also added land.[9] Although he was prominent in many civic matters, John Griswold's public activities were evidently confined to Lyme, where he was a justice of the peace and served on a committee charged with hiring a schoolmaster and building two schoolhouses.[10] Known as "Judge John," he was a man of great wealth and much esteemed for wisdom and integrity. No doubt these traits and his vast inheritance made him eligible in 1713 to marry Hannah Lee, the daughter of Thomas Lee, the largest landholder in Lyme after John's father.[11] The first of their eleven children was a son, the fourth Matthew Griswold, born on March 25, 1714.[12] In years to come his career would enhance the public esteem for three generations of Griswolds and place it among those familiar surnames associated with leadership in Connecticut through the trying years of the imperial crisis, the Revolution, and the early republic.

Just how important Matthew Griswold's first twenty years in Lyme were in making the statesman of later years is difficult to determine. His only formal education may have been the rather rudimentary instruction available in one of Lyme's two schools, held for four months of the year in rooms rented in private houses on both sides of the Black Hall River. Or perhaps he attended one of the two new district schools built in 1725, but most likely he studied at the school west of the Black Hall River.[13]

No doubt other events in Lyme had a strong influence on Griswold's development. By 1727 the town had three ecclesiastical societies, with Black Hall a part of the First Society.[14] When the religious revival known as the Great Awakening enveloped Connecticut, the three churches of Lyme were all affected in varying degrees, and the First Society received revivalist preachings with great enthusiasm. Beginning in March 1731, its minister was Jonathan Parsons, who married Matthew's sister, Phoebe, on December 14 of that year. The officiating clergyman was Rev. George Griswold, Matthew's uncle, and, from 1724 to 1761, the minister of Lyme's Second Society. The couple were the parents of the revolutionary patriot and soldier Samuel Holden Parsons.[15] Soon after his appointment, Parsons renounced the Saybrook Platform, which had Presbyterianized Connecticut's ecclesiastical organization.[16] When he heard the great revivalist George Whitefield preach in 1740, he announced immediately his conversion.[17] Parsons changed his mode of preaching to the revivalist style, the effects of which, according to his own account, were that "great numbers cried aloud in the anguish of their souls. Several stout men fell as though a cannon ball had been discharged, and a ball had made its way through their hearts. Some young women were thrown into hysteric fits."[18]

The influence of his preaching is evident in the addition of 150 new members to his church between April 1741 and February 1742.[19] Among the many saved was Matthew Griswold, who became a church member on June 7, 1741.[20] Evidence of the permanence of Griswold's conversion is clear in the remarks of the Reverend Lathrop Rockwell delivered at the time of Griswold's death:

> He was a firm believer in revelation, and the system of grace and salvation by a crucified Savior. By a virtuous godly life, he exhibited charitable evidence of the sincerity of his profession, which he adorned with the graces of humility, meekness and charity. He exhibited in his conduct the real fruits of religion, which excited in his own breast a rational hope of future happiness.[21]

Opponents of the revival in Lyme's First Church, known as Old Lights, organized a successful movement to expel the Reverend Mr. Parsons.[22] No member of the Griswold family, however, is on record as an advocate of Parsons's removal.[23] Parsons's dismissal was only a temporary setback for the New Light faction, as supporters of the revival were called, because the even more liberal and outspoken Stephen Johnson became minister of the First Society in 1746.[24] Some opposition to his ministry appeared in 1759, but the following year a committee including Matthew Griswold decided not to terminate Johnson's ministry.[25] The increasing membership under his generally popular leadership and the significant number of New Lights in the First Society's church government illustrate the revivalists' continued dominance in Lyme's First Church.[26]

Matthew Griswold's New Light affiliation is apparent in the date of his church membership and possibly in his continued prominence in the affairs of Lyme's First Society. He was clerk of the society from 1742 through 1748, a member of the society committee in 1760, and moderator for the society meetings in December 1760 and January 1766. He belonged to other society committees until the mid-1760s, when the burgeoning imperial crisis began to demand a greater portion of his time.[27] No doubt Matthew's New Light leanings were reinforced by his uncle, the Reverend George Griswold, who in "the great revival of 1740," it was said, was in "full accord with his neighbor, Jonathan Parsons. . . ."[28]

It is hardly surprising that Matthew Griswold, as an eastern Connecticut New Light, would be devoted to the patriot cause as the town of Lyme and the colony of Connecticut responded to British attempts of imperial reorganization during the 1760s. The Great Awakening, along with other issues, divided Connecticut along east-west lines and placed many of her citizens in direct opposition to their rulers. The Old Lights, concentrated in western Connecticut, sought to restrain the advance of the New Lights, concentrated in the east, in their assault upon Connecticut's religious order, and aroused the easterners to organize resistance during the next twenty years.[29] When the hated stamp tax was imposed in 1765, Matthew Griswold and other eastern Connecticut New Lights were prepared to resist once again with similar religious fervor.[30]

The years of conflict with Great Britain were more than two decades away, however, when Matthew Griswold's religious conversion coincided with thoughts about marriage. At first his attentions went to a young lady from Durham. At that time he was merely a good-looking young farmer, and she thought she might hold him in reserve while hoping to get a better offer from a young physician. Aware of the situation, young Matthew pressed the lady for a decision. When she told him she needed more time, he was said to have responded, "Madam, you may have your lifetime." She, indeed, took her lifetime, for she never married.[31]

Naturally diffident and shy, Matthew Griswold must have become somewhat silent and reluctant to declare his love a second time. He was rescued from this predicament by his second cousin, Ursula Wolcott of Windsor. She realized that he would one day be the possessor of a fine house and much property in addition to the already distinguished name and would, no doubt, make a fine husband. After a series of visits to Black Hall, Ursula decided she had to take the initiative. When she met him from time to time about the house, she reputedly asked, "What did you say, Cousin Matthew?" He invariably replied, "Nothing." Finally, meeting him on the steep, narrow, winding staircase, she again asked, "What did you say, Cousin Matthew?" "Oh, nothing," he again answered. "Well, it is time you did," Ursula insisted. Matthew did, and the couple were married on November 10, 1743.[32]

Matthew and Ursula were the parents of seven children, five of whom reached adulthood. The death of their first child, Ursula, in infancy was, doubtless, a shock to the young couple. The death of their second child, Hannah, on December 15, 1755, at the age of only nine years and seven months also severely saddened her parents.[33] On the following day Matthew Griswold expressed his sorrow to his father-in-law and revealed his deep paternal love, strong religious faith, and determination to rise above adversity. Death had taken from her parents, he wrote, "a dear and tender child who on account of some enviable qualities which as I imagined appeared in her in an uncommon degree with a most exemplary and dutiful behavior . . . extremely endeared her to her parents. . . ." He described the child's "calm and serene temper of mind" because she had made her "peace with God." The bereaving father concluded:

> Indeed the satisfactory account she gave how she had seen herself a sinner and of the love of God manifested to her soul and a sense of her love to God, and willingness to part with the world with the surprising unshaken fortitude of mind with which she was carried through the agonies of death afford us unspeakable comfort, but to human nature the blow is violent and the wound deep. I beg your prayers to almighty God that we might be supported under this bereaving stroke, and not

murmur or repine at the dispensation of heaven and by such undutiful behavior make this chastisement a new occasion of sin.[34]

Matthew Griswold encouraged the practice of virtue and religion in the lives of his children. More than twenty years later he wrote to give advice to his son, Matthew, while the young man was a student at Yale College. After informing his son that the family, "through Divine Goodness," was in good health and explaining that the enclosed thirty-dollar bill was for the purchase of a ticket in the continental lottery, the solicitous father concluded:

> I hope you will pursue your studies with diligence and industry. But above all keep holy the Sabbath Day and pay all possible regard to religion; a virtuous life is the only foundation upon which you can depend to be comfortable here and happy in the coming world, the joy of your friends and a blessing to the world.[35]

The Griswolds indeed set the proper parental example, the proof of which lay in their offspring's own accomplishments.

Matthew Griswold, however, did not rely on the achievements of his ancestors and relatives for a distinguished public career. While still in his late twenties he undertook the study of law. Notwithstanding Matthew's lack of formal education, President Stiles of Yale College said that he "fitted for college" and "studied law *proprio marte,* bought him the first considerable law library in Connecticut . . . a great reader of law."[36] Securing a legal education in mid-eighteenth-century Connecticut was difficult since there were few trained lawyers in the colony. Aspiring lawyers most often read Thomas Wood's *Institutes* and Coke's *Institutes,* while actual training was acquired by following the law courts and listening to trials.[37] Matthew successfully met the challenge and was admitted to the bar by the New London County Court in November 1742.[38]

Griswold's law practice, generally speaking, was a successful one, perhaps because he was, according to the Reverend Lathrop Rockwell, "sincere in all his professions of friendship," which brought him "the confidence and esteem of a numerous and extensive acquaintance."[39] Soon after admittance to the bar, he represented the Town of Lyme before the County Court in a case against New London. He was also an agent for Lyme when it successfully opposed in court a group of petitioners who wanted to build a highway in the town. In November 1743 Griswold was appointed king's attorney for the county of New London, a position he served with "integrity and reputation" until 1766. As Griswold's legal reputation grew, other appointments were offered. He was made an agent for New London County in 1754, 1757, and 1762.[40] With William Samuel Johnson, another prominent attorney, he represented the town of Plainfield in Windham County before the General Assembly during its May 1757 session.[41]

Much of Griswold's practice apparently dealt with the collection of debts and the settling of estates. He was asked by Thomas Cushing of Boston, for example, to obtain all available information on a late Mr. Winthrop's deed to his son in London, a document Cushing suspected may have been a contrivance to defraud the late Winthrop's creditors.[42] Unfortunately, Samuel Avery was being sued for debt while at the same time employing Griswold to collect debts owed him.[43] Griswold advised Avery to pay his creditors whatever he could: if "the gentlemen see their money is coming," Griswold suggested, "they will be more contented, though but part of it."[44]

Among the many indications of Griswold's legal prominence was the great quantity of his correspondence with William Samuel Johnson, one of Connecticut's recognized leaders at the bar by mid-century.[45] Another indication of respect for an attorney's professional ability was measured by his popularity as a teacher.[46] Just how many lawyers Griswold trained is difficult to determine, but his nephew, Samuel Holden Parsons, studied law under his uncle Matthew and was admitted to the bar in 1759.[47] Griswold's law collection, about two hundred books by 1790, reflected the broadening and deepening interests of his later career and indicated he was one of a comparatively new group of legal specialists in Connecticut.[48] Considering his professional prestige, his law library, and his professional association with Connecticut's most eminent attorneys, it is hardly surprising that Matthew Griswold would be called to public service.

Griswold began his new career as early as 1739, when Connecticut's General Assembly appointed him captain of the south company or trainband in the Town of Lyme.[49] He was first elected to serve in the General Assembly as a deputy for Lyme in October 1748. The citizens of Lyme conferred this honor again in May 1751 and every year from 1754 through 1759, for both the regular and special sessions of the General Assembly.[50] While a member of the Assembly, upon the death of Samuel Lynde he was appointed an overseer of the Mohegan Indians "to lease out the lands, oversee, order and take care of the estate and affairs of the said Indians."[51] He held this position until October 1769.[52] As an overseer and a member of the committee for the defense of the colony in the notorious Mohegan case, a dispute over lands in eastern Connecticut, Griswold wrote some lengthy remarks to William Samuel Johnson, also a defender of Connecticut's interest in the case.[53]

These remarks give some indication of Griswold's views on property rights: "If we consider the foundation of the Indian title at the time of the first coming of the English into America," he wrote, "it must fall vastly short of coming up to those transactions by which absolute property is acquired . . . by the laws of nations." He went on:

> They [the Indians] wandered up and down from place to place like vagabonds in the earth, never secured lands and when they set down in one place they soon removed to another without leaving the least trace or footsteps of any claim to future improvement. This evidently was their immemorial practice. Nor could their rambles in hunting which mainly consisted in only a transient walking upon the ground give life to absolute property.

Because the English, with the Indians' permission, came and built houses, cleared and fenced in the land, and declared "to the world they designed to secure them to their posterity," they, and not the Indians, had established their rights to the property. Would turning "many hundred families out of doors into the state of beggars and giving the Indians the benefit of their houses and improvements for which they never labored," asked Griswold, be "doing justice to the faithful subjects of the king?"[54] While acknowledging little understanding of Indian customs, he nonetheless believed faithful subjects of the English sovereign had a right to the fruits of their labors. For over a century the Griswold family had improved and enjoyed the land and buildings of Black Hall while remaining faithful to their king. When the right was threatened, not by Indian claimants, but by royal power itself, Matthew Griswold would again join in the protest.

Public service in both colonial and early national Connecticut was dominated by old established families, successful merchants, large landowners, and prominent attorneys. Both seniority and faithful, efficient service were traditionally rewarded by successive elections and by promotion to more prestigious offices.[55] By returning Matthew Griswold to the General Assembly for more than a decade, the citizens of Lyme had already recognized these attributes in their representative. Recognition by voters beyond the bounds of Lyme was evident as early as 1749, when Griswold was considered for nomination to the prestigious Council, the colonial legislature's upper house.[56] More than the Lower House, the twelve-member Council represented Connecticut's aristocracy, which the method of election reinforced.[57] In 1753 and 1754 Griswold received even more votes for nomination to the Council and finally in 1755 was actually nominated and placed twentieth on the list, with 970 votes.[58] He was again nominated in 1756, 1757, and 1758 with a steadily increasing popular vote placing him higher each year on the nomination list.[59] In May 1759, with 1,740 votes, he was finally elected to the Council.[60]

Each year for ten consecutive years the citizens of Connecticut elected the assistant from Lyme to the Council with an ever increasing popular vote at both nomination and election times. Very often he outpolled all others on the nomination list, including even the governor and deputy governor, as well as at May elections.[61] Griswold never betrayed the trust of Connecticut's citizens, and attended all regular and special sessions during his decade of service.[62] He served on several committees during his tenure, including those which considered amending Connecticut's laws in 1764 and the committee which each year counted votes.[63]

More than anything else, Griswold's patriotism during the decade of impending revolution gained him the deep respect and gratitude of all of Connecticut's citizens. When news of the Stamp Act first reached the colony in 1765, there was immediate resistance. Town meetings, newspapers, and Congregational ministers led the verbal attack.[64] New Light minister Stephen Johnson was one of the first spokesmen in Lyme and published five articles in the *New London Gazette* attacking the Stamp Act as a violation of colonial rights.[65] Lyme's citizens responded by passing an anti–Stamp Act resolution which closely resembled Johnson's arguments and phraseology. A large delegation of Lyme's citizens was among the five hundred men who met Jared Ingersoll at Hartford to demand his resignation as Connecticut's stamp distributor.[66] Surely Matthew Griswold shared the sentiments and perhaps even participated in these actions of his fellow townsmen, actions which must have encouraged him to further resistance as a member of the Council.

In spite of Connecticut's overt resistance to the Stamp Act, Gov. Thomas Fitch, from Norwalk, had agreed to take the required oath to carry out the provisions of the act. When the assistants, who were to administer the oath, were informed of Fitch's decision, Matthew Griswold and other Council members from eastern Connecticut withdrew from the Council chamber, leaving only four assistants to administer the oath. Eastern Connecticut Whigs, frustrated in previous decades in their religious and economic aspirations by western Connecticut's control of the executive branch of the government, intended to use this patriotic issue to remove their old opponents. In March 1766 a colony-wide meeting of the Sons of Liberty, an organization in which Griswold had been active, was held at Hartford. The meeting chose Deputy Gov. William Pitkin as its candidate for governor and Council member Jonathan Trumbull as its candidate for deputy governor. Both Pitkin and Trumbull were elected to the colony's two top offices while the four assistants who administered the oath to Governor Fitch were turned out.[67] Matthew Griswold was, of course, reelected to the Council, and in the fall of 1766, next to Hezekiah Huntington, received the largest number of popular votes for nomination since he first entered the list more than ten years earlier. In the May 1767 election he surpassed all candidates in popular votes.[68] With the large mandate in his reelection, and the victory of the eastern Connecticut New Light Whigs in the election of 1766, Matthew Griswold was secure in his continued leadership of resistance against British violations of American rights.

Victory at home was even more meaningful upon repeal of the Stamp Act in February 1766. When the news reached Connecticut, church bells were rung, small arms and cannon shot, a letter of thanks sent to the king, a day of thanksgiving proclaimed, and pledges of loyalty to Britain renewed.[69] Griswold was on the committee appointed to assist Governor Pitkin in preparing the letter of thanks.[70] An early draft of the address composed by Griswold conveys his joy at the repeal of the act and reveals to some extent the basis for his objections to the Stamp Act. After acknowledging the loyalty of the governor and company of Connecticut to His Majesty, Griswold expressed relief that the American colonies were "relieved from a great and heavy burden and enabled to carry on and promote their trade and commerce with Great Britain to a great advantage."[71] The address which was finally sent, an elaboration of Griswold's sentiments, was apparently drafted by a newly elected assistant and Griswold's law colleague, William Samuel Johnson.[72]

The repeal of the Stamp Act and the political victory of the eastern Whigs in the election of 1766 did not mean peace within Connecticut or in its relations with Great Britain. Another issue exacerbating Connecticut's east-west split and placing the east in even greater opposition to imperial authority during the 1760s and early 1770s was the western land claims of the Susquehannah Company. Established in Windham in 1753, it was composed of eastern Connecticut's leading citizens, who had used the Connecticut charter's sea-to-sea clause to persuade the General Assembly in 1755 to approve the company's establishment of a settlement along the banks of the Susquehanna River in northern Pennsylvania. Resistance came immediately from the Penns, who registered protests with the government of Connecticut and Parliament. Partly on the basis of these remonstrances, objections to the project developed within Connecticut. Governor Fitch led the opposition with a proclamation warning the company not to begin settlement in Pennsylvania, an act, he warned, which would anger the Penns and the Indians and incur royal displeasure.[73]

Appreciating the need for migration from populous, overcrowded eastern Connecticut, Matthew Griswold generally sympathized with the Susquehannah Company's claims.[74] As early as 1752 he signed a petition of Joseph Blackleach and others to the General Assembly for the right to settle lands west of the Hudson.[75] When Eliphalet Dyer, a company leader since 1753, presented a petition to the General Assembly in January 1769, asking for rights to Pennsylvania lands, Griswold, along with Roger Sherman, served as a Council representative on a joint committee with the Lower House to confer on the matter. Neither Griswold nor Sherman could persuade the members of the Lower House to grant the petition.[76] The company unsucessfully continued to pursue its claims during the next several months.[77]

Governor Pitkin died on October 1, and the efforts of the Susquehannah Company during the previous year helped to determine the Assembly's choice of Pitkin's successor. Fitch's supporters had been attempting to return him to the governorship since 1766. In the special October election Deputy Governor Trumbull, a member and strong supporter of the Susquehannah Company, received a majority on the first ballot. Fitch then sought the second position and gained forty-two votes, considerably more than his nearest rival, Matthew Griswold, who had only twenty-six. Fitch, however, lacked the necessary majority. On the third ballot Fitch and Griswold tied with fifty-four votes each. Not until the fourth ballot did Griswold emerge as the colony's new deputy governor with seventy-two votes compared with Fitch's forty-seven.[78]

While Connecticut's citizens expected the deputy governor to succeed to the governorship, Griswold's election to the second position and Eliphalet Dyer's defeat surprised everyone. One observer explained it this way:

> I happened to be at New Haven when these matters were transacted and we were most of us I mean the *Second House taken in;* not one word was said of Mr. Griswold, very little of Col. Huntington but all seemed determined to have our friend Dyer to take Mr. Trumbull's post, but our acquaintance Samuel Parsons of Lyme proved himself a better politician than all the rest of the colony and brought in his uncle Griswold to the disappointment of many and the mortification of others. Col. Huntington's friends seem much disappointed. Col. Dyer and his are really out of temper. The day before the vote half the Assembly congratulated him on the fair prospect they were sure he had to the second post which with his having only 8 votes made the mortification the greater. I believe he plainly sees that it is not the intent of the Assembly or the major party that he shall get any higher. . . .[79]

Dyer's prominence in the eastern Connecticut radical camp had outshone Griswold's to some extent, for Dyer, unlike Griswold, had been a delegate to the Stamp Act Congress and the Susquehannah Company's leading spokesman for several years, particularly during 1769.[80] Dyer, therefore, appeared to be the logical choice among Connecticut's Whigs for deputy governor. His widely publicized activities in the company's behalf instead cost him the western votes necessary for victory.[81] What machinations in the Assembly Samuel Holden Parsons was able to perform are difficult to determine, but his efforts may have influenced the election's outcome. With Dyer's eight votes on the first ballot clearly indicating his defeat, Parsons, one of Lyme's delegates to the Assembly's October session and a Pennsylvania landowner, still desired the election of a deputy governor favorable to his own interests.[82] Even William Samuel Johnson, aware of Griswold's prowess in the legal profession, and serving as the Susquehannah Company's agent in London, expressed his surprise at

Dyer's defeat and Griswold's victory.[83] Although Johnson believed that Hezekiah Huntington might even have had a better chance, he asked, "Who can account for the different turns of men's minds or the various motives men are influenced by on such occasions?"[84] To Dyer himself Johnson wrote that while Dyer's "merit and services justly entitled" him to the second seat, Johnson still valued "Mr. G. very highly for his integrity, assiduity . . . and ability."[85]

Despite the strengthening of the Whigs in the election of 1769, geographic, religious, and political divisions remained intact.[86] As deputy governor, Matthew Griswold gave additional prestige to the continued efforts of the Susquehannah Company.[87] He once served as a liaison between Governor Trumbull and company officers, including Dyer, to convey the impression that Trumbull, a prominent company member, and company officers had no regular contact except by official correspondence.[88] Griswold advised the governor to plead the company's case "forthwith without the loss of time . . . delay might prejudice the affair and disappoint the people of the colony."[89] When the colonial legislature formed a committee to reach an agreement with Pennsylvania, Griswold joined other Whigs and company supporters, including Dyer and Parsons.[90]

Reacting to the failures of the committee's mission, the legislature, in a special session in January 1774, extended its jurisdiction over the Susquehannah settlements and created the new township of Westmoreland.[91] A committee was also formed, to which Matthew Griswold belonged, to help the governor to "pursue and prosecute the claim and title of this colony to the lands lying within the boundaries of the grant and charter of the colony west of the Delaware River" and to advance Connecticut's case in Great Britain.[92] Western Connecticut conservatives reacted violently. They feared the colony's charter was in jeopardy and identified the company's backers with the so-called radicals who came to power in 1766. The conservatives organized a convention to meet in Middletown in March, ostensibly to consider the Assembly's assumption of the Susquehannah Company's claims, but actually to remove the expansionist Whigs from office.[93] Fear of this maneuver led some company members to lobby for Matthew Griswold and other incumbent company supporters like Governor Trumbull, Dyer, and Parsons.[94] The convention delegates prepared their own lists of "western" candidates for governor, deputy governor, and assistants, with two lists containing Griswold's name.

With this divisive tactic, the conservatives obviously hoped to increase their chances.[95]

Despite the conservatives' efforts at Middletown, the eastern Connecticut Whigs carried the election.[96] The voters of Lyme clearly indicated their position by returning Governor Trumbull and their own Matthew Griswold with 137 and 165 votes respectively while giving only 3 to ex-Governor Fitch.[97] As a New Light opponent of the Stamp Act and supporter of the Susquehannah Company, Griswold aligned himself with the dominant forces in prerevolutionary Connecticut. With imperial relations steadily worsening and violent conflict more and more imminent, Connecticut's voters understood the importance of strong leadership during the burgeoning crisis and elected their magistrate deputy governor every year until independence was achieved in 1783.[98]

The only major duty required of the deputy governor in Connecticut was to replace the governor during absence or incapacity and to serve, ex officio, on the Council. Beginning in 1741 the deputy governor was also chief judge of the Superior Court.[99] In this last capacity Matthew spent the major portion of his time during the years before Lexington and Concord.[100] He was chosen judge of the Superior Court each year beginning in October 1765, and became chief judge in October 1769, a position he held until 1783.[101] According to the Reverend Mr. Rockwell, Griswold's legal training and practice eminently qualified him for his judicial role:

> As he had devoted himself to the study and practice of law, as his professional employment, he acquired a large fund of political knowledge, which is highly important, and indispensably necessary, to discharge the duties of this office with propriety. . . . Not being biased by the undue influence of others, nor actuated by any selfish, unlawful motives, he administered justice impartially, and his decisions were founded in truth and equity. He, therefore, filled this office with dignity; did honor to himself; and justly acquired respect and esteem.[102]

Griswold's high regard for the law and his sense of compassion and justice were displayed in a letter to Governor Tryon of New York requesting the pardon of Felix Meigs, a Connecticut man under sentence of death in the neighboring colony for counterfeiting money. Meigs, wrote Griswold, was from a respectable family who along with his wife and children deserved compassion. Being "ignorant and undesigning," Meigs could only have been drawn into a counterfeiting scheme by an "artful man" and could have been, according to Griswold, at most an accessory to the crime. Therefore, Griswold concluded, mercy could be shown "without injury to the law, and is rather doing honor to it, as it always rather wishes to save than to destroy."[103]

Service on the Superior Court was demanding, sometimes requiring material sacrifice. Worldly comforts were never Matthew Griswold's motive for public service, but he had a family to consider. He and other Superior Court judges presented petitions to the General Assembly at both its May and October sessions in 1773 explaining their need for greater financial remuneration. According to the petition, business of the court had so increased that it consumed the major portion of the justices' time, kept them from other responsibilities, and forced them to rely on the emoluments of their office, savings, or inheritances for family support. A man's obligation to the public should not require him "to neglect that well known Christian obligation." Making public service a lucrative calling would lead to temptation, they admitted, but to require service "at the expense of individuals renders the government and their officers comtemptible."[104]

Matthew Griswold nevertheless remained faithful to Connecticut's ideal of public service while upholding his obligations to his family. Surely the deputy governor's salary of £100 the Assembly voted him each year could not alone have sustained his dedication through the trying years of revolution.[105] Not even the pomp and circumstance of public office could entice him. He advised against the wearing of scarlet robes by Superior Court judges, believing such a practice would set an "ill example" and was likely to "excite in the apprehension of the people the appearance at least of such a levity of mind in the judges as would naturally tend to disengage them from that attention the importance of their service requires."[106] Griswold never neglected the obligations of public servants. His attention to social welfare made him an ideal member of the General Assembly's joint committee established in 1773 to consider the "state of education and learning" at Yale College and to "devise the most effectual measures to render the institution most extensively useful and the support thereof permanent and lasting. . . ."[107] He had displayed his concern for Connecticut's religious and educational institutions some years earlier when he contributed a substantial sum to the Yale College chapel fund.[108] Long before the end of his distinguished public career Yale College acknowledged Griswold's faithful service as deputy governor and judge of the Superior Court by awarding him the degree of Doctor of Laws in 1779.[109]

As British-colonial relations worsened during the early and mid 1770s, Matthew Griswold's attentions turned more often to the problems between the colonies and Great Britain. He was intensely aware of the threat of British actions to the self-governing colony of Connecticut and colonial rights in general when, as chief judge of the Superior Court, he received from the governor and company of Rhode Island a request for advice on how to respond to the king's decision to have prisoners arrested and tried in England after the destruction of the revenue schooner *Gaspee*.[110] As a lawyer Griswold surely understood the dangerous precedent in the royal command, but he might also have agreed with another justice, William Samuel Johnson, who feared the ever more frequent discussions of colonial rights and Parliamentary power might provoke open hostilities between the colonies and the mother country.[111]

Perhaps these concerns materialized when Connecticut's Sons of Liberty intensified their intimidation of those with Tory sympathies after the Boston Tea Party and the implementation of the Coercive Acts intended to punish Boston.[112] While Matthew Griswold consistently supported Connecticut's Whigs, the violent outbursts throughout the colony disturbed him. He deplored the kidnapping and imprisoning of David Ingersoll, a Tory, from Great Barrington, Massachusetts, in Canaan, Connecticut. When about thirty persons accompanied those arrested to the trial, Griswold, on circuit in Litchfield, observed the absence of hostilities: "The spirit of the people in this county in general appears to condemn such disorders and profess a firm resolution to support the administration of civil government in this colony and avoid disturbances of the public peace."[113] Nevertheless, the chief judge found it advisable to postpone trying the offenders until the next term.[114] Perhaps Griswold and other prominent magistrates were unable to condone the usurpation of their functions by popular committees and mobs and to justify popular license regardless of motives. In spite of his leadership in the eastern Connecticut Whig camp, Griswold continued to favor restraint. Yet as moderator of a town meeting in Lyme he demonstrated his sympathy for Boston's plight when the meeting resolved to aid the citizens of that city by a subscription for "the relief of the poor people of Boston."[115]

Once the news of the battle of Lexington and Concord reached Lyme on April 21, 1775, however, Griswold committed himself to the patriot cause.[116] At the May 1775 meeting of the General Assembly Griswold and other prominent eastern Connecticut patriots were among the first members appointed to the Council of Safety established to assist the governor when the Assembly was not in session.[117] In many hundreds of meetings between 1775 and 1783 Griswold and the Council of Safety transacted a wide variety of public business. It interviewed congressmen, made military appointments, listened to pleas of townsmen for coastal defense, considered requests for trading outside Connecticut, allocated war supplies, filled requests for troops and provisions for the Continental Army, and consulted with colony and Continental military commanders about troop movements.[118] Griswold's attendance at these deliberations at Governor Trumbull's "War Office" in Lebanon throughout the war years illustrates well his devotion to the patriot cause.[119] At certain times Governor Trumbull specifically requested the presence of the deputy governor when the Council had some particularly important matters before it.[120] On one occasion he was sent by the Council with two others to investigate the mutiny aboard the brigantine *Minerva*.[121]

A year before independence was declared on July 4, 1776, Governor Trumbull summoned Griswold to a special meeting of the General Assembly called to confront the new and special problems of warfare.[122] At that session in July 1775, the deputy governor was appointed to several committees concerned with the reinforcement of troops in Boston and measures for procuring troops and commissioning officers in Connecticut.[123] At the request of the governor, the Council of Safety in October 1775 appointed Griswold to go to Cambridge, Massachusetts, to meet with a committee of the Continental Congress and other representatives from the New England states to confer with General Washington on the reestablishment of the Continental Army "for the defense of the invaded rights of the united colonies."[124] From Cambridge Griswold reported British threats to destroy towns in New Hampshire, Rhode Island, and Connecticut wherever "any armed force appears to oppose the ministerial troops."[125]

At times during the years of conflict Matthew Griswold could hardly meet the demands placed upon him. As chief judge of the Superior Court he was sometimes unable to attend meetings of the Council of Safety. He explained to the governor "sundry capital cases" were pending at the Superior Court in Fairfield, which adjourned in a few days. One or more of the appointed judges were missing, Griswold explained, and "the public as well as individuals expect cases of life and death should be tried and determined by the judges specially appointed for that service when it can be done without great inconvenience." Therefore he assumed Trumbull would excuse his attendance at the Council of Safety.[126] In another instance, Griswold informed Trumbull attendance at the Council of Safety would be a greater disservice to the public "than to stop the court here."[127] As a lawyer who defended American rights, Griswold fully understood that they could hardly be sacrificed by the demands of a war being fought in defense of those rights.

As deputy governor throughout the war Griswold also regularly attended meetings of the General Assembly.[128] When younger members of the legislative body failed to appear for special sessions, Griswold appeared in Hartford even in mid-January. He once chided the governor for his own absence and seemed concerned in May 1780 when no provision had been made for the place of the Assembly's October session, which usually met in New Haven, a location he believed "would not be thought expedient" at the time.[129] The regular journeys to Hartford and New Haven and on the circuit of the Superior Court must have been somewhat of a strain for a man in his mid-sixties. It would be much more convenient for him, he advised, if court sessions in Hartford coincided with sessions of the Assembly and if at least four or five days notice of the court's sessions were given.[130]

From the outbreak of the war patriots in exposed towns along the sound lived in great fear of British attack. The fears of Matthew Griswold, living at Black Hall, where the Connecticut River flowed into the sound, could hardly have been more justified. As early as June 23, 1775, a British ship attempted to capture a schooner grounded on the bar at the mouth of the Connecticut River.[131] According to Governor Trumbull's son, it was perhaps during this encounter, which occurred "just before the Deputy Governor's door," that "the old gentleman rallied his neighbors, put himself at their head and exchanged several shots" with the enemy ship.[132] About two months later another British man-of-war attempted to steal some cattle at Black Point.[133] This event and an earlier encounter prompted Griswold in September to describe clearly the plight of Lyme's citizens to Governor Trumbull and to request the stationing of troops in the town. The governor and Council responded by sending a company to Lyme "under the direction of the Deputy Governor and civil authority of that town" to "keep up and maintain proper watches and guards in such manner and place as they shall direct, for the present."[134] A more permanent arrangement was made in October when the General Assembly voted to make these troops part of the regular establishment. In April 1776 the number at Lyme was raised from fifteen to thirty, at least until the end of the year.[135]

Griswold's fears of an enemy attack were not assuaged by these measures. Two years later he enclosed orders from Governor Trumbull to the commanding officer at New London regarding protection of the mouth of the Connecticut River. He explained that the enemy's armed ships were cruising the sound and attacks were expected in Lyme at any moment.[136] In the following year the Council of Safety voted to increase defenses at Stonington and the adjacent coast and to reinforce the troops at Black Hall and Long Point in Lyme.[137] Evidently such measures failed in Lyme because Griswold soon complained again that the enemy landed at Black Point and carried off some sheep. No harm, however, "by the protection of a kind Providence," came to Griswold's family. The ships remained offshore for several days, he reported, and again, because of the "threatening danger," asked for more assistance in "regulating and disposing of the guards along this shore for the safety of the people and their property. . . ."[138] Although the number of troops seemed sufficient, Griswold feared a lack of provisions and suggested using a barrel or two of Irish beef reserved for the governor and Council or sending some sheep to the commissary at New London.[139]

While Connecticut escaped British occupation, the state suffered considerable damage from four attacks. There was a devastating assault on Danbury in 1777, an attack on the salt works at Greenwich in 1779, a series of raids in July 1779 on New Haven, Fairfield, and Norwalk, and finally, a particularly brutal attack in 1781 led by Benedict Arnold on New London and Groton.[140] Matthew Griswold was not selfishly concerned only with the fate of his native Lyme but was very much aware of British movements in western Connecticut. While the human and physical destruction appalled him, he was especially disgusted with the Tories' interception of a warning to Danbury's citizens about the impending attack and subsequent participation of Tories in the general fighting.[141] The implementation of his order to have British Capt. John Thomson and his apprentice, James Marsfield, transferred to the governor's custody in Lebanon must have assured Griswold of sufficient resistance to British aggression.[142] He believed the governor would "pursue every proper measure relative to them."[143]

A "small privateer belonging to the enemy," however, caused Griswold constant anguish. Privateers, he learned, attacked in the night and ladened themselves "with provisions — all valuable cargoes — the property of the people of this state." They would then refit and "return here for the purpose of plundering." Moreover, he added, "These privateers are (as we are informed) principally manned by Tories from this state acquainted with every creek and harbor and it seems if no step is taken the navigation of the sound must be given up and the people on the shore, where there is no guard, very much exposed."[144] Griswold suggested to the governor and Council of Safety that an armed vessel, small enough to navigate the harbors, be sent to cruise the sound. Since it seemed the state provided insufficient protection for the coastal areas, Griswold looked with favor at the proposal of Branford's citizens to build a "row galley at their own cost" with the expectation of state aid for guns and rigging. He hoped such a plan "may be pursued with all possible expedition as the best measure in addition to the provisions already proposed," and he heartily recommended it to the governor and Council of Safety.[145]

News during the summer of 1779 of British preparation of a large fleet at New York reportedly bound on "expeditions eastward" prompted a series of suggestions to Governor Trumbull from Griswold. He had heard about the British offers to enlistees of high wages and "the whole of the plunder they may take." Even worse, the fleet would be manned with Tories "whose rage and malice seems to have no bounds." The plan of the British, according to Griswold, was to "ravage the coast of this state," with New London as their particular object. His recommendations included having militia units along the coast, "arranged under the proper officers, with signals to direct them where to repair, and to run to the relief of the place attacked." He also recommended "immediate care be taken to provide a competent number of cartridges, and deposited in the most convenient places," and orders "issued for a view of arms once in a few days . . . so they be kept in constant repair."[146]

Fears of a devastating British attack on Connecticut's shore were not immediately realized except for the particularly brutal raid on New London and Groton in September 1781 which cost the Americans over eighty lives.[147] Griswold was in New Haven for a session of the Superior Court when he heard the horrible tale at 3 A.M., and he immediately consulted the other judges and "sundry of the inhabitants" to decide on a plan of action. Without loss of time, Griswold and the others sent express news to Connecticut's western towns of New London's tragedy and directed the commanding officers there to "exert themselves to the utmost of their powers in their several departments to put the people in the best posture of defense and transmit the intelligence to the adjacent towns." Griswold also sent an order to Brigadier General Ward "to fix posts of intelligence between New Haven and New London." He ordered Colonels Cook and Sabin each to send 100 men for the defense of New Haven in case of attack and to issue full orders to officers under their command to have troops "in constant readiness to march at a moment's warning to any place that may be attacked."[148] Neither his advanced age nor the suddenness of the emergency overtaxed the stamina or judgment of Connecticut's deputy governor.

The independence of the United States could hardly have been won by Connecticut alone, and from the outset of the conflict Matthew Griswold was aware of the necessity of intercolonial cooperation. He had already attended a meeting in Cambridge in 1775 to talk with congressional representatives, and throughout the war years Connecticut's representatives to the Continental Congress kept him informed of Continental affairs.[149] He was disturbed, however, because in Lyme "the levies for the Continental Army have made but slow progress" because of a smallpox epidemic, but in most Connecticut towns, he wrote Oliver Wolcott, the Continental quotas had been met.[150] The difficulties of a coordinated Continental effort were apparent to Griswold when he had to explain to George Washington the problem of delay in paying Connecticut troops sent to fight in a New York campaign. The effect, he informed Washington, was unfortunate because men declined "to enlist till they are paid their former wages."[151] More than a year after the Cambridge meeting attended by

Griswold, Wolcott complained to the deputy governor: "Establishing the new army . . . I fear will be attended with much difficulty, notwithstanding all the encouragement offered the men for enlisting." There were still the problems of uniforms and medical care. To Wolcott the problems were "too perplexing to point out any particular way in which it can be done," but, he went on to say, "it is certain we must have an army, otherwise we shall be reduced to the most unhappy condition." Congress was so sparsely attended, Wolcott lamented, that little could be done. At the war's end he wrote again to Griswold: "The present state of our finances renders it improbable that any immediate pay can be made to the army," but he praised his native state for its "liberal payments" in attempting to alleviate the shortage of money.[152]

Griswold's steadfast exertions in behalf of American independence made it difficult for him to understand why others committed to the cause lacked his devotion: "It seems there is nothing wanting on the part of the Americans but virtue and exertion under a common blessing of Divine Providence to make useful defense against the unjust demands of the British Ministry." "As the means of defense by the favors of heaven are put into our hands," he went on, "it is shocking to see that the laws of self-preservation have so little influence upon so many of our people that they stupidly neglect to use the powers they are [in] possession of to prevent their own ruin."[153]

Almost all of Connecticut's citizens used their powers well in behalf of the American cause. Unfortunately, the area possessed a contingent of Tories, located mostly in western towns, amounting to about six percent of the adult male population. The General Assembly enacted legislation against them, but for the most part there was no protracted patriot-Tory conflict, and by 1777 they were treated with tolerance.[154] Griswold held Tories in both fear and contempt, and as chief judge of the Superior Court he had ample opportunity to preside over their trials. Punishment of Tories varied according to the gravity of their crimes, and the chief judge reported to Wolcott the Court's sentence of execution for treason of one individual and fines and imprisonment of others.[155] Lyme also had Tories, but they were mainly absentee landlords. A few who belonged to the old families moved to either New York or Nova Scotia, which aroused suspicion of them.[156] One Lyme Tory, however, Elisha Beckwith, delayed his departure until 1781, when he was jailed in Hartford for the treasonous act of joining the British at New York. While imprisoned, the Assembly censured him because he "manifested the malignity of his heart" in letters to Griswold "replete with insults, threats and abuses for a supposed opposition made by him [Griswold] to his [Beckwith's] exchange to which he thought himself entitled insinuating that His Honor was not safe in his present situation."[157] Griswold must have been somewhat chagrined to receive two blistering, threatening letters from a Tory angrily blaming him for opposing an exchange between prisoners of war.[158]

Threats to Griswold's safety came not only from Tories. Family reminiscences illustrate further the risks to personal safety Griswold endured in behalf of American independence. When some British soldiers crossed the fields toward Black Hall, he reputedly jumped into a meal chest and was covered with bags. His wife, Ursula, invited the soldiers to search the house, but they found nothing. In another incident Griswold was pursued by a band of British soldiers and escaped by running up the lane to a nearby house where Hetty Marvin was sprinkling homespun linen on the grass to bleach. Griswold then hid under the linen and told the little girl not to tell the soldiers he was there. When the soldiers asked if His Honor had passed that way, the child answered he had not, "which was strictly true, as he had not *passed*."[159]

Only a few months before the independence of the United States was officially recognized by the Treaty of Paris in September 1783, Matthew Griswold wrote to his brother-in-law, Oliver Wolcott, that the prospect of peace seemed "to spread a general joy through this state." He went on, however, to note some qualifications. Traders, Griswold explained, "lament the effect it [peace] may have on their interests in trade; but the farmers who compose the main body of the people will soon feel the salutary effects of so desirable a blessing." The "illicit" traders would be compelled "to look for bread some other way." Many articles of commerce had fallen in price, and many Connecticut citizens had "a great aversion to pay taxes." A drought in eastern Connecticut the previous summer had worsened the problem.[160]

With these comments Griswold exhibited a perceptive understanding in postrevolutionary Connecticut of a complex situation which would have a direct effect on his own political career. The general consensus with which Connecticut's citizens had entered the conflict with Great Britain deteriorated as tensions developed between the area's mercantile community and its farmers. Connecticut's merchants, it seems, had fared rather well during the war through a lucrative trade with French and Danish possessions in the Caribbean: they had received special permits from Governor Trumbull and the Council of Safety, and had ignored the state embargo. Some simply traded directly with the enemy. Connecticut's farmers, on the other hand, experienced acute economic distress. Most of them were unable to produce a sufficient surplus to participate in the provisions trade and to meet the ever rising prices of manufactured goods. Disturbed by the inability of the state government to establish consistent price regulations, the farmers constantly complained about the "great pests of society," the merchants who were able to turn wartime scarcity to their own benefit. Governor Trumbull had been one of those merchant "pests" who identified with mercantile interests during the war years. A charge of illicit trade with the enemy proved untrue, but it added to his unpopularity and was reflected in the elections of 1780, 1781, and 1783, when Trumbull was denied a popular majority but was returned to office by the General Assembly. The problem of reelection and exhaustion from his wartime labors led to the governor's decision not to seek office in the elections of May 1784.[161]

As deputy governor, it would have been natural for Matthew Griswold to succeed Trumbull in the gubernatorial office, but his name was missing from the top twenty on the nomination list in 1783.[162] Actually his popular vote for deputy governor had steadily declined in both the nomination lists and the May elections during the last years of the Revolutionary War. In May 1780 he failed to receive a majority and was returned to office by the General Assembly. In the election of May 1784, with only 2,192 votes, he again failed to receive a popular majority and was placed in the governorship only by the Assembly's vote.[163] Samuel Huntington, however, was elected directly by the freemen as Connecticut's new deputy governor.[164]

A possible explanation for Griswold's declining popularity was that he suffered from the same kind of disaffection the public had for Governor Trumbull. As deputy governor, Griswold generally supported Trumbull's policies, which the people then construed to be his own. Trumbull, for example, had favored a pay bonus for Revolutionary War officers and a national impost which Connecticut's farmers viewed only as an additional tax burden. Another reason behind

Griswold's loss of public support was his age. His constituents wanted younger leadership dissociated with the sufferings and deprivations of war. By 1784 Matthew Griswold was seventy and considered too feeble to assume the duties of the governorship. He was returned to office only once, in May 1785.[165] In May 1786 he failed again to achieve a popular majority, and the General Assembly chose Deputy Governor Huntington as his successor and Oliver Wolcott as deputy governor.[166] William Williams observed a year after the event that "Governor Griswold remains exceedingly offended that he was discarded last year."[167] Perhaps to reconcile his brother-in-law to his fate, Wolcott tried to explain what happened. Griswold lost the election not because of "false and insidious insinuations to the injury of . . . moral character," but instead "from an apprehension that . . . want of health would render the office very burdensome . . . and less beneficial to the state, than [the] former administration had been."[168]

Whatever the state of his health, the magistrate from Lyme rendered competent service during the two years he held Connecticut's highest office. The governorship was one of little power but commanded great respect and honor. Its responsibilities allowed the incumbent to serve mainly as "the communicating medium between the state, the central government and other states."[169] As governor, Griswold continued to employ his legal talents as president of the Supreme Court of Errors established in 1784 but was barred by law from his place on the Superior Court.[170]

At the opening of each session of the General Assembly the governor delivered an address on the state's progress since the last meeting with recommendations on certain policies.[171] The only extant example of Governor Griswold's addresses is the one he delivered at the end of the session in May 1785. According to custom, he thanked the Assembly members for their excellent services during the past session. He then urged them "in the most pressing manner by precept or example in all . . . several departments to use . . . utmost endeavours to promote piety and virtue, industry and frugality, justice and benevolence to mankind. Frown upon every vice and impress the duty of our obedience to the laws." Finally he urged them to "cultivate that harmony that has so happily taken place in the state and is so essentially necessary to the wealth of a people." Not to do this, he warned, would bring down upon Connecticut's citizens the righteous judgment of almighty God.[172]

The absence of Governor Griswold's speeches in the official archives and newspapers can perhaps be explained by a long letter received by the governor soon after he delivered his closing address to the session in May 1784. The writer began by questioning the propriety of publishing the address. He then praised the governor for achievement in high office through honesty, candor, and strong natural abilities, qualities which would surely be recognized by posterity. Why, the writer questioned, did Griswold at the end of his life, long after the body and mind had lost their vigor, attempt to enhance his excellent reputation by literary accomplishments? "Your Excellency never shone in the middle stage of life either as a graceful speaker or an easy writer, and can the setting sun shine with more lustre?" he asked again. More was expected from the state's chief magistrate than from the common citizen, and publication of the address would appear to the people to be only a "foible of old age." Perhaps the content of the address would have offended certain of Connecticut's citizens because publication was a novelty, and "there exists a large party in this state who have violently opposed Your Excellency's election and who are waiting with anxiety to take advantage of everything new or uncommon in Your Excellency's administration to your disadvantage."[173] Very likely the governor made certain statements on those issues contributing to Connecticut's postwar political factionalism and may have offended those who had opposed his reelection. Perhaps the suggested forthrightness of the 1784 address explains to some extent the platitudinous nature of the one delivered in 1785.

As the "communicating medium between the state, the central government and other states," Governor Griswold received and answered many official letters.[174] Most of them warranted only a cursory response while others required action from the General Assembly. When there was a request from Congress in June 1784 for 165 officers and troops to help man some posts on the new nation's frontier, Governor Griswold consulted with others about the extent of his own power to make the military appointments, whether to convene a special session of the General Assembly or whether to wait for the Assembly to act on the appointments at its regular October session.[175] Lieutenant Governor Huntington and others advised Griswold to wait until the General Assembly's October session, at which time that body appointed the officers and troops.[176] Congressional reliance on the imperfect procedures of the various states for raising troops was just one example among many allowing Governor Griswold to perceive the weakness of the national government, which had few powers under the Articles of Confederation.

The inadequacies of the Articles of Confederation were again made clear to Governor Griswold as he tried to settle the Wyoming Valley land controversy which continued for months during his two years in office. According to the ninth article, Congress was the court of appeal in all disputes concerning interstate boundaries or territorial jurisdiction. The decision of judges appointed by Congress to hear such disputes was final and conclusive. Both Pennsylvania and Connecticut brought suits, and a panel of judges at Trenton in 1782 awarded jurisdiction to Pennsylvania but left ownership of the land unsettled. Thus a whole new issue was raised. Largely because of the violence which erupted between Pennsylvanians and the Connecticut settlers, President Dickinson of Pennsylvania was unable to secure legislation guaranteeing the Connecticut settlers' use of the soil they occupied.[177]

Governor Griswold sent to Dickinson a resolution from the General Assembly redressing the grievances of the Connecticut settlers. In his accompanying letter he told Dickinson the settlers were encouraged by Connecticut's leaders to "put themselves under the protection of [his] government and to have confidence in the justice and humanity of [his] state for a confirmation of their just rights and possessions." These "flattering prospects," however, had vanished, Griswold lamented, and repeated testimonies of violence against the Connecticut settlers continued to reach the governor. Finally, Griswold concluded, the whole question of soil rights must not be settled by violence but by a "legal and constitutional trial and decision."[178]

Griswold's old friend, William Samuel Johnson, was appointed by the General Assembly as a delegate to Congress to represent Connecticut's interests in this matter.[179] Johnson was prepared to attend Congress but wrote Griswold, "I am not in cash of my own for such an undertaking."[180] According to the Articles of Confederation, each state was responsible for the support of its own congressional representatives. Griswold then informed Johnson of the need to canvas the state to raise funds for the delegate. The governor requested the state treasurer and sheriffs "to pursue every proper and legal measure that belongs to [them] so as to bring so much into the treasury as to answer the present occasion."[181] Griswold was powerless to do anything else. The Assembly finally provided Johnson with a sufficient sum, and by the end of the congressional session in 1785, Johnson had contributed significantly to the solution of the Wyoming Valley problem. Connecticut ceded all of her western territories except the Western Reserves south of Lake Erie.[182]

In his Thanksgiving proclamations Governor Griswold suggested prayers for the perpetuation of the "federal union" and prayed "that civil discord and internal dissensions, or whatever tends to disturb the happiness, peace and prosperity of the nation may be prevented."[183] Perhaps he was really thinking of congressional difficulties in raising troops, settling interstate disputes, and the violence in the Wyoming Valley. Connecticut's congressional delegation kept him informed on national questions. He surely understood Connecticut's problems in both interstate and international commerce, the shortage of specie, and the general fear of social anarchy after Shay's Rebellion.[184] A strong national government with powers to deal with these problems was the obvious solution. He complained, "The scarcity of cash renders the collection but slow: we flatter ourselves that what may be had in that way with some assistance from an impost which we presume the states will not be so stupid as to delay." These comments demonstrate Griswold's understanding, at least from Connecticut's point of view, of why the national government should have the power to tax.[185] Unanimous approval for amending the Articles of Confederation had made a congressional impost impossible.[186] Griswold believed a national impost would help pay Connecticut's huge public debt, eliminate the need for state imposts, put the trade of all states on an equal footing, and transfer the state's public securities into a surplus of fluid capital for investment.[187]

Along with other Connecticut nationalists, Griswold looked hopefully to the general convention called at Philadelphia in May 1787, "to render the Constitution of the federal government adequate to the exigencies of the union."[188] Connecticut sent three nationalist delegates — Roger Sherman, Oliver Ellsworth, and William Samuel Johnson — to participate.[189] In session the delegates rejected the Articles of Confederation and wrote a new constitution.[190] On October 29, Connecticut's General Assembly issued a formal call for a ratifying convention and ordered towns to hold meetings on the second Monday in November to select their delegates. Each town was to choose as many delegates as it had representatives in the Assembly, and these delegates were to meet in Hartford on the first Thursday in January.[191] The citizens of Lyme elected Matthew Griswold, at the age of nearly seventy-four, just a year and a half after his retirement as governor, and William Noyes as their delegates to the convention; the convention promptly selected the former governor as its president.[192] Sherman, Johnson, and Ellsworth argued eloquently on behalf of the Constitution, and when the final vote of 128 to 40 approved the establishment of the new government, Griswold, along with Noyes, cast his vote with the majority. As presiding officer, perhaps Griswold contributed a good measure of the "decorum and propriety" which characterized the sessions. It was also Matthew Griswold's duty, as well as his pleasure, to inform the president of Congress of Connecticut's ratification of the Constitution. He reported that the citizens of the state would "do all in their power to promote the establishment of so salutary a plan of government."[193] Considering his large contribution to the founding of the new nation, the General Assembly in 1789 appropriately asked Griswold to help prepare an address to Pres. George Washington and to be one of the dignitaries to greet him upon his arrival at New Haven.[194]

With his long and distinguished public career finally at an end, Matthew Griswold returned to farming his 400 acres at Black Hall. According to Pres. Ezra Stiles of Yale, the farm was a prosperous one, with 100 head of cattle, several fields of hay, and many acres under the cultivation of corn, wheat, and oats.[195] Griswold's tranquil life was seemingly threatened, however, when his house narrowly escaped a fire which destroyed his barn "by means of a candle being carried into it."[196]

Retirement from public life provided time for intellectual pursuits as well as for farming. In 1790 Ezra Stiles wrote that the old governor was "in perfect health of body and mind, lame, yet vigorous." With a "fine library of well chosen books," amounting to several hundred volumes, he had ample opportunity to sustain his intellectual vitality.[197] An example of his scholarly efforts, which give additional insight into his religious and social attitudes, is found in his anonymous essay of 1795 entitled "Remarks on Liberty and the African Trade." A curious defense of slavery by a "revolutionary patriot," it is based on the Calvinist doctrine of original sin after Adam's fall.

According to Griswold, the Africans fell into heathen despotism but in Connecticut were "placed under the government of a master who is bound to provide necessaries sufficient for their comfort in life, [and] are protected by law from cruelty and oppression." Slavery was not worse than death, Griswold explained, because life is a "state of trial and probation" for the eternal happiness which God granted as a favor to fallen humanity. If a father were in bondage, Griswold went on, so too must be the son for *"political privileges are hereditary."* To free all slaves "at one blow" would dissolve the legal right of the master to the service of his slaves, who were legally purchased and provided with the necessities of life. Setting free those "as ought to be restrained would tend to sap the foundations of civil government." He agreed with measures already taken to prevent further importation of slaves into Connecticut, but he insisted that liberty consists "in nothing else than in a spirit of obedience to the divine law."[198] Continuing the argument used in the Mohegan controversy, Griswold used his own perception of property rights and his religious beliefs to rationalize the existing relationship between master and slave as the one best able to serve the interests of the two races and conform to the divine will.

Perhaps in retirement Griswold also had time to reflect more deeply on the role of government in religious affairs when studying the volumes of election sermons he had collected over the years. In writing to the Reverend Levi Hart concerning the election sermon in 1785, the governor included with his letter several volumes of these sermons preached during the past several decades. Griswold wanted the sermons to guide the parson but noted that they generally revealed no consensus "respecting the right of the civil power to interpose in matters of religion." Some sermons, he wrote, conflicted directly with others on that point. The several preachers, he concluded,

> are all something out of the way. To admit the right of the civil power to control the right of conscience would be injurious to religion and tend to unhinge a true spirit of Gospel obedience. So on the other hand as social worship directly tends to promote the civil interests of a people in the strongest manner, it seems to be an object within the jurisdiction of the civil magistrate to make provision for the support of it.

The conflict between one's conscience and the needs of the social order was one which Griswold could not yet resolve, and in the end he could give no advice of his own to the Reverend Mr. Hart.[199] Ten years later in his discourse on slavery, however, he argued for the limitation of the powers of civil government to secular affairs.[200]

Griswold's remarks were germane to one of the most sensitive issues in Connecticut during the last decade of his life. Growing numbers of dissenters challenged the Congregational establishment, and the relationship of church and state became, as it had been during the Great Awakening, an important political issue largely responsible for the development of political parties in early national Connecticut.[201] President Stiles in 1785 requested the old governor to donate the election sermons to Yale College, but Griswold declined for the present. He did not want them stored in a library but wanted them to be used by ministers in preparing sermons. "Besides," he added, "I have a fondness for the perusal of those sermons: The more I become acquainted the more it generates my esteem of their importance." His plan was to turn the sermons over to Yale upon his death.[202]

Griswold supported religious institutions throughout his life, and with the pressures of public life behind him he had more time to participate in the governance of Lyme's First Church. He was moderator at several society meetings in 1787 and 1788 and from 1789 to 1793 served on several committees formed to call and receive new pastors.[203]

Old friends and members of his family must have contributed to Matthew Griswold's contentment during his final years. He was no doubt pleased to hear of the birth of a new grandson from his son Roger, who hoped the new addition to the family "will not disgrace his ancestors."[204] But there was also reason for concern and sorrow. In 1798 Roger was representing Connecticut in the national Congress as an ardent Federalist, and the news of his fight in Philadelphia with Matthew Lyon, Republican of Vermont, must have provoked great anxiety in the elder Griswold. Roger assured his father he was in "no more danger of receiving personal violence in this city" than in Connecticut.[205] The saddest experience was the sudden death of Ursula, his wife of almost forty-five years, in April 1788. The "funeral solemnities were attended by a numerous concourse of relatives and friends." Matthew Griswold lost a worthy companion who "exemplified the virtues of the Christian, and was the affectionate wife and the tender parent."[206] The old man expressed sorrow to his son Roger, to whom he reported the family to be in usual health. He continued:

For my own part [I] feel myself in the train of painful mourners. Lost my companion (your kind mother), much deserted by my old acquaintances who are dispersed in almost every town in this state, which places me in a gloomy situation. I hope we may be enabled to make a religious improvement of this distressing visitation of Divine Providence, that this awakening call may sensibly affect our minds with a sense of the infinite importance of being ready and prepared for [the] dying hour.[207]

Griswold's feeling of desertion was surely somewhat relieved by written condolences from family and friends such as Ursula's brother, Oliver Wolcott, and President Stiles of Yale.[208] Thus he in turn offered appropriate words of consolation upon the death of his sister Lucia to his brother-in-law Elijah Backus. Griswold believed the "afflictive dispensations of Divine Providence call aloud upon all surviving friends to afford all the consolation in their power." Beyond this, he added, "we are all in the hands of that Benevolent Being who is able and willing to repair the greatest temporal loss more than ten thousand fold."[209] When his own death came on April 28, 1799, Griswold's survivors surely received consolation from the many who had been so well served by this distinguished magistrate.[210]

Matthew Griswold of Lyme is perhaps best known for his ardent patriotism during the Revolutionary War, but the course of his life exhibited more than this. It exemplified the sober values of the citizens of eighteenth-century Lyme as well as of the colony and state of Connecticut. In his funeral oration based on Proverbs 10:7, "The Memory of the Just is Blessed," the Reverend Lathrop Rockwell, pastor of Lyme's First Society, represented Griswold as the epitome of these qualities. Rockwell described the many services performed by the deceased in behalf of his family, town, state, and nation, and concluded, "The whole tenor of his conduct was happily designated with fidelity, integrity, uprightness, and a high regard for the good of his constituents."[211] These values personified in men like Lyme's revolutionary magistrate contributed to the place the United States has among the democracies of the modern world.

Notes

1. Edward Elbridge Salisbury, *The Griswold Family of Connecticut, with Pedigree* (privately printed, 1884), I:121–29; Albert E. Van Dusen, *Connecticut: A*

Fully Illustrated History of the State from the Seventeenth Century to the Present (New York: Random House, 1961), p. 44.

2. Adeline Bartlett Allyn, *Black Hall: Traditions and Reminiscences* (Hartford: Case, Lockwood and Brainard Co., 1908), pp. 8–9.

3. Salisbury, *Griswold Family*, I:129–32; May Hall James, *The Educational History of Old Lyme, Connecticut, 1635–1935* (New Haven: Yale University Press, 1939), pp. 17–22, 47.

4. Salisbury, *Griswold Family*, I:131–32; John D. Little, "Lyme 1765–1783: Portrait of an Eastern Connecticut Town during the Revolutionary Period" (Honors essay, Southern Connecticut State College, 1975), p. 36.

5. Other children of the couple were Elizabeth, b. about 1652; John, who died young; Sarah, b. 1655; and Anna, b. 1656. Salisbury, *Griswold Family*, I:135–36.

6. Ibid., I:138.

7. James, *Educational History*, p. 57.

8. Phoebe, b. 1684; Elizabeth, b. 1685; Sarah, b. 1687/88; Matthew, b. 1688; John, b. 1690; George, b. 1692; Mary, b. 1694; Deborah, b. 1696; Samuel, b. 1697; Patience, b. 1698; Thomas, b. 1700.

9. Salisbury, *Griswold Family*, I:135–52.

10. Glenn E. Griswold, *The Griswold Family: England–America* (Rutland, Vt.: Tuttle Publishing Company, 1943), II:130, 131; James, *Educational History*, p. 74.

11. Griswold, *Griswold Family*, II:130.

12. The other ten were Phoebe, b. 1716; Thomas, b. 1718; Hannah, b. 1724; Lucy, b. 1726; Sarah, b. 1728; Clerine, b. 1731; Clarina, b. 1732/33; Deborah, b. 1735; John, b. 1739; Lydia, b. 1742. Ibid., p. 131; Barbour Collection, Connecticut Vital Records, Lyme, L–2, 197, Connecticut State Library (hereafter cited as CSL).

13. James, *Educational History*, pp. 73–74.

14. Ibid., p. 72.

15. Franklin Bowditch Dexter, *Biographical Sketches of the Graduates of Yale College* (New York: Henry Holt and Company, 1885–1911), I:169, 389; Allen Johnson and Dumos Malone, eds., *Dictionary of American Biography* (New York: Charles Scribner's Sons, 1928–36), XVI:270 (hereafter cited as *DAB*).

16. Richard L. Bushman, *From Puritan to Yankee: Character and the Social Order in Connecticut, 1690–1765* (Cambridge: Harvard University Press, 1967), p. 152.

17. Dexter, *Biographical Sketches*, I:389.

18. Mary Hewitt Mitchell, *The Great Awakening and the Revivals in the Religious Life of Connecticut* (New Haven: Yale University Press, 1934), pp. 12–13.

19. Dexter, *Biographical Sketches*, I:389.

20. Old Lyme, First Congregational Church Records, I:36, CSL.

21. Lathrop Rockwell, *Sermon Delivered at the Funeral of His Excellency, Matthew Griswold, Esq.* (New London: S. Green, 1802), p. 15.

22. James, *Educational History*, p. 87.

23. Little, "Lyme," p. 25.

24. Ibid., pp. 27, 29; Dexter, *Biographical Sketches,* I:739.

25. James, *Educational History,* p. 90; Old Lyme, First Congregational Church Records, Ecclesiastical Society Meetings, 1721–1876, p. 119, CSL.

26. Little, "Lyme," pp. 28–29.

27. Old Lyme, First Congregational Church Records, Ecclesiastical Society Meetings, pp. 53, 58, 60, 69, 72, 78, 85, 95, 117, 118, 119, 120, CSL.

28. Dexter, *Biographical Sketches,* I:169.

29. Oscar Zeichner, *Connecticut's Years of Controversy, 1750–1776* (Chapel Hill: University of North Carolina Press, 1949), p. 24; Van Dusen, *Connecticut,* p. 118; Bushman, *Puritan to Yankee,* pp. 238–39.

30. Bushman, *Puritan to Yankee,* pp. 220–66.

31. Allyn, *Black Hall,* pp. 42–43; Salisbury, *Griswold Family,* II:233; Griswold, *Griswold Family,* II:136–37.

32. Allyn, *Black Hall,* pp. 43–44; Salisbury, *Griswold Family,* II:234; Griswold, *Griswold Family,* II:137; *DAB,* VIII:9.

33. Other children were Marian, b. 1750; John, b. 1752; Ursula, b. 1754; Matthew, b. 1760; and Roger, b. 1762. Griswold, *Griswold Family,* II:137.

34. Matthew Griswold to Roger Wolcott, Lyme, December 16, 1755, William Griswold Lane Collection, Yale University Library (hereafter cited as W. G. Lane, Yale).

35. Matthew Griswold to his son, Lyme, November 8, 1779, Griswold, *Griswold Family,* II:135.

36. Ezra Stiles, Itineraries, V:243, Beinecke Library, Yale University.

37. George C. Groce, *William Samuel Johnson: A Maker of the Constitution* (New York: Columbia University Press, 1937), pp. 16–20.

38. New London County Court Records, Trials-Dockets, XX, CSL.

39. Rockwell, *Sermon,* p. 15.

40. Ibid., p. 13; New London County Court Records, Trials-Dockets, XXI, cases 136, 201; XXII, case 47; XXIV; "Connecticut Archives" (hereafter cited as "Arch."), Finance and Currency, IV:13a, 27a, 37, 153; V:16.

41. Sylvie Turner, ed., *Journal Kept by William Williams* (Hartford: Connecticut Historical Society, 1975), p. 38.

42. Thomas Cushing to Matthew Griswold, Boston, July 9, 1750, W. G. Lane, Yale.

43. William Butler to Matthew Griswold, New York, September 15, 1760; Samuel Avery to Matthew Griswold, Groton, March 8, 1762, W. G. Lane, Yale.

44. Matthew Griswold to Samuel Avery, Norwich, March 30, 1762, W. G. Lane, Yale.

45. Groce, *Johnson,* pp. 15–33; *DAB,* X:131; William Samuel Johnson to Matthew Griswold, Stratford, July 24, 1753, December 13, 1754, January 16, 1755, August 5, 1756; Matthew Griswold to William Samuel Johnson, Lyme, July 6, 1762, W. G. Lane, Yale.

46. Groce, *Johnson,* pp. 25–26.

47. *DAB,* XIV:270.

48. Stiles, Itineraries, V:243; Groce, *Johnson,* pp. 27–31.

49. J. Hammond Trumbull and Charles J. Hoadly, eds., *The Public Records of the Colony of Connecticut* (Hartford: Case, Lockwood and Brainard Company, 1850–90), XIII:259.

50. Ibid., IX:381; X:2, 291, 326, 335, 406, 447, 468, 554, 598; XI:115, 174, 221, 244.

51. Ibid., X:306.

52. Ibid., XIII:261.

53. Zeichner, *Controversy*, pp. 45, 79; *Connecticut Courant*, December 8, 1766.

54. Matthew Griswold to William Samuel Johnson, [1766], William Samuel Johnson Papers, III:30, Connecticut Historical Society (hereafter cited as CHS).

55. Chester McArthur Destler, *Joshua Coit: American Federalist, 1758–1798* (Middletown, Conn.: Wesleyan University Press, 1962), p. 27.

56. Matthew Griswold received 162 votes, placing him thirty-third in a list of thirty-seven each with more than 100 votes. Connecticut General Assembly, I, CHS.

57. Richard J. Purcell, *Connecticut in Transition: 1775–1818* (Middletown, Conn.: Wesleyan University Press, 1963), pp. 125–26.

58. In 1753 Griswold placed twenty-fourth with 314 votes in a list of forty. Connecticut General Assembly, I. In 1754 he was twenty-sixth with 453 votes in a list of thirty-nine. Connecticut Secretary of State, CHS; *Colony Records,* X:413.

59. In 1756 he was seventeenth with 1,488 votes. Connecticut General Assembly, I, CHS. In 1757 he came in seventeenth. *Colony Records,* XI:65. In 1758 he placed fifteenth with 1,834 votes, more than all other nonincumbents. Connecticut General Assembly, I, CHS.

60. Jonathan Trumbull, Sr., Papers, Diary and Account Book, 1759–62, CHS; *Colony Records,* XI:246.

61. October 1760, thirteenth in seniority, 2,782 votes, second in popularity. Connecticut Secretary of State, CHS. October 1761, twelfth in seniority, 3,019 votes, second in popularity. Connecticut General Assembly, I, CHS. October 1762, eleventh in seniority, 2,831 votes, first in popularity. Connecticut General Assembly, I, CHS. October 1766, fourth in seniority, 3,724 votes, second in popularity. Connecticut General Assembly, I, CHS. May 1767, fourth in seniority, 4,402 votes, first in popularity. Franklin Bowditch Dexter, ed., *Itineraries and Correspondence of Ezra Stiles* (New Haven: Yale University Press, 1916), pp. 465–66. October 1767, fourth in seniority, 3,539 votes, first in popularity. Connecticut General Assembly, I, CHS. May 1768, fourth in seniority, 4,632 votes, first in popularity. *Connecticut Courant,* May 16, 1768. October 1769, 4,315 votes, first in popularity. Connecticut Secretary of State, CHS. *Colony Records,* XI:246, 368, 494; XII:3, 122, 243, 342, 453, 547.

62. *Colony Records,* XI:366, 435, 478, 568, 612; XII:1, 73, 120, 188, 227, 230, 294, 340, 409, 412, 451, 493, 540, 545, 605; XIII:1, 91, 122, 168, 234.

63. "Arch.," Civil Officers, second series, IV:132; V:25a, 35a, 44a, 49a, 59a, 68a, 75a. Griswold also served on committees dealing with judges and

justices, private petitions, and the expense account of the treasurer. XI:26a, 78a, 92b; I:72a, 77a;V:80a.

64. Zeichner, *Controversy*, pp. 50–52.

65. For complete document see Part Two.

66. Zeichner, *Controversy*, pp. 53–54; Dexter, *Biographical Sketches*, I:739; Little, "Lyme," pp. 45–46.

67. Zeichner, *Controversy*, pp. 56–59, 70–75. Christopher Collier, *Roger Sherman's Connecticut: Yankee Politics and the American Revolution* (Middletown, Conn.: Wesleyan University Press, 1971), pp. 85–86.

68. *Colony Records*, XII:453; Connecticut General Assembly, I, CHS; Dexter, ed., *Itineraries*, pp. 465–66.

69. Van Dusen, *Connecticut*, p. 128.

70. *Colony Records*, XII:466–67.

71. Matthew Griswold, Address to the King, W. G. Lane, Yale.

72. Zeichner, *Controversy*, pp. 74–75; William Samuel Johnson, Address to the King [May 1766], William Samuel Johnson Papers, CHS.

73. Zeichner, *Controversy*, pp. 30–33.

74. Bushman, *Puritan to Yankee*, pp. 122–23.

75. Julian P. Boyd and Robert J. Taylor, eds., *The Susquehannah Company Papers* (Ithaca: Cornell University Press, 1962–70), I:9–15 (hereafter cited as *SCP*).

76. *SCP*, III:53–56, 233–34; Richard Thomas Warfle, "Connecticut's Critical Period: The Response to the Susquehannah Affair, 1769–1774" (Ph.D. diss., University of Connecticut, 1972), p. 16.

77. Warfle, "Connecticut's Critical Period," pp. 38–60.

78. Zeichner, *Controversy*, pp. 121–22; Glenn Weaver, *Jonathan Trumbull: Connecticut's Merchant Magistrate* (Hartford: Connecticut Historical Society, 1956), pp. 133–34; Connecticut Secretary of State, October 1769, CHS.

79. Joseph Chew to William Samuel Johnson, December 9, 1769, *SCP*, III:207–8.

80. Warfle, "Connecticut's Critical Period," pp. 73–75.

81. Joseph Chew to William Samuel Johnson, December 9, 1769, *SCP*, III:208.

82. *Colony Records*, XIII:169; Clifford K. Shipton, *Sibley's Harvard Graduates: Biographical Sketches of Those Who Attended Harvard College* (Boston: Massachusetts Historical Society, 1968), XIV:50.

83. Warfle, "Connecticut's Critical Period," p. 71.

84. William Samuel Johnson to Joseph Chew, Westminster, February 13, 1770, *SCP*, IV:25.

85. William Samuel Johnson to Eliphalet Dyer, February 27, 1770, *SCP*, IV:34.

86. Warfle, "Connecticut's Critical Period," p. 76.

87. Purcell, *Transition*, p. 124.

88. *SCP*, IV:n. 2, pp. 184–85.

89. Matthew Griswold to Jonathan Trumbull, Windham, September 18, 1771, *SCP*, IV:263–64.

90. *Colony Records,* XIV:161.

91. Zeichner, *Controversy,* p. 146.

92. *Colony Records,* XIV:217.

93. Zeichner, *Controversy,* pp. 146–51.

94. Benjamin Stevens and others to Zebulon Butler and Nathan Denison, Canaan, April 1, 1774, *SCP,* VI:155–56.

95. Zeichner, *Controversy,* p. 155; Article by Colonist, *SCP,* VI:218–20; Ebenezer Gray to Jonathan Trumbull, Fairfield, April 26, 1774, *SCP,* VI:229–30.

96. Zeichner, *Controversy,* p. 156.

97. Joseph Trumbull to Jonathan Trumbull, Norwich, April 16, 1774, *SCP,* VI:214–15.

98. "Arch.," Civil Officers, V:84a, 98a, 107a, 113a, 119b, 126a, 149b, 158bc, 174a, 182a, 190ab, 193a.

99. There were five justices on the Superior Court who adjudged all crimes, the punishment of which related to life, limb, or banishment. Superior Court judges were also sent on three circuits into which Connecticut was divided, each judge appearing twice a year in every county. Purcell, *Transition,* pp. 119, 131.

100. Little, "Lyme," p. 44.

101. *Colony Records,* XII:414, 455, 548; XIII:5, 171, 237, 286, 416, 573; XIV:74, 255; XV:5, 273; Charles J. Hoadly, et al., *Public Records of the State of Connecticut* (Hartford: Case, Lockwood and Brainard Company and the State of Connecticut, 1894–1967), I:222; II:4, 252; III:6; IV:133; V:111.

102. Rockwell, *Sermon,* p. 14.

103. Matthew Griswold to Governor Tryon, New Haven, August 24, 1772, W. G. Lane, Yale.

104. Matthew Griswold and others to the General Assembly of Connecticut, May, October 1773, "Arch.," Miscellaneous, first series, III:301a, 304a. The other petitioners on both petitions were Eliphalet Dyer, Roger Sherman, and William Pitkin. William Samuel Johnson signed the May petition and Samuel Huntington the October petition.

105. *Colony Records,* XIII:354, 410, 502, 566, 656; XIV:66, 152, 211, 322, 386; XV:82, 175, 398.

106. Matthew Griswold to Jonathan Trumbull, Lyme, February 13, 1769, Jonathan Trumbull Papers, III, CHS.

107. *Colony Records,* XIV:36.

108. List of subscribers to the Yale College Chapel Fund, Beinecke Library, Yale University.

109. *Connecticut Journal,* September 15, 1779; Diploma, September 6, 1779, W. G. Lane, Yale.

110. Darius Sessions and others to Matthew Griswold and others, Providence, December 25, 1772, W. G. Lane, Yale.

111. Zeichner, *Controversy,* p. 138.

112. Ibid., pp. 171–76.

113. Matthew Griswold to Jonathan Trumbull, Litchfield, August 20, 1774, Jonathan Trumbull Papers, IV:20, CSL.

114. Ibid., New Haven, August 30, 1774, IV:21.

115. "Extracts from Lyme Revolutionary Records, 1774–1784," p. 3, CSL. For complete document, see Part Two, pp. 54–55.

116. Little, "Lyme," p. 54.

117. *Colony Records*, XV:39.

118. Rupert Charles Loucks, "Connecticut in the American Revolution" (M.S. thesis, University of Wisconsin, 1959), pp. 116–17.

119. *Colony Records*, XV:39, 177, 315; *State Records*, I:53–57, 80–82, 152–57, 166, 168, 212–14, 216, 213–16, 318–19, 321–27, 329–31, 336, 338–39, 341–43, 345–47, 349–55, 357–62, 364, 384–86, 397–99, 450–55, 456, 509–11, 513–18, 566–71, 573; II:87–90, 97–99, 211–14, 219–20, 246, 344–68, 396, 435–40, 498–506, 511–12, 541; IV:88–129, 239–85, 325–41; V:82–106, 189–201, 249–51.

120. Jonathan Trumbull to Matthew Griswold, Lebanon, September 3, 1776, W. G. Lane, Yale; Lyme, November 27, 1778, Jonathan Trumbull Papers, VIII:261, CSL; Lebanon, March 28, 1783, Jonathan Trumbull Papers, IV, CHS.

121. *Colony Records*, XV:176–77.

122. Jonathan Trumbull to Matthew Griswold, June 23, 1775, Jonathan Trumbull Papers, III, CHS.

123. "Arch.," Revolutionary War, first series, I:209, 350.

124. Jonathan Trumbull to Matthew Griswold, Lebanon, October 5, 1775, W. G. Lane, Yale; *Colony Records*, XV:132; *Connecticut Courant*, October 20, 1775.

125. Matthew Griswold to Jonathan Trumbull, Cambridge, October 20, 1775, W. G. Lane, Yale.

126. Ibid., Lyme, November 27, 1778, Jonathan Trumbull Papers, VIII:261, CSL.

127. Ibid., Hartford, September 8, 1780, XII:282.

128. *Colony Records*, XV:1, 90, 185, 269, 410; *State Records*, I:60, 89, 219, 365, 408, 410, 469, 521; II:1, 122, 130, 170, 221, 249, 402, 448, 514; III:1, 300, 371; IV:1, 130, 285; V:13, 107, 202, 252, 315, 430.

129. Matthew Griswold to Jonathan Trumbull, Hartford, January 13, 17, September 8, 1780, Jonathan Trumbull Papers, XI:26, 33; XII:202, CSL.

130. Matthew Griswold to Charles Chauncey, Lyme, November 10, 1779, Chauncey Family Papers, Yale University.

131. Little, "Lyme," p. 57.

132. Jonathan Trumbull, Jr., to Joseph Trumbull, Lebanon, July 17, 1775, Joseph Trumbull Collection, CSL.

133. Little, "Lyme," p. 57. For complete document see Part Two.

134. *Colony Records*, XV:123.

135. Ibid., pp. 128, 142, 256.

136. Matthew Griswold to the Commanding Officer at New London, Lyme, July 11, 1778, W. G. Lane, Yale.

137. John Tyler to Governor Trumbull, Headquarters, New London, July 21, 1779, Jonathan Trumbull Papers, X:41, CSL.

138. Matthew Griswold to Jonathan Trumbull, Lyme, July 28, 1779, Jonathan Trumbull Papers, X:53, CSL.

139. Ibid., July 9, 1780, XII:204.

140. David M. Roth, "Connecticut in the American Revolution," *Connecticut Review 9* (1) (November 1975):12–13.

141. Matthew Griswold to Oliver Wolcott, East Windsor, May 3, 1777, Oliver Wolcott, Sr., Papers, I:45, CHS.

142. Matthew Griswold to Captain Elisha Lee, Lyme, July 14, 1778, Jonathan Trumbull Papers, VIII:162, CSL.

143. Matthew Griswold to Governor Trumbull, Lyme, July 14, 1778, Jonathan Trumbull Papers, VIII:163, CSL.

144. Ibid., New Haven, November 30, 1778, VIII:268.

145. Ibid., February 25, 1779, IX:56.

146. Ibid., Lyme, August 3, 1779; Salisbury, *Griswold Family*, II:223–24.

147. Roth, "Connecticut in the American Revolution," pp. 12–13.

148. Matthew Griswold to Governor Trumbull, New Haven, September 7, 1781, Jonathan Trumbull Papers, IV, CHS. For complete document see Part Two.

149. Samuel Huntington to Matthew Griswold, Philadelphia, August 30, September 7, 1776, W. G. Lane, Yale; Oliver Wolcott to Matthew Griswold, Philadelphia, April 3, 1777, Oliver Wolcott, Sr., Papers, I:40a, CHS; Samuel Huntington to Matthew Griswold, Philadelphia, March 5, 1781, Roger Sherman to Matthew Griswold, Philadelphia, August 14, 1781, Salisbury, *Griswold Family*, II:225–26.

150. Matthew Griswold to Oliver Wolcott, East Windsor, May 3, 1777, Oliver Wolcott, Sr., Papers, I:45, CHS.

151. Matthew Griswold to George Washington, Fairfield, June 25, 1776, W. G. Lane, Yale.

152. Oliver Wolcott to Matthew Griswold, Philadelphia, November 18, 1776, January 22, 1783, Burnett, *Letters of Members of the Continental Congress* (Gloucester, Mass.: Peter Smith, 1963), I:158–59; VII:20.

153. Matthew Griswold to Oliver Wolcott, East Windsor, May 3, 1777, Oliver Wolcott, Sr., Papers, I:45, CHS.

154. Roth, "Connecticut in the Revolution," pp. 10–11.

155. Matthew Griswold to Oliver Wolcott, East Windsor, May 3, 1777, Oliver Wolcott, Sr., Papers, I:45, CHS.

156. Little, "Lyme," p. 54; James, *Educational History*, p. 100.

157. *State Records*, IV:31.

158. Elisha Beckwith to Matthew Griswold, [1781], "Arch.," Revolutionary War, first series, XXIII:336, 337.

159. Allyn, *Black Hall*, pp. 42, 47.

160. Edmond S. Morgan, *The Birth of the Republic, 1763–1769* (Chicago: University of Chicago Press, 1956), pp. 86–87; Matthew Griswold to Oliver Wolcott, Lyme, April 19, 1783, Oliver Wolcott, Sr., Papers, III:151, CHS.

161. David M. Roth, *Connecticut's War Governor: Jonathan Trumbull* (Chester, Conn.: Pequot Press, 1974), pp. 70–76.

162. Collier, *Sherman,* p. 218.

163. Connecticut Secretary of State; Oliver Wolcott, Sr., Papers, I:109; Jonathan Trumbull Papers, Diary 1780–85, CHS.

164. Collier, *Sherman,* p. 218.

165. *State Records,* VI:3.

166. Griswold received 2,160 popular votes, Huntington 1,701, Wolcott 1,049, and 943 were scattered. "Arch.," Civil Officers, second series, V:233.

167. William Williams to Mary Williams, Hartford, May 12, 1787, Williams Papers, CHS.

168. Oliver Wolcott to Matthew Griswold, Litchfield, November 22, 1788, Salisbury, *Griswold Family,* II:227.

169. Purcell, *Transition,* pp. 117–18.

170. *State Records,* V:323.

171. Purcell, *Transition,* p. 117.

172. Matthew Griswold, Address to the Council and House of Representatives, May 1785, W. G. Lane, Yale.

173. Address to Governor Matthew Griswold, unsigned, [May 1784], W. G. Lane, Yale.

174. Many are scattered throughout the W. G. Lane Collection, Yale.

175. *State Records,* V:445; Matthew Griswold to Richard Law, Lyme, July 6, 1784, Ernest Law Papers, CHS; Matthew Griswold to Lieutenant Governor Huntington, Lyme, July 21, 1784, Emmet Collection, 2495, New York Public Library.

176. Samuel Huntington to Matthew Griswold, Litchfield, August 4, 1784, W. G. Lane, Yale; *State Records,* V:445.

177. Groce, *Johnson,* pp. 113–17.

178. Matthew Griswold to [John Dickinson], Lyme, December 20, 1784, *SCP,* VIII:161–63.

179. Groce, *Johnson,* p. 118.

180. William Samuel Johnson to Matthew Griswold, Stratford, November 27, 1784, Burnett, *Letters,* VII:616–17.

181. Matthew Griswold to William Samuel Johnson, Lyme, November 22, December 7, December 10, 1784, William Samuel Johnson Papers, II:84, 87, 89, CHS.

182. Ibid., December 18, 1784, William Samuel Johnson Papers, II:88, CHS; Groce, *Johnson,* pp. 123–27.

183. Governor Matthew Griswold, Thanksgiving Proclamations, 1784, 1785, Beinecke Library, Yale University.

184. Philip H. Jordan, Jr., "Connecticut Politics during the Revolution and Confederation 1776–1789" (Ph.D. diss., Yale University, 1962), chs. 5–9. Connecticut Delegates to the Governor of Connecticut, New York, April 12, 1786, Burnett, *Letters,* VIII:339–40.

185. Matthew Griswold to William Samuel Johnson, Hartford, March 3, 1785, William Samuel Johnson Papers, CHS.

186. Forest McDonald, *E Pluribus Unum: The Formation of the American Republic, 1776–1790* (Boston: Houghton Mifflin Company, 1965), pp. 16–17, 20–22, 141–42, 144–45.

187. Gaspare John Saladino, "The Economic Revolution in Late Eighteenth Century Connecticut" (Ph.D. diss., University of Wisconsin, 1964), pp. 174–75, 197; Forest McDonald, *We the People: The Economic Origins of the Constitution* (Chicago: University of Chicago Press, 1958), pp. 139–40.

188. Morgan, *Birth,* p. 130.

189. Van Dusen, *Connecticut,* p. 176.

190. Morgan, *Birth,* pp. 130–44.

191. *State Records,* VI: 355–56.

192. Ibid., pp. 550, 553.

193. Ibid., pp. 553–73.

194. "Arch.," Revolutionary War, first series, XXXVII:299.

195. Ezra Stiles, Itineraries, V:243. On an additional page Stiles lists Matthew Griswold's farm stock for the year 1790: 23 hogs, 8 yoke oxen, 17 fat cattle, 25 cows, 3,000 pounds of cheese, 400 pounds of butter, 8,000 pounds of beef, 400 bushels of oats, 500 bushels of corn, 100 loads of English hay, 500 pounds of flax, 45 bushels of wheat, 120 bushels of rye, and 105 sheep. Itineraries, V:268.

196. *Connecticut Courant,* March 26, April 2, 1792.

197. Stiles, Itineraries, V:243.

198. Salisbury, *Griswold Family,* II:230–33.

199. Matthew Griswold to Reverend Levi Hart, Lyme, February 7, 1785, Simon Gratz Collection, American Judges, Case 3, Box 28, Historical Society of Pennsylvania.

200. Salisbury, *Griswold Family,* II:231.

201. Purcell, *Transition,* chs. 2, 6–9.

202. Matthew Griswold to President Stiles, Lyme, March 16, 1785, Beinecke Library, Yale University.

203. Old Lyme, First Congregational Church Records, III:54, 55, 60, 61, 62, Ecclesiastical Society Meetings, 1721–1876, pp. 173–77, CSL.

204. Roger Griswold to Matthew Griswold, Norwich, November 2, 1789, W. G. Lane, Yale.

205. Ibid., Philadelphia, March 19, 1798, Griswold Family Papers, Yale University.

206. *Connecticut Courant,* April 14, 1788.

207. Matthew Griswold to Roger Griswold, Lyme, May 20, 1788, W. G. Lane, Yale.

208. Oliver Wolcott to Matthew Griswold, Litchfield, November 22, 1788, Salisbury, *Griswold Family,* II:227; Ezra Stiles to Matthew Griswold, Yale College, November 3, 1788, W. G. Lane, Yale.

209. Matthew Griswold to Elijah Backus, Lyme, December 17, 1795, W. G. Lane, Yale.

210. *Connecticut Courant,* May 6, 1799.

211. Rockwell, *Sermon.*

The Upper House in Early Connecticut History

BRUCE STARK

DURING the colonial and early national periods Connecticut had her share of controversies. There were nevertheless few deep-seated and prolonged conflicts between executive and legislative powers and between the coastal areas and the backcountry. The colony therefore developed with relative ease and stability. She had a high degree of social, economic, and religious homogeneity and an enduring system of government based on the Fundamental Orders and the charter granted by Charles II in 1662. For these reasons Connecticut was often called the land of "steady habits."[1]

Historians have called attention to the colony's unusual political system, which combined frequent election for all important positions with long tenure in office for those elected. Unfortunately, they have not systematically analyzed this governmental system. In this essay Connecticut's Upper House, whose members were called assistants, will be examined in terms of historical background and evolution, the election laws and their implementation, and eighteenth-century politics as it affected the Council.

Connecticut's government was first defined in the Fundamental Orders adopted by the General Court, composed of members from Hartford, Windsor, and Wethersfield, on January 14, 1638/39. Twice a year, in April and September, the General Court or Assembly was to meet.[2] At the April session, called the "Court of Election," the governor and six additional magistrates were elected by the freemen of the commonwealth, who gathered in person to choose them.[3] In addition to the magistrates each of the three towns elected four deputies, who together with the governor, deputy governor, and magistrates made up the General Court. According to the Fundamental Orders, no person could be elected governor two years in succession. Until 1660, when this provision was changed, the governor and deputy governor often alternated in office. The General Court exercised supreme power, except for the election of magistrates, which was reserved for the freemen. The writ of the General Court was equally wide under the Charter of 1662, although no laws contrary to those of England could be enacted.[4]

In February 1644/45 the General Court resolved that in the future no law was binding unless it had the approval of a majority of both deputies and magistrates. As each group had a veto over the other, this act presaged the formal division of the two bodies, which occurred in October 1698.[5] The Fundamental Orders fixed the number of magistrates at seven, and for the next three years a governor, a deputy governor, and five magistrates were chosen. In 1642, as an attempt was apparently made to ensure at least one magistrate from each town, the total reached eight and in 1643 ten. Thereafter the number ranged from a low of eight in 1646, six magistrates plus a governor and deputy governor, to a high of sixteen in 1658.[6] The number of magistrates and deputies increased as the colony grew and added new communities.

Besides making up part of the General Court, the magistrates exercised judicial responsibilities.[7] Within individual towns they tried criminal and civil cases involving fewer than forty shillings and punished drunkenness, lying, and theft. These men also composed the membership of the Particular Court. In February 1637/38, even before the creation of a permanent form of government, the General Court ordered that a "particular court" be held the next May to try two persons accused of misdemeanors. This court, consisting of the governor or deputy governor and two magistrates, met quarterly in Hartford. The Particular Court had jurisdiction over all subjects of legal controversy. It heard appeals from local town courts, and its decisions were appealable to the General Court, which had supreme judicial authority.[8]

The Charter of 1662 produced few significant changes. Gov. John Winthrop, Deputy Gov. John Mason, and seventeen other men were constituted a "body corporate and politic . . . by the name of governor and company of the English colony of Connecticut in New England in America." The king empowered the company to make all reasonable and necessary laws for the government of the colony, as long as they were in accord with the laws of England. In May and October the assistants and the freemen of the company elected by the freemen of the towns, not exceeding two from each town, were to hold a general meeting or assembly to consult and advise on the business of the company. The General Assembly, consisting of the deputies present, the governor or the deputy governor, and at least six assistants, had full governing powers. On the second Thursday in May the governor, deputy governor, and assistants were elected for the year ensuing by the freemen present and voting in Hartford.[9]

Connecticut's charter also was responsible for the extinction of New Haven Colony, another experiment in the effort to create a Bible commonwealth in New England. Despite resistance from some political leaders the New Haven General Court voted on December 13, 1664, to join Connecticut. In May 1665 four of the leading men of the former colony were elected assistants, one of whom, William Leete, succeeded John Winthrop as governor.[10]

After 1665 Connecticut's government changed little. A law passed in 1670 ended the requirement for freemen to appear in person at Hartford to choose their governor, deputy governor, and assistants. To ensure honest and efficient management of election by proxy, another act directed the freemen in each town to gather on the last Tuesday in April to cast their votes. The constables and local deputies or commissioners were given the responsibility of taking the votes and delivering them to the capital on election day.[11] In October 1698 the General Assembly was formally separated into two houses. The first, made up of the governor, or in his absence the deputy governor, and the assistants, was known as the Upper House. The other was made up of the deputies from the towns and called the Lower House. The governor presided over the Upper House and the Speaker, chosen by the deputies, over the Lower House.[12]

The twelve assistants in the Upper House continued to exercise important judicial responsibilities. Many of the highest ranking military officers in the colony were members of the Council, and virtually all governors and deputy governors were drawn from the Upper House.[13]

The governor's office was one of dignity, respect, and influence but of little direct power. He had no veto and little patronage power, but he was responsible for all official correspondence with the British government and other colonies. He issued proclamations, determined days of fast and thanksgiving, and reprieved condemned criminals until the next meeting of the General Assembly. He had no power to dissolve the legislature but when necessary called special sessions on fourteen days notice. He presided over the Council and had a "casting voice" whenever an "equi vote" occurred. An act of the legislature in 1672 made him general of all the colony's military forces, and in 1750 he was officially given the title of captain-general and commander-in-chief. During the colonial period he was referred to as "His Honor" or "the Honorable," and in 1777 officially titled "His Excellency." Except for Gurdon Saltonstall, who was a minister in New London prior to his election, every governor from the adoption of the Charter to 1817 first served as deputy governor.[14]

The duties of the deputy governor were more limited. He acted as governor in the latter's absence or sickness, had a voice in the Council, provided the governor was present, and was lieutenant general of all military forces. From 1712 until 1785, the deputy governor served as chief judge of the Superior Court.[15] All vacancies in the deputy governorship from the time of the Charter until 1796 were filled from the ranks of the assistants. Most often the man promoted was not the senior assistant but a younger and more vigorous individual. If he outlived his superior or his superior resigned or was defeated for reelection, the deputy governor could expect to succeed him. The official title of Connecticut's second citizen was changed to lieutenant governor in 1784.[16]

Since the assistants were the best known, most experienced, and most influential individuals within the colony, they often commanded its militia regiments. In October 1739 the legislature reorganized the military establishment and increased the number of regiments from five to thirteen. The chief officers in each regiment were colonel, lieutenant colonel, and major. The field officers in both the First Regiment, from the Hartford area, and the Second Regiment, from the New Haven area, were all incumbent assistants.[17] Ten members of the Council held high ranks in the military establishment, as did eleven future assistants, one former assistant, and three persons nominated but never elected to the Upper House.[18] The colony's military establishment in 1762, still composed of thirteen regiments, had seven assistants among its chief officers, three future assistants, and two former ones.[19] The Assembly created twelve more regiments by independence so the percentage of councillors among their chief officers declined. But eight of the assistants in May 1776 filled high military positions.[20]

Members of the Upper House retained significant judicial responsibilities. A Court of Assistants replaced the Particular Court. Created in October 1665, it was made up of at least seven assistants and met twice a year in Hartford, a week before the May and October sessions of the General Assembly. The Court of Assistants had original jurisdiction over all cases relating to life, limb, or banishment and appellate jurisdiction in all other cases. According to the law code of 1672, membership in the court consisted of at least six assistants together with the governor or deputy governor as presiding officer.[21]

In May 1711 legislation established the Superior Court to replace the Court of Assistants. The chief judge — the governor or in his absence the deputy governor — and four assistant judges were appointed annually by the General Assembly to hold court in March and September in each of the four counties. The deputy governor presided as chief judge in all except two years between 1711 and 1785 and, although the law did not specify that the assistant judges be assistants, thirty-three of thirty-five were.[22] An act of 1784, effective May 1785, barred the governor, lieutenant governor, assistants, members of the Lower House, and delegates to Congress from sitting on the Superior Court. At the same time, the legislature created the Supreme Court of Errors, whose members were the lieutenant governor and the Council. Although the 1784 act prohibited assistants from simultaneously sitting on the Superior Court, eighteen of twenty-four new members of the Superior Court between 1785 and 1818 previously sat on the Council.[23]

County courts were established in October 1665. Each court consisted of three assistants, if that many lived in the county, or at least one assistant and two commissioners. The Assembly reorganized the county courts in January 1697/98. The new county courts were headed by a judge appointed by the legislature assisted by three or four justices of the peace, designated "of the Quorum." The law did not require that the judge of the county court be an assistant, but in May 1698 all the men chosen were members of the Council.[24] This trend continued. In Hartford, New Haven, Fairfield, and New London counties between 1698 and 1776, there were thirty-nine judges of the County Court, of whom thirty-five were assistants. The four judges who never belonged to the Upper House served ten years in all.[25] The tenure of judges of the Superior Court invariably terminated with the end of their service on the Council, but judges of the County Court sometimes continued in that position.[26]

Plural officeholding was the rule among assistants. Of those elected in 1762, three were on the Superior Court, four were judges of the County Court, five were judges of Probate, and seven filled high militia ranks. Before the end of their service in the Upper House, three others became members of the Superior Court, one attained field rank in the militia, one became judge of the County Court, and one judge of Probate.[27] Positions on the Superior Court and County Court were monopolized by members of the Council and seem to have been largely reserved for them. Other offices fell to members of the Upper House — for example, judge of Probate and field rank in the militia — because they were prominent members of Connecticut's ruling class, not because they were assistants.

Constitutionally the two houses of the legislature were equal, but actually the Council had more influence.[28] When disagreements broke out between the two houses, the Lower House generally deferred to the Council.[29] The Upper House was more influential because its members, including the governor and deputy governor, were the most prominent individuals in the colony. Moreover, the Council was a smaller and more intimate body, whose members enjoyed long tenure in office.

Upon election assistants bore heavy responsibilities and exercised great powers. They stood for election twice a year. In September each freeman cast twenty votes for his nominees for the Council. The twenty candidates receiving the most votes were officially nominated to run for the Council. The following April the freemen elected the governor, deputy governor, and twelve assistants from the list of nominees.[30]

Orders Two and Three of the Fundamental Orders defined the method of electing magistrates. No person could be chosen magistrate unless he had been nominated for that post at the preceding General Court. On election day the secretary first read the names of all nominees, and then the assembled freemen made a choice in turn from among all persons placed in nomination. As a name was read, each freeman in favor of the man wrote the nominee's name on a slip of paper. If he chose not to vote for that man, he cast a blank paper.

The nominees who received "more written papers than blanks" were elected magistrates for the coming year. If six individuals, the minimum number required for the Upper House, did not receive more written papers than blanks, those with the most votes, up to the number of six, were declared elected.[31]

The Charter permanently fixed the number of assistants at twelve, but the method of choosing them was altered by a May 1670 act of the General Assembly. This law required the secretary to send to each town the list of individuals nominated by the General Assembly at its October session. The constable published the list, and on the last Tuesday in April the freemen gathered to vote. The constable read the names of all persons placed in nomination, and from among that number the freemen first cast their votes for governor. Next they voted for deputy governor, secretary, and treasurer; then for the Council. They began "with he that first stands in nomination, and bring in their votes for him . . . and so they shall proceed for every person, till they have past through the whole nomination." As before, every freeman wrote the name of the person voted for on paper and cast a blank if he did not want to vote for that individual.[32] Although nothing is stated in the 1670 act or the law codes of 1672, 1702, and 1715, no freeman was supposed to vote more than twelve times. The law code of 1750 permitted "no one freeman to vote for more than twelve of the number in nomination to the assistants."[33]

The General Assembly passed a new election law in October 1689. Previously nominations were made by the legislature, but this act directed freemen to meet on the third Tuesday in March and vote for twenty nominees for election as assistants. On the last Tuesday in March the votes were counted in Hartford, and the twenty persons receiving the most votes were placed before the freemen on the last Tuesday in April. Thereafter voting was carried out in the manner described in the 1670 law, except that the votes for treasurer and secretary were taken last. According to the Fundamental Orders, all magistrates had to receive more ballots than blanks. The 1689 law rescinded the provision requiring more written ballots than blank ones for election and simply declared election for the twelve persons receiving the most votes.[34]

An October 1692 law took the privilege of nomination away from the freemen and returned it to the General Court, but in 1697 the Assembly reversed itself. The freemen of the towns were to convene on the third Tuesday of September. After choosing his deputies to attend the October session of the legislature, each freeman was to "give in his vote or suffrage for twenty persons (their names being fairly written upon a piece of paper) whom he judges qualified to stand in nomination for election in May next."[35] Another modification of the election laws was made in December 1707. The General Assembly granted the freemen the right to choose a governor and deputy governor from among all freemen in the colony instead of limiting the choice to the twenty nominees.[36] A final change took place in the first half of the eighteenth century. To ensure a maximum of twelve votes, each freeman was given only twelve instead of twenty pieces of paper.[37]

Scholars commenting on the method of electing councillors and on their long tenure focus on three factors which they believe gave incumbents advantages over aspirants. Richard J. Purcell points out that freemen, when faced with choosing among the twenty nominees, were given just twelve slips of paper. If they wanted to vote for any nonincumbents, they had to save one or more of their twelve ballots, thereby proclaiming themselves in revolt against the "standing order."[38] Jackson Turner Main notes that whenever an assistant died, the vacancy was filled by the remaining members of the Upper House, who chose a replacement. Main believes this was an important factor in making the Council "a nearly self-perpetuating oligarchy."[39] Charles S. Grant, in addition to Purcell and Main, emphasizes the method of voting. The poll began with the man that stood first in nomination and proceeded in order down the list until it was completed. This gave incumbents "an almost insuperable advantage." The procedure was "an electoral gimmick," which in the absence of intense political passions ensured the reelection of all incumbent councillors.[40]

Purcell oversimplifies the process and underestimates the importance of two elections every year. In September each freeman could vote for any number of men up to twenty to stand in nomination for the Council. Because no lists of candidates were published, the freemen could vote for anyone, but they tended to choose those with familiar names. Despite local popularity or unpopularity, the best-known men in the colony were usually renominated. In spring the freemen, after voting for governor and deputy governor, could vote for twelve persons from among the remaining list of nominees. Incumbents were generally reelected, and unsuccessful nominees usually received substantial voter support. Thus those who voted for nonincumbents were not necessarily misguided.[41]

The General Assembly had the right to fill vacancies whenever they occurred in the magistracy.[42] The legislature exercised this power seven times at the death of a governor or deputy governor, but only four times when there was a vacancy on the Council.[43] Upon reestablishment of Connecticut's Charter government in May 1689, the legislature appointed Samuel Willys and Fitz-John Winthrop to fill two vacancies in the Upper House. In July 1691 the Assembly elected Caleb Stanly as assistant to replace William Joanes, who was chosen deputy governor. Four assistants were appointed in May 1785 to replace four councillors who had resigned to continue as Superior Court judges. In May 1786 James Wadsworth was appointed assistant in place of Oliver Wolcott, newly elected lieutenant governor. All other vacancies remained unfilled until the next election.[44]

In the election of magistrates colony law directed the freemen to begin with the first nominee and proceed in order to the twentieth and last name.[45] Operating to the distinct advantage of incumbents was the unwritten interpretation of the law. By tradition, incumbents

TABLE 1

Nominations, October 1761[46]

The Honorable Thomas Fitch, Esq.	2574
Honorable William Pitkin, Esq.	2664
Roger Newton, Esq.	1480
Ebenezer Silliman, Esq.	2920
Jonathan Trumbull, Esq.	2901
Hezekiah Huntington, Esq.	3205
Andrew Burr, Esq.	2211
John Chester, Esq.	2603
Benjamin Hall, Esq.	2619
Daniel Edwards, Esq.	2473
Jabez Hamlin, Esq.	2768
Matthew Griswold, Esq.	3019
Shubael Conant, Esq.	2548
Elisha Sheldon, Esq.	2584
Col. Phineas Lyman	1703
Col. Eliphalet Dyer	2327
Mr. Roger Sherman	1722
Col. Robert Walker	1369
Capt. Jabez Huntington	1100
Mr. David Rowland	956

were listed in order of seniority and nonincumbents by popular vote.

On the nominations list the governor and deputy governor occupied the top two places. The next twelve places were filled by sitting assistants, and the final six by nonincumbents. The order of incumbents was determined by seniority, measured not by total years on the Council but from the date of first election. Hezekiah Huntington, for example, was first chosen assistant in 1740. He lost his seat in 1743 and did not regain it until 1748. Thus he was senior to Andrew Burr, first elected to the Upper House in 1746.[47] If more than one man were elected for the first time the same year, the person receiving the most votes on that occasion was placed ahead and always remained ahead on the list.[48] Nominees were placed according to their popularity unless they formerly served on the Council. In such cases they ranked ahead of all other nominees, regardless of votes received. This explains why the name of Phineas Lyman appeared before those of Eliphalet Dyer and Roger Sherman. To enjoy the advantages of incumbency on the nominations list an assistant had to be among the top twenty. Thus Roger Newton, first elected in 1736 and the senior assistant in October 1761, ranked number three in that election although he was seventeenth by popular vote.[49]

The advantages of incumbency were considerable, although it is worth noting that Roger Newton lost his Council seat the next election to Eliphalet Dyer.[50] The manner of listing nominations is a factor of some importance in explaining the long tenure in office of councillors. Of equal importance is the fact that the government generally served the interests of the populace and thus earned the support of

TABLE 2

Vacancies on the Council

Decade	No.	Death	Defeat	New position	Resigned
1700–09	7	2	4	1	0
1710–19	6	4	2	0	0
1720–29	11	6	2	2	1
1730–39	5	1	4	0	0
1740–49	7	2	4	1	0
1750–59	8	2	4	2	0
1760–69	10	3	5	2	0
1770–79	6	4	1	0	1
1780–89	15	2	3	8	2
	75[53]	26	29[54]	16[55]	4

most of the people.[51] Between 1700 and 1789 there were seventy-four newly elected assistants. The typical assistant served 13.6 years, and if years of service as governor and deputy governor are included, the average was 15.8 years.[52] Assistants relinquished their seats for other reasons besides death or senility, however.

Only thirty-five percent of all assistants died in office, thirty-nine percent were defeated for reelection, and twenty-one percent moved on to new positions. Many assistants lost their posts, though some had a great deal of seniority, and this demonstrates the flexibility of Connecticut's electoral system.

Assistants lost their seats for three reasons. Some took unpopular stands on important issues. Old Light Gov. Thomas Fitch and councillors Ebenezer Silliman, John Chester, Benjamin Hall, and Jabez Hamlin were dislodged in 1766 because they swore to uphold the Stamp Act.[56] For a handful of others the crucial factor was personal unpopularity unconnected with larger issues. Phineas Lyman (1716–74) was elected assistant in 1752 but ousted in 1759. He was a major general commanding Connecticut forces in the French and Indian War. In the spring of 1759 the war was still unsuccessful and costly in both manpower and material, and the freemen reacted by rejecting the colony's most visible symbol of the war.[57] For others there is no simple explanation, but a hint is evident in the fact that the average service for assistants defeated for reelection was 16.6 years, three years longer than the mean for all assistants. Evidently, freemen turned out those who no longer seemed useful. John Sherman (1651–1730), for example, after serving as assistant for ten years, lost his Council seat in May 1723, when he was seventy-two. John Hamlin (1658–1733) lost his in 1730 after serving on the Council for thirty-six years. Samuel Eells (1666–1753) was defeated in 1740 after thirty-one years.[58]

The typical assistant was 46.6 years old when first elected, and all except three chosen between 1700 and 1789 were natives of Connecticut.[59] Over the course of a century a greater number of these men had college degrees and were lawyers. Twenty-three assistants were elected between 1700 and 1729, and only four had college degrees, all from Harvard, and just four were lawyers. Twenty-four of thirty-one councillors elected from 1760 to 1789 graduated from college, twenty-one from Yale, and eighteen were members of the bar. Most came from well-to-do backgrounds. Their fathers were most often large landowners, businessmen, or ministers.[60] Before becoming assistants virtually all had distinguished themselves in the militia or in a lesser office such as deputy to the General Assembly or justice of the peace. Prior to election an average assistant served 15.3 terms in the Lower House.[61] Sixty-nine of seventy-four had been appointed justices of the peace, and fifty-two held militia positions.[62]

The career of Matthew Griswold (1714–99) offers a good example of the qualities helpful for election to the Upper House. His father, John Griswold (1690–1764), was elected to the legislature twenty-eight times, was judge of the Quorum for New London County for twenty-nine years, and was nominated assistant fifteen times between 1740 and 1754. John Griswold's reputation proved distinctly advantageous to his son's future political career. Inspired by the religious fervor of the Great Awakening, Matthew Griswold joined the First Church in Lyme on June 7, 1741. He studied law and began practicing before the New London County Court in February 1739/40. Admitted to the bar in November 1742 and chosen king's attorney for New London County three years later, he combined a busy and successful private practice with public service. In October 1739 he was elected captain in the militia, went first to the legislature in October 1748, and was appointed overseer of the Mohegans in 1754. The next year he was placed in nomination for the first time and in May 1759 elected assistant, replacing Phineas Lyman. A moderate New Light and Son of Liberty, Griswold was genuinely popular and often led the poll. Upon Governor Pitkin's death in October 1769, he was chosen deputy governor, much to the surprise of contemporary political observers. His election, managed by his politically astute nephew Samuel Holden Parsons, was a function of popularity and availability. Griswold served as deputy governor and chief judge of the Superior Court until 1784, when he succeeded Jonathan Trumbull as governor, but he was defeated for reelection two years later. His active political career ended in January 1788 when he presided over Connecticut's ratifying convention. Griswold's political success resulted from a combination of factors: a well-known family name, a successful legal career, personal popularity, and capable service in various offices.[63]

Connecticut history during the eighteenth century is best understood if divided into three segments: 1700–40, when the issues centered on land development and economic policy; 1740–65, when political controversies revolved around the Great Awakening and its aftermath; and 1765–88, the age of the American Revolution.

At the turn of the century the colony was plagued by bitter disputes over control of the Quinebaug lands in eastern Connecticut. The leaders of one group were Fitz-John and Wait Winthrop supported by the Reverend Gurdon Saltonstall of New London. Opposition leadership rested in the capable hands of James Fitch of Norwich, assistant from 1681 to 1698 and 1700 to 1709. Both groups sought to control for their own profit the distribution and sale of territory in eastern Connecticut, including part of New London County and almost all of Windham County. Before the victory of the Winthrop faction, the struggle to control the Quinebaug lands led to factionalism and open, bitter political controversies. The disputes abated after 1724 but produced a decline of respect for civil authority and prepared the way for more serious controversies following the Great Awakening.[64] Most quarrels occurred at the local level, in the courts, or in wrangling over appointments, but changes in the makeup of the Upper House also reflected divisions within the colony. James Fitch lost his Council seat in 1698. He regained it in 1700, replacing Richard Christophers of New London, who may have been a Winthrop ally, and lost it again in 1709. Samuel Mason of Stonington, a supporter of Fitch, lost his seat in 1703 after twenty years in office. The voters rejected four other assistants between 1700 and 1719, but in only one case was there a possible connection with the Winthrop-Fitch controversy. Daniel Wetherell of New London was not reelected in 1710 after nineteen years in office.[65]

Two assistants, Joseph Curtice and John Sherman, lost their seats during the 1720s.[66] Since both were over seventy, perhaps their age prompted the freemen to favor younger, more vigorous individuals. In the next decade four assistants were permanently denied reelection and one, future governor Thomas Fitch, temporarily lost his seat. John Hamlin, after thirty-six years in office, did not return in May 1730. Matthew Allyn and John Hooker failed to gain reelection in May 1734.[67] Both were aged and had lost popular esteem. But their defeat coincided with a sectional controversy over a land bank, the New London Society for Trade and Commerce. This organization was promoted by traders from eastern Connecticut who wanted paper money to foster economic growth and expansion. Their inflationary program aroused opposition from established merchants in western Connecticut and the Hartford area. As soon as it became known that the company was issuing bills of credit, the General Assembly, called into special session by Governor Talcott in February 1732/33, declared this practice illegal. The company collapsed soon after one vessel was shipwrecked and another captured by the Spanish. Political repercussions followed. Two assistants, Allyn and Hooker, both from the Hartford area and closely connected with Governor Talcott, were voted out of office; and in October 1734, for the first and only time, John Curtis, former treasurer of the society, was placed in nomination.[68]

In 1739 and 1740 four councillors lost their seats. Edmund Lewiss was defeated in May 1739 and Samuel Eells, John Burr, and Roger Newton the next year.[69] Although all had lost popularity and lived in the western part of the colony, their defeat is hard to understand. Eells and Newton resided in Milford, Burr in Fairfield, and Lewiss in Stratford.[70] Perhaps continuing sectional differences regarding economic policy give a partial explanation. This simultaneous defeat of three incumbents deeply disturbed the Council. In May 1740 the Upper House passed but the Lower House rejected "an act against fraud and clandestine dealing in the choice of the Governor and Council." The intent of the bill was to prevent distribution of lists of nominees to the voters.[71]

With the Great Awakening came a new era in Connecticut's religious and political history. Inaugurated by George Whitefield, the Awakening permeated the entire colony, especially the eastern part, including Windham and New London counties. The New Lights favored the revival, but their emotional fervor and rejection of the principles of the Half-Way Covenant and the Saybrook Platform antagonized conservatives who controlled the religious and political establishments. The government firmly allied itself with opponents of the revival by a 1742 statute that outlawed itineracy and another of 1743 that partially repealed the colony's Act of Toleration.[72]

After attempting to silence their opponents legally, the Old Lights worked to defeat outspoken supporters of the Awakening. Elisha Williams, former rector of Yale College and judge of the Superior Court, was not reappointed judge by the legislature in May 1743; and Councillor Hezekiah Huntington from Norwich, a supporter of the revival, was defeated for reelection by John Bulkley, an Old Light.[73]

In votes for nomination in individual towns local popularity always exerted great influence, but the Great Awakening controversy added another dimension, religious support or nonsupport for a candidate. The votes for nomination for several towns are extant for autumn 1745. John Bulkley, an Old Light favorite, received strong voter support in the conservative towns of Kent, New Milford, and Stratford in the western half of the colony, but less in the eastern revivalist towns of Coventry and Groton. Former councillor Hezekiah Huntington and Elisha Williams won favor in Coventry and Groton but received few votes in more conservative areas.

TABLE 3[74]

Votes for Nomination, September 1745

	Coventry	Groton	Kent	New Milford	Stratford
Nathaniel Stanly	34	8	0	37	62
Joseph Whiting	3	0	29	5	3
John Bulkley	3	34	28	43	94
Hezekiah Huntington	39	47	1	6	35
Elisha Williams	38	47	0	7	3

Two assistants, Joseph Whiting, an Old Light of New Haven, and Nathaniel Stanly, possibly a New Light of Hartford, lost their seats on the Council before the end of the decade, in 1746 and 1749 respectively. The popularity of both had declined, but their demise was probably hastened by partisan sentiments.[75]

During the next decade and a half, while religious dissent and the strength of New Lights increased, six other councillors were defeated for reelection. At least two incumbents were rejected for reasons unconnected with the religious struggle. Gov. Roger Wolcott and Gurdon Saltonstall of New London, the former governor's son, were not reelected in 1754 as a result of the Spanish ship case. A disabled Spanish snow landed at New London in November 1752 laden with gold and silver valued at 400,000 Spanish dollars. While in port a large portion of the treasure disappeared. Believing Wolcott and Saltonstall had been negligent and fearing the colony would have to make up the loss, the people of Connecticut turned these men out of office. Phineas Lyman lost in 1759 because he was associated in the public mind with a costly and unsuccessful war.[76]

Other incumbents who gave up their seats were James Wadsworth, Jonathan Huntington, Thomas Wells, and Roger Newton. Newton, defeated by Eliphalet Dyer in 1762, belonged to the Old Light faction, and perhaps James Wadsworth did also. No clear political identification is discernible for Jonathan Huntington and Thomas Wells, who may have favored the New Lights. Huntington came from Windham in New Light-dominated eastern Connecticut, Wells from Glastonbury. The latter lost his seat in 1761 but did not appear on a New Light purge list circulated in 1759.[77]

Throughout the 1750s political labeling became more common, and magistrates in office were increasingly disturbed by the New Light challenge. In May 1756 the legislature passed "An Act to Prevent Bribery and Corruption in the Election of Members of the General Assembly," and in March 1761 former governor Roger Wolcott warned against party ambitions hidden "under the paint of religion." In addition he admonished the voters to choose "according to [their] judgment, and not the judgment of another."[78]

Although the New Lights failed to defeat their conservative adversaries until the Stamp Act election of 1766, they usually commanded a majority in the Lower House by 1760. The Council, however, remained a bastion of conservatism. New Lights represented a powerful but heterogeneous coalition. In addition to supporting revived religion, the eastern party favored expansionary economic policies and promoted the territorial claims of the eastern-organized and -controlled Susquehannah Company. New Lights had tried, unsuccessfully, for a decade to defeat Old Light Gov. Thomas Fitch and his allies in the Upper House. Passage of the Stamp Act in 1765 gave them their opportunity. Popular hostility to the Stamp Act, enhanced by the extralegal activities of the Sons of Liberty, was intense. Three eastern veterans of the French and Indian War, Israel Putnam of Pomfret, Hugh Ledlie of Windham, and John Durkee of Norwich, directed their activities. Supporting them were easterners of standing such as Councillors Matthew Griswold of Lyme, Jonathan Trumbull of Lebanon, Eliphalet Dyer of Windham, and Jabez Huntington of Norwich. Local militia leaders led the shock troops of the Sons of Liberty, but the larger political goals of the eastern party were managed by New Light politicians who favored western expansion. The opportunity to expel their long-detested Old Light opponents arose when an Old Light from New Haven, Jared Ingersoll, accepted the post of stamp distributor for Connecticut; and Governor Fitch, with four allies on the Council — Ebenezer Silliman, John Chester, Benjamin Hall, and Jabez Hamlin — swore to obey the Stamp Act.[79] The Sons of Liberty called a series of meetings throughout eastern Connecticut during the late fall and winter of 1765–66 to "animate & strengthen in the people an aversion & abhorrence of stamping oppression." On March 25 and 26, 1766, at a general meeting in Hartford of Sons from all parts of the colony, the delegates united behind a ticket made up of individuals supporting Connecticut's rights and liberties. When votes were counted on election day, the Sons of Liberty had won a decisive victory. Deputy Gov. William Pitkin, the radicals' gubernatorial candidate, was elected governor by a "majority so great, votes not counted." Councillor Jonathan Trumbull of Lebanon was chosen deputy governor, and six new assistants were elected.[80]

The victory of the eastern party in 1766 was never reversed, and those responsible for the triumph led Connecticut into revolution. But the followers of former governor Fitch sought to return him to office by waging a series of aggressive campaigns in every election between 1767 and 1774. Indeed, the electoral battles fought by the two factions in the wake of the Stamp Act were unmatched in Connecticut history. Old Lights made a vigorous effort in 1767 to oust the radicals. Observers believed Pitkin would be reelected because "the Old Lights are not awake yet," but they hoped that Silliman and Hamlin would "have a resurrection." Such dreams proved false. Pitkin easily defeated Fitch, 4,777 to 3,481, but Silliman came within one hundred votes of ousting Joseph Spencer.[81]

The 1768 election was not nearly as close, perhaps because passage of the Townshend Acts reminded the voters of the issues that divided them. Governor Pitkin polled 5,033 votes and Fitch only 2,835. Ebenezer Silliman polled six hundred fewer votes than Joseph Spencer, the least popular incumbent. But conservatives in the General Assembly nearly elected Fitch chief justice of the Superior Court over Deputy Governor Trumbull. They again supported Fitch for governor in 1769, and again Pitkin was reelected. Trumbull, however, failed to gain a majority of votes for deputy governor, and conservatives tried in vain to place Fitch in that office.[82]

Old Lights had another opportunity when Pitkin died on October 1, 1769. The legislature easily chose Trumbull governor over Fitch by a vote of seventy-two to forty-eight, but four ballots were required before Matthew Griswold was elected deputy governor over Fitch and several other opponents. Fitch polled 42 votes on the first ballot and Griswold 26 out of 125 cast. The 1770 election was especially hard fought. Trumbull polled 4,700 votes, Fitch 4,266, and 805 were scattered among other persons.[83]

Two things are noteworthy about elections during this period: the political sophistication of the voters and the deep split between east and west. In October 1769 Fitch, Silliman, Chester, and Hamlin held positions fourteen through seventeen on the ballot. Only in positions eighteen through twenty were new persons listed.[84] With the elevation of Matthew Griswold to deputy governor, the voters had to elect a new person to replace him. In May 1770 they selected Zebulon West of Tolland, listed eighteenth among nominees. He polled 2,838 votes, 450 more than Thomas Fitch. Clearly, the freemen understood the electoral system and possessed both the perspicacity and shrewdness to elect a Son of Liberty over a conservative.[85]

Fairfield County was the conservative bulwark, while the strength of the New Lights centered in New London and Windham counties. A preliminary nominations list for October 1770 amply demonstrates the division within the colony.

TABLE 4

Votes for Nomination, October 1770[86]

County	Trumbull	West	Fitch	Silliman
Hartford	899	865	459	454
New Haven	385	468	513	434
New London	499	430	85	80
Fairfield	140	112	607	519
Windham	618	721	11	3
Litchfield	389	497	304	231
Total	2,930	3,093	1,979	1,721

The voting strength of radicals in the east continued to frustrate conservatives.

The most divisive issue in Connecticut between 1769 and 1774 was the Susquehannah affair. Organized in Windham in July 1753, the Susquehannah Company won support from land-hungry farmers and prominent politicians, most of whom were allied with the eastern

New Lights. Opponents of the company, including Governor Fitch, belonged to the Old Light party. Initial efforts to settle the territory along the Susquehanna River were frustrated by an Indian massacre and a proclamation prohibiting further settlement by Governor Fitch. The issue remained quiescent until 1769, when a more favorable political attitude at home encouraged new efforts to establish Connecticut's claim. The Upper House, many of whose members were shareholders, and Governor Trumbull supported the company, but the Lower House resisted until October 1773. Then the Assembly resolved to "assert their claim . . . to those lands contained within the limits and boundaries of the charter of this colony, which are westward of the Province of New York." In January 1774 the inhabitants of the territory were constituted into a distinct town called Westmoreland and made part of Litchfield County.[87]

The final effort by anti-Susquehannah followers of Thomas Fitch to regain control of the colony occurred in 1774. Trumbull's victory over Fitch was so decisive, with a majority of about two to one, that the votes were not counted. For the Council the assistant with the fewest votes still polled 1,500 more than Fitch. Three months later, in July 1774, Thomas Fitch died. The defeat of conservatives in a campaign waged over territorial expansion meant far more than approval of Susquehannah. "For that defeat ensured Whig control of the provincial government during the grave months when the colonies were to be engaged in their last controversy with Britain."[88]

From 1774 to 1780 politics remained relatively calm. The divisions of the preceding decade ended with the deaths of conservative leaders and preparation for the War of Independence.[89] Two assistants, however, lost their seats because the voters suspected they were Tories. James Abraham Hillhouse of New Haven, elected assistant in May 1773, was not returned in 1775 after he offered protection to the notorious Tory Samuel Peters. William Samuel Johnson, an Anglican, was defeated in 1776 because he refused to take up arms against Britain.[90]

In 1780 the political climate began to change, and the campaigns of the 1780s were much more heated. In May for the first time since 1770 Governor Trumbull failed to receive an electoral majority, and his son-in-law, William Williams, lost his Council seat. The governor's popularity abated because of his opposition to price controls and the people's war-weariness. Although Williams favored price controls, he was so closely identified with Trumbull and a vigorous war effort that he was caught in the backlash.[91] The next year the governor's popularity declined still further, and he polled only 2,636 votes out of 6,802 cast. In 1782, however, with the war almost won, Trumbull gathered 3,026 votes compared with 3,006 scattered among several opponents.[92]

The ending of the war brought new factionalism set off by the Continental Congress when it proposed to reward the officer corps of the Continental Army. In 1780, with the war at its lowest ebb, Congress promised half pay for life to all Continental officers who agreed to serve until the end. This measure aroused such hostility that Congress in 1782 commuted half pay for life to five years full pay plus three months back pay. Commutation was condemned as "unconstitutional, injurious, impolitic, oppressive, & unjust." Among farmers, who had assumed the burden of wartime taxation, inflation, and economic hardship, the idea of special rewards for a privileged cast of officers seemed unconscionable. Nationalists and merchants, on the contrary, favored commutation.[93] Governor Trumbull, a merchant and the embodiment of nationalism, fared poorly in the election of 1783. Out of a total of 7,091 votes, he polled 2,309, only 129 more than William Pitkin. Although easily reelected by the legislature, the opponents of commutation in the fall of 1783 provided the most serious challenge to the standing order since the Stamp Act election. Representatives from about fifty towns met at Middletown in September to coordinate strategy and plan changes in the makeup of the nationalist Upper House. Their initial efforts were quite successful. Both the governor and deputy governor were left off the nominations list along with Eliphalet Dyer and Abraham Davenport, two of the most senior assistants. Five new men, all opponents of commutation, appeared on the nominations list. The vigor of the anticommutation movement died out by the 1784 election, and just one of seven nonincumbents supported by the Middletown Convention was elected.[94]

Although the issue of commutation disappeared, new issues arose between nationalists and localists. Nationalists, led by Trumbull and a majority of the Council, represented established leadership determined to preserve the status quo. Wishing to strengthen national authority, they had the support of merchants, Continental security holders, and former Continental Army officers. Localists represented ambitious politicians and the interests of state creditors and hard-pressed farmers. They disliked the Society of Cincinnati, a nationalist organization of former members of the officer corps of the Continental Army, because of its elitist character. Nationalists, Continental creditors, and the Society of Cincinnati wanted to sell sight unseen Connecticut's Western Reserve, the northern portion of the future state of Ohio, in 5,000-acre tracts, and to allow Continental securities for payment. Localists, who controlled the Lower House, wanted to keep the Western Reserve to benefit Connecticut farmers. They wanted to have the area surveyed before settlement and to prohibit payment in Continental securities.[95]

After adoption of the new Constitution, the nationalist faction emerged victorious. But elections from 1784 to 1788 were hard fought, and ten new assistants were chosen. Three were elected in 1784, two to replace defeated incumbents, and one to replace Samuel Huntington, who became lieutenant governor. An act of May 1784, operative the next year and supported by localists, prohibited the same person from sitting on both the Superior Court and the Council. In May 1785 four nationalist assistants resigned from the Upper House in order to continue on the Superior Court. A fifth new assistant was chosen to replace Jabez Hamlin, who had resigned. In 1786 one new assistant was elected to replace Oliver Wolcott, who was elevated to the post of lieutenant governor after the defeat of Governor Griswold for reelection. After Connecticut's adoption of the Constitution in 1788, James Wadsworth, an arch-localist, lost his seat to the young nationalist John Chester.[96] The localists ultimately lost the war, but several of their leaders gained election to the Council, and the makeup of the Upper House changed drastically in response to popular pressures.

The tenure in office for assistants was long, averaging 13.6 years, and because of the structure of the nominations list incumbents enjoyed real advantages over nonincumbents. Once elected, a councillor could expect to be returned to office year after year, but enough assistants were defeated to teach them that tenure was not permanent. During the course of the eighteenth century the length of service for assistants declined. Those elected between 1700 and 1759 averaged 15.5 years in office; those elected between 1760 and 1789 averaged 8.76 years.[97] This decline was not caused by a greater frequency of electoral defeats. Prior to 1784 the office of assistant was considered the most desirable, but with the prohibition of simultaneous service in the Upper House and Superior Court and with election to the United States Congress customarily leading to resignation from the Council or denial of reelection, many more individuals were elevated to the Upper House. The rate of turnover was higher in the twenty years from 1780 through 1799 than in any other in Connecticut history, when thirty were newly elected assistants. Between 1800 and 1817 twenty-one new assistants were chosen, so the rate of turnover continued to be high. Flexibility disappeared with the rise of a two-party system, however. The majority Federalists tightened their control over government, and since party candidates were selected by caucus and party managers persuaded freemen to vote exclusively for incumbents, the political system became more rigid.

James Kirby Martin recently defined several variables for measuring political democracy. First, the voters must have some voice in selecting candidates for nomination. Second, elected officials must be sensitive to public opinion. Third, politicians must realize that their tenure in office will be limited unless they maintain an identity of interests with their constituents, and, finally, the voters must understand the difference between candidates and issues and use their franchise accordingly. According to Martin few of these qualities of political democracy are completely operative today.[98] Although it would be incorrect to say that Connecticut politics in the eighteenth century was democratic, all the variables noted above are applicable at least part of the time. Freemen in Connecticut not only elected their magistrates but nominated them in September elections. Elected officials were sensitive to public opinion, which helps to explain both their long tenure in office and the respect government usually earned. Whenever assistants lost the support of a majority of the voters, they were not returned to office. Moreover, events of the 1760s and 1770s reveal that the freemen had a clear understanding of political issues and the candidates' platforms.[99]

Connecticut enjoyed a republican form of government, one chosen by the freemen but acting in a paternalistic way to govern in the best interests of the people. The Upper House was unlike that of any other colony except Rhode Island. Before independence the typical council was an appointive body, and its members remained overwhelmingly loyal to the Crown. The Council of Connecticut was not transformed by the revolutionary experience as were the upper houses in other states. The typical postrevolutionary senator represented a district, not the state at large, and he was sometimes elected on a different voter-qualification basis than members of the lower house.[100]

Whether Connecticut's government was based on the ideal of deference depends on how it is defined. If a deferential society is one in which higher governmental positions are held by the better-educated and more wealthy persons of an elevated social position, it was deferential. If, however, the highest governmental positions are controlled by a small elite regardless of the political views of ordinary men, if little or no choice is given the voters, and if most important offices are appointive, then the government was not deferential, at least when compared with that of Virginia. Nor did Connecticut's government pattern itself on Whig ideals of mixed government.[101] Although it had a chief executive and an Upper House, the Council did not represent or aim to represent a different order of society from the Lower House. Moreover, the governor, deputy governor, and Council were elected annually by the freemen, and the governor possessed little executive authority. Instead of a balanced mixed government, Connecticut relied on the principle of legislative supremacy. The Council, on which the governor and deputy governor sat, was nevertheless the more influential of the two houses. The government of Connecticut was responsible and responsive to the will of the majority, though not to its whims.

Notes

1. See Christopher Collier, "Steady Habits Considered and Reconsidered," *Connecticut Review* V (April 1972):28–37.

2. J. Hammond Trumbull and Charles J. Hoadly, eds., *The Public Records of the Colony of Connecticut* (Hartford: Case, Lockwood, and Brainard Co., 1850–90), I:20–25, 140. The Court of Election was altered from the second Thursday in April to the third Thursday in May in 1646.

3. The Fundamental Orders did not specify eligibility for being a freeman, but Connecticut's law code of 1672 specified that an aspirant had to present himself to the General Assembly with a certificate from the selectmen of the town of his residence, and that he be a person "of an honest, peaceable and civil conversation." In addition, he had to be at least twenty-one years old and possess an estate in housing or land worth at least twenty pounds. A person so qualified was presented to one General Court and admitted at the follow-

ing one. The property qualification for freemanship was revised in the code of 1702. A freeman had to possess a "freehold estate to the value of forty shillings per annum, or forty pounds personal estate." Further legislation in October 1729 gave the responsibility of admission to freemen's meetings in each town. *Colony Records,* I:21; VII:259–60; *The Book of the General Laws for the People within the Jurisdiction of Connecticut* (Cambridge: Samuel Green, 1673), Caleb Stanly copy, Connecticut State Library, p. 26; *Acts and Laws of His Majesties Colony of Connecticut in New-England* (Boston: Green and Allen, 1702), p. 40.

4. *Colony Records,* I:20–25, 347; II:8; Dwight Loomis and J. Gilbert Calhoun, *The Judicial and Civil History of Connecticut* (Boston: Boston History Company, 1895), pp. 112, 114, 116.

5. *Colony Records,* I:119; IV:267.

6. *Colony Records,* I:27, 46, 64, 71, 84, 137, 314.

7. The members of the Upper House of the legislature were called *magistrates* until 1662. The Charter designated them *assistants* and fixed their number at twelve. The word *assistant* was first used in October 1651, when the General Court designated three men "assistants to join with the magistrates for the execution of justice in the towns by the sea side." After 1662 these assistants to the magistrates were called *commissioners.* In January 1697/98 new legislation created the office of justice of the peace. *Colony Records,* I:226–27, 336, 400, 402; II:4, 38; IV:235–37.

8. Loomis and Calhoun, *Judicial and Civil History,* pp. 125–28, p. 155; *Colony Records,* I:12, 71, 81, 126–27, 336.

9. *Colony Records,* II:3–9.

10. Albert E. Van Dusen, *Connecticut* (New York: Random House, 1961), pp. 72–74.

11. *Colony Records,* II:131, 133–34.

12. Ibid., IV:267.

13. Between 1665 and 1796 only one governor or deputy governor failed to serve on the Council. In December 1707 the Reverend Gurdon Saltonstall of New London was chosen governor by the General Assembly to replace Fitz-John Winthrop, deceased. *Colony Records,* V:38; *Dictionary of American Biography* (New York: Charles Scribner's Sons, 1928–36), VIII, pt. 2:317–18 (hereafter cited as *DAB*).

14. Loomis and Calhoun, *Judicial and Civil History,* pp. 112–16; Richard J. Purcell, *Connecticut in Transition: 1775–1818* (Middletown, Conn.: Wesleyan University Press, 1963), pp. 117–18; *Book of General Laws,* p. 28.

15. The act creating the Superior Court in May 1711 designated the governor or in his absence the deputy governor as chief judge. In May 1712 Deputy Gov. Nathan Gold was chosen chief judge, and with the single exception of 1713 the Assembly always chose the deputy governor to be chief judge. *Colony Records,* V:241, 332, 385, 430; Loomis and Calhoun, *Judicial and Civil History,* pp. 137–38.

16. Loomis and Calhoun, *Judicial and Civil History,* pp. 115–16; *Colony Records,* VIII:277; *Acts and Laws of the State of Connecticut in America* (New London,

Conn.: Timothy Green, 1784), p. 27; Charles J. Hoadly et al., *The Public Records of the State of Connecticut* (Hartford: Case, Lockwood, and Brainard and the State of Connecticut, 1894–1967), V:107, 317; Leonard W. Labaree, *Conservatism in Early American History* (New York: New York University Press, 1948), p. 21.

17. *Colony Records,* VIII:272, 279.

18. Ibid., VIII:279–81.

19. Ibid., VIII:272, 277–81; XI:632–33; XII:3.

20. *Colony Records,* XII:88, 347, 459; XIII:9, 519; XIV:264, 332, 393, 422; XV:43, 272, 285; *State Records,* I:134.

21. *Colony Records,* II:28–29; *Book of General Laws,* p. 17.

22. Thirty-one were members of the Upper House before serving on the Superior Court, two were appointed before election to the Upper House, and two others, Elisha Williams and Joseph Fowler, were never assistants although both were nominated for the post. Loomis and Calhoun, *Judicial and Civil History,* pp. 127–28, 161; *Colony Records,* VIII:287, 366, 446; X:244, 394, 490; XI:4, 117, 274.

23. *Colony Records,* V:238–39, 241; *State Records,* V:323–24; VI:4–5; Loomis and Calhoun, *Judicial and Civil History,* pp. 137–39.

24. *Colony Records,* II:35; IV:235–36, 244, 261.

25. Ibid., V–XV passim. The total terms were 316, 79 years multiplied by 4.

26. For example, Roger Newton, assistant from 1736 to 1740 and from 1742 to 1762, served as judge of the New Haven County Court from 1738 until his death in January 1771.

27. *Colony Records,* IX:632–33; XII:3–5, 347, 414, 454–55; XIII:5, 237.

28. On this point the author agrees with Richard J. Purcell and disagrees with Oscar Zeichner. Purcell, *Transition,* pp. 120–25; Oscar Zeichner, *Connecticut's Years of Controversy, 1750–1776* (Charlotte: University of North Carolina Press, 1949), p. 5.

29. "Connecticut Archives," Civil Officers, first series, I–III passim (hereafter cited as "Arch.").

30. For brief descriptions of election procedures see Zeichner, *Controversy,* p. 240n; Labaree, *Conservatism,* p. 21; Jackson Turner Main, *The Upper House in Revolutionary America* (Madison, Wis.: University of Wisconsin Press, 1967), p. 81; and Charles S. Grant, *Democracy in the Connecticut Frontier Town of Kent* (New York: Columbia University Press, 1961), pp. 122–27.

31. *Colony Records,* I:21–22.

32. Ibid., II:133–34.

33. Ibid., II:133–34; *Book of General Laws,* p. 23; *Acts and Laws* (1702), p. 31; *Acts and Laws of His Majesties Colony of Connecticut in New-England* (New London: Timothy Green, 1715), pp. 31–32; *Acts and Laws Passed by the General Court or Assembly of His Majesty's English Colony of Connecticut in New-England in America* (New London: Timothy Green, 1750), p. 46.

34. *Colony Records,* IV:11–12. According to Richard Bushman the altered method of counting votes worked to the advantage of incumbents. Richard L.

Bushman, *From Puritan to Yankee* (Cambridge: Harvard University Press, 1967), p. 90.

35. *Colony Records,* IV:81, 223–24.

36. Ibid., V:39.

37. *Acts and Laws* (New London: Timothy Green, 1750), p. 46; Purcell, *Transition,* p. 125.

38. Purcell, *Transition,* p. 125.

39. Main, *Upper House,* p. 81.

40. Main, *Upper House,* p. 81; Grant, *Kent,* pp. 123–26; Purcell, *Transition,* pp. 125–27; *Laws of 1750,* p. 46.

41. The two largest collections of votes for nomination and election for the period before 1790 are those of Connecticut, Secretary of State, and Connecticut, General Assembly, I, at the Connecticut Historical Society (hereafter cited as CHS).

42. The operating statute provided that "if there be want of assistants by occasion of death or otherwise, after the election, such want shall or may be supplied and made up by the General Courts election or appointing some suitable person or persons to supply such want according to Charter." The revision of the laws in 1750 substituted the word "officers" for "assistants." Main is incorrect in his assertion that vacancies were filled by the governor and other assistants. According to the statute, vacancies could only be filled by the entire General Assembly. *Book of General Laws,* p. 17; *Acts and Laws* (1702), p. 23; *Acts and Laws* (1750), p. 28; Main, *Upper House,* p. 81.

43. Governors and deputy governors were replaced on seven occasions at the October or special sessions of the legislature between 1665 and 1790: in July 1691, December 1707, October 1723, October 1724, October 1741, November 1750, and October 1769. *Colony Records,* IV:54; V:38; VI:414–15, 484–85; VIII:416; IX:585; XIII:246.

44. Ibid., III:250; IV:54; *State Records,* VI:4–5, 144–46.

45. *Colony Records,* II:134; *Book of General Laws,* p. 22; *Acts and Laws* (1702), p. 31; *Acts and Laws* (1750), p. 46.

46. Connecticut, General Assembly, I, CHS.

47. *Colony Records,* VIII:286, 512; IX:188, 349–50.

48. Jonathan Trumbull and Hezekiah Huntington were both elected assistants for the first time in May 1740. Trumbull gathered 2,298 votes and Huntington 2,191. Trumbull's larger vote ensured him precedence over Huntington. Connecticut, Secretary of State, CHS; *Colony Records,* VIII:286.

49. *Colony Records,* VIII:28.

50. Ibid., XIII:3.

51. Grant believes the colony's rulers gave "the freemen a benevolent, paternalistic rule which seemed to satisfy them." Grant, *Kent,* pp. 126–27.

52. Using different parameters, Labaree found that the average assistant was elected and reelected fourteen times. The mean length of service for elected magistrates in Connecticut was longer than that for appointed ones in Virginia. Labaree, *Conservatism,* pp. 21–22.

53. An individual is counted only when first elected, and not a second time

if defeated and then reelected. Thus, seventy-four persons were newly elected assistants, and seventy-five vacancies occurred. Richard Christophers was first elected assistant in 1699 and defeated for reelection in 1700. He regained his seat in 1703 and served until his resignation in 1723.

54. Nine persons who lost their Council seats later regained them. If they are added to the total of defeated legislators, then thirty-eight of seventy-five assistants were defeated for reelection. Included among this number were such distinguished figures as Gov. Roger Wolcott; Gov. Thomas Fitch; Hezekiah Huntington; Gov. Jonathan Trumbull; William Williams, the Signer; and William Samuel Johnson, Founding Father.

55. The careers of eleven governors and deputy governors ended during this period. Six died in office, three were dislodged by the voters, and two resigned.

56. Van Dusen, *Connecticut*, p. 128; Zeichner, *Controversy*, pp. 56–58, 73–75.

57. Franklin Bowditch Dexter, *Biographical Sketches of the Graduates of Yale College* (New York: Henry Holt and Company, 1885–1911), I:603–06; *Colony Records*, X:345, 470, 600; XI:95, 226, 353, 503, 618.

58. Thomas Townsend Sherman, *Sherman Genealogy* (New York: Tobias A. Wright, 1920), p. 134; H. Franklin Andrews, *The Hamlin Family* (Exira, Iowa: the author, 1900), p. 25; Frank Farnsworth Starr, *The Eells Family* (New Haven: Morehouse and Taylor, 1903), pp. 120–23, 132; "Arch.," Civil Officers, first series, I:361; II:116; Connecticut, Secretary of State, CHS; *Colony Records*, VI:367–68; VII:253, 268; VIII:263, 286.

59. Timothy Pierce, assistant 1728–48, was born in Woburn, Massachusetts. Elisha Sheldon, assistant 1761–78, came from Northampton, and Roger Sherman, councillor 1766–85, was born in Newton. Frederic Beech Pierce, *Pierce Genealogy* (Worcester, Mass.: Press of Chas. Hamilton, 1882), p. 37; Dexter, *Biographical Sketches* I:418; *DAB*, IX, pt. I:88.

60. Main, *Upper House*, pp. 82–84, 180; Dexter, *Biographical Sketches*, I–III passim.

61. Twelve was the median number of terms served. Election to the Lower House has not been counted if it coincided with election to the Council.

62. *Colony Records*, III–XV passim; *State Records*, I–VI passim.

63. Glenn E. Griswold, *The Griswold Family* (Rutland, Vt.: Tuttle Publishing Co., 1935), pp. 130–31, 134–37; *DAB*, IV, pt. 2:9–10; Old Lyme, Connecticut, First Congregational Church Records, I:36; New London Court Records, Trials-Dockets, XIX, February 1739/40:244; XX, November 1742, November 1745; XXI–XXII passim; *Colony Records*, VII:259; IX:384; X:306, 413; XI:246; Connecticut, General Assembly, I, CHS; Joseph Chew to William Samuel Johnson, December 9, 1769, William Samuel Johnson Papers, II:4, CHS.

64. Bushman, *Puritan to Yankee*, pp. 83–103.

65. *Colony Records*, IV:341–42, 406; V:89, 142–43, 206.

66. Ibid., VI:305, 367–68; "Arch.," Civil Officers, first series, I:361.

67. *Colony Records*, VII:268, 483; VIII:28.

68. Ibid., VII:483, 522; Bushman, *Puritan to Yankee*, pp. 124–27; Dexter, *Biographical Sketches*, I:203–5.

69. Newton recaptured his seat in 1742.

70. *Colony Records*, VIII:222, 286; Connecticut, Secretary of State, CHS; Selections from the M.H.S. Trumbull Papers (microfilm, CHS); Starr, *Eells Family*, pp. 120–23; Clair Alonzo Newton, *Newton Families of Colonial America* (Napierville, Ill.: the author, 1949), II:236–37; Charles Burr Todd, *A General History of the Burr Family*, 4th ed. (New York: the author, 1902), pp. 26–30; Donald Lines Jacobus, *History and Genealogy of the Families of Old Fairfield* (Fairfield, Conn.: Tuttle, Morehouse, and Taylor, 1930), p. 379.

71. "Arch.," Civil Officers, first series, II:399.

72. Zeichner, *Controversy*, pp. 21–25; Bushman, *Puritan to Yankee*, pp. 183–91.

73. *DAB*, X, pt. 2:257; *Colony Records*, VIII:446, 512–13.

74. Robert J. Dinkin, "The Nomination of Governor and Assistants in Colonial Connecticut," *Connecticut Historical Society Bulletin* XXXVI (1971):92–96.

75. *Colony Records*, IX:188, 414–15; Dinkin, "Nomination of Governor," p. 93.

76. Roland Mather Hooker, *The Spanish Ship Case* (New Haven: Yale University Press, 1934), pp. 3–26; *Colony Records*, X:198, 243; XI:180, 246.

77. *Colony Records*, X:3; XI:3, 494; XII:3; Zeichner, *Controversy*, p. 253n.

78. *Colony Records*, X:496; Zeichner, *Controversy*, pp. 25, 252n; *New London Summary*, March 20, 1761.

79. Zeichner, *Controversy*, pp. 25–77; Bushman, *Puritan to Yankee*, pp. 245–66; Christopher Collier, *Roger Sherman's Connecticut* (Middletown, Conn.: Wesleyan University Press, 1971), pp. 31–59; Edmund S. and Helen M. Morgan, *The Stamp Act Crisis* (New York: Collier Books, 1962), pp. 280–300.

80. William Williams to Mr. Lyman, December 25, 1765, the Historical Society of Pennsylvania; *Connecticut Courant*, March 31, 1766; *Connecticut Gazette* (New Haven), May 10, 1766; *Colony Records*, XII:411, 453–54. Four assistants were chosen to replace defeated incumbents, one to replace Jonathan Trumbull, and one to fill a vacancy.

81. John Devotion to Ezra Stiles, April 22, 1767, June 6, 1767, Franklin Bowditch Dexter, ed., *Itineraries and Correspondence of Ezra Stiles* (New Haven: Yale University Press, 1916), pp. 462–66.

82. *New London Gazette*, May 20, 1768; Zeichner, *Controversy*, p. 121.

83. Connecticut, Secretary of State, CHS; Zeichner, *Controversy*, p. 121–22.

84. Votes for nomination October 1769: Fitch, 2,242; Silliman, 1,904; Chester, 1,655; Hamlin, 1,980; Zebulon West, 3,191; Oliver Wolcott, 2,882; Nathan Whiting, 1,117.

85. Connecticut, Secretary of State, CHS.

86. Ibid.

87. Julian Boyd, *The Susquehannah Company: Connecticut's Experiment in Expansion* (New Haven: Yale University Press, 1935), pp. 5–37; *Colony Records*, XIV:160–61, 217–18.

88. Connecticut, Secretary of State, CHS; Zeichner, *Controversy*, pp. 155–58.

89. John Chester died in September 1771; Benjamin Hall in January 1773; Fitch in July 1774; and Ebenezer Silliman on October 11, 1775. The last Old Light, Jabez Hamlin, was reelected assistant in May 1773. Clifford K. Shipton, *Biographical Sketches of Those Who Attended Harvard College* (Boston: Massachusetts Historical Society, 1945), VII:26; Dexter, *Biographical Sketches*, I:250, 357; *Connecticut Courant*, January 12, 1773; *Colony Records*, XIV:73.

90. Margaret P. Hillhouse, *Historical and Genealogical Collections Relating to the Descendents of Rev. James Hillhouse* (New York: Tobias A. Wright, 1924), pp. 53–55, 423; Dexter, *Biographical Sketches*, I:763; Governor Joseph Trumbull Collection, IV:413, 457, Connecticut State Library.

91. Collier, *Sherman's Connecticut*, pp. 179–80; *State Records*, III:5–6; Connecticut, Secretary of State, CHS.

92. Jonathan Trumbull, Sr., Papers, Diary, 1780–85, CHS.

93. Collier, *Sherman's Connecticut*, pp. 210–18; Philip H. Jordan, Jr., "Connecticut Politics during the Revolution and Confederation, 1776–1789," (Ph.D. diss., Yale University, 1962), pp. 157–85, 215–20; Instructions to Col. Wm. Williams & Capt. Daniel Tilden, 1782, Williams Papers, CHS.

94. Collier, *Sherman's Connecticut*, pp. 218–19; *State Records*, V:313, 317; *Connecticut Gazette* (New London), April 9, 1784; Jonathan Trumbull (1710–84), Diary, 1784, Connecticut State Library.

95. Jordan, "Connecticut Politics," pp. 187–90, 251–68.

96. *State Records*, V:317, 323–24; VI:4, 144, 146, 398; "Arch.," Civil Officers, second series, V:233; *The New Haven Gazette and the Connecticut Magazine*, May 15, 1788, p. 7.

97. Sixteen persons served in the Upper House during the 1790s and thirteen in the first decade of the nineteenth century. Councillors elected in the 1790s spent an average of 9.4 years in office and those elected the following decade 6.9.

98. James Kirby Martin, *Men in Rebellion* (New Brunswick, N.J.: Rutgers University Press, 1973), pp. 7–8.

99. Purcell, in disapproval, notes that from 1639 to 1818, 185 persons were chosen councillors from just forty-five towns and 108 represented eight towns — Hartford, Windsor, Fairfield, New Haven, New London, Norwich, Wethersfield, and Litchfield. These figures are misleading. In the early years of settlement only a small number of towns existed, so the Council contained several representatives from Hartford, Windsor, Wethersfield, Fairfield, and New Haven. These eight communities were among the most populous, as well as the commercial centers of Connecticut. Five were also county seats, centers of political activity. Purcell, *Transition*, p. 126.

100. See Main, *Upper House*, and Martin, *Rebellion*.

101. J. R. Pole, "Historians and the Problem of Early American Democracy," *American Historical Review* LXVII (April 1962):626–46.

Patterns of Officeholding in the Connecticut General Assembly: 1725–1774

HAROLD E. SELESKY

CONNECTICUT occupies a unique place among the thirteen colonies that rose against Great Britain in 1775. Without altering their existing forms of government, the people of Connecticut joined the rebellion, saw it to a successful conclusion, and eventually united with their neighbors in an unprecedented experiment in political democracy. The royal charter of 1662 granted the colony virtual autonomy in internal affairs, and no extralegal conventions were needed to organize resistance to British authority. Connecticut's participation in the War of American Independence is significant because its people made the decision to resort to arms within an orderly and adaptable framework of popular government.

In the past twenty-five years several historians have reexamined the reasons behind that decision. Rejecting the view that the colony was a "land of steady habits," Oscar Zeichner and Richard Bushman have analyzed and emphasized the issues which deeply and bitterly divided Connecticut.[1] They have demonstrated that financial affairs in the 1720s, religious revivals in the 1730s and 1740s, the desire for western lands in the 1750s and 1760s, the Stamp Act in 1765/66, and, to a lesser extent, freedom from imperial control in the 1760s and 1770s divided the colony. These disputes gradually destroyed the stability of the conservative old order.

According to Bushman, "The assumption had always been that 'Gentlemen of approved Capacity and Fidelity' were to remain in office, however unpopular their actions, so long as their character was unimpeached."[2] This attitude changed as the government grappled with the problems confronting it. Many people became dissatisfied with the solutions enacted by the ruling oligarchy, and they organized to elect men more sympathetic to their views. The idea that the people could hold their leaders accountable for their decisions transformed the character of the political system. Officials who flouted the public will were denied reelection. The process culminated in 1766 when men who shared the widespread popular determination to resist more firmly the tightening of imperial regulations won control of the government.

Bushman and the others base their analyses almost exclusively on the comments of partisan contemporaries contained in books, pamphlets, letters, and diaries, because few others recorded their ideas about government or the performance they expected from the men they elected. Historians assume that the new attitudes about politics were accompanied by a fundamental shift in voting behavior, but without basic voting data, they can only infer that Connecticut experienced a democratic revolution in the years before 1775. Occasionally they abstract the career of an individual or the upheaval of a particular event to illustrate the ideas about officeholding they believe were characteristic of the society.[3] A more complete understanding of these ideas is derived by examining the careers of all the men who served in the legislature between 1725 and 1774. Patterns can be established, and their evolution under the pressure of events documented. An analysis of officeholding in the General Assembly can show how the people of Connecticut manipulated their institutions of government to achieve their objectives and, by inference, reveal some of their assumptions about the nature of government.

For purposes of analysis the records of service compiled by Connecticut's legislators have been summarized in ten five-year intervals beginning in 1725.[4] While the history of Connecticut cannot be divided neatly into five-year periods, several intervals do have strong unifying themes. In 1740, for instance, the colony raised troops for Britain's abortive assault against Carthagena. But the economic and manpower burden imposed by that venture was small compared with the tumult of a religious revival which wracked Connecticut between 1740 and 1745. The Great Awakening generated a storm of controversy in the colony's religious and political life and created divisions which lingered on long after the last outburst of revival energy. In 1745, Connecticut joined its neighbors in the ambitious scheme to reduce Louisbourg, an investment of men and money which bore fruit when the fortress eventually fell to the New Englanders.

The Great War for Empire began a decade later in 1755 and with it came a heavy burden on Connecticut's resources. The colony contributed substantially to the series of annual campaigns which culminated in a British victory in North America in 1759. Even while the fighting was still in progress, British statesmen laid plans to shore up the weak points of imperial control which the stress of war had revealed. One of their principal measures, the Stamp Act, forced a response unprecedented in the colony's history; it has been argued that the Stamp Act crisis of 1765/66 initiated the chain of events which led inexorably to rebellion in 1775.

Some of the other periods are not as sharply defined. For example, it is not entirely evident that the post–Stamp Act period ended in 1769 and the final prerevolutionary period began in 1770. Though this division into periods does tend to blur changes occurring in any single year, it is a useful means of identifying and focusing on patterns of officeholding.

Political authority in Connecticut was vested in a three-part General Assembly, the entire membership of which was subject to semiannual review by the voters.[5] The governor and his deputy acted as the Assembly's executive agents and, unlike their counterparts in neighboring royal colonies, had no veto power over its decisions. The Council of twelve assistants had been erected into a separate house of the General Assembly in 1698, an arrangement which enabled it to exercise a restraining influence on some of the more audacious plans developed in the Lower House. The deputies, two from each town, formed the largest part of the Assembly.[6]

The people of Connecticut possessed a unique system for choosing their governor, deputy governor, and assistants. Every freeman voted twice, first to create the slate of candidates and again to elect from that list the fourteen men in whom he had most confidence. The freemen cast their ballots for the nomination list at their local town meetings each September, and the results were tabulated at the regular session of the Assembly in October. The top twenty vote-getters were then declared in nomination for the governorship, the deputy governorship, and the twelve places on the Council. The incumbent governor and deputy governor customarily headed this list, followed by the incumbent assistants in order of seniority and then by the nominees ranked by number of votes received. The next April the freemen voted for their leaders, and the winners were sworn into office in May. Thus the voters had two opportunities in each year to reject unsatisfactory legislators.[7]

This procedure, repeated annually for over a century and a half, paradoxically produced an extraordinary record of stability and continuity (Table One). The average tenure of the thirty-eight men first elected to the Council between 1725 and 1774 was 15.6 years. The average number of assistants who won reelection each year (Column 2) never dropped below 10.8 men, a rate most clearly expressed as one of ninety percent retention of incumbents and ten percent turnover (Column 3). These figures must be used carefully, for in the case of the 1765–69 period all six new men entered in a single year, 1766. While this unprecedented fifty percent turnover appears to mark a political revolution, the figures for 1770–74 demonstrate that the voters reelected these new incumbents with the same consistency as they had their predecessors in earlier years.

A comparison of the average number of assistants with prior service (Column 5), whether in the previous year or before, with the average number with immediate prior service (Column 2) shows that an individual was likely to win reelection each year until death, severe disability, or a grave error in judgment removed him from office. On a few occasions — twice in 1740–44, and once each in 1745–49, 1750–54, and 1770–74 — a man did return to high office after an absence of at least one year.[8] Service on the Council is analyzed in Columns 6, 7, and 8 according to the length of time since an individual's first term. In 1725–29, for instance, of the average of 11.0 men with prior service, 6.8 had entered within the preceding decade. Less than half that number, 3.2 per year, had remained on the Council for eleven to twenty years. Only 1.0 man in each year had served more than two decades.[9] As might be expected, fewer men were drawn from years increasingly distant from the current session.

The distribution shown in 1725–29 did not continue, however. Gradually the balance shifted as more men served for more years. In the 1740s over half the assistants (fifty-four percent in 1740–44 and fifty-eight percent in 1745–49) were veterans of more than eleven years on the Council. The pattern of 1725–29 returned during the 1750s and again in 1770–74 after a decade of abrupt changes. In the early 1760s the Council was endowed with abundant experience, including a greater percentage of men with over twenty years of service

TABLE ONE
Assistants

| | 1 | 2 | | 3 | 4 | | 5 | | 6 | | 7 | | 8 | |
| | Total Assistants | Assistants with Immediate Prior Service | | Turnover | New Assistants | | Total Assistants with Prior Service | | Assistants with 1 to 10 Years Prior Service | | Assistants with 11 to 20 Years Prior Service | | Assistants with 21 or More Years Prior Service | |
Years	Average Number	Average Number	Percent	Percent	Average Number	Percent	Average Number	Percent	Average Number	Percent*	Average Number	Percent*	Average Number	Percent*
1725–29	12.0	11.0	92	8	1.0	8	11.0	92	6.8	62	3.2	29	1.0	9
1730–34	12.0	11.2	93	7	0.8	7	11.2	93	7.4	66	2.2	20	1.6	14
1735–39	12.0	11.6	97	3	0.4	3	11.6	97	6.4	55	3.0	26	2.2	19
1740–44	12.0	11.0	92	8	0.6	5	11.4	95	5.2	46	4.8	42	1.4	12
1745–49	12.0	11.2	93	7	0.6	5	11.4	95	4.8	42	5.0	44	1.6	14
1750–54	12.0	10.8	90	10	1.0	8	11.0	92	5.6	51	4.2	38	1.2	11
1755–59	12.0	11.4	95	5	0.6	5	11.4	95	6.4	56	4.4	39	0.6	5
1760–64	12.0	11.2	93	7	0.8	7	11.2	93	5.4	48	2.8	25	3.0	27
1765–69	12.0	10.8	90	10	1.2	10	10.8	90	9.0	83	0.4	4	1.4	13
1770–74	12.0	11.2	93	7	0.6	5	11.4	95	8.6	76	2.2	19	0.6	5

*Percentages in Columns 6, 7, and 8 are based on Column 5 equaling 100%.

NOTE: The figures are the actual averages for the five-year periods, while the percentages are rounded off to the nearest whole number. Decimals indicate differences not otherwise apparent, as in Column 2 of Table One and Column 2 of Tables Four and Five. Trends can be spotted and comparisons made most easily through the percentage figures.

than in any period since 1725. The upheaval caused by the Stamp Act altered dramatically this state of affairs. Between 1765 and 1769 fewer than one in four assistants (actually seventeen percent) had as much as eleven years tenure. Curiously, this crisis had greater impact on the careers of those with eleven to twenty years of service than among those with longer tenure.

Overemphasis on the pattern of low turnover in high office can obscure the fact that new men were continually elected to the Council, with at least one new assistant every four years. Moreover, substantial changes could occur within a relatively short period. For example, the five new men for 1725–29 (an average of 1.0 per year) plus the four for 1730–34 (0.8 each year) represented a seventy-five percent turnover within a decade. The reelection of incumbents was balanced by the steady introduction of new men. This pattern is due partly to the large constituency electing the assistants and partly to attitudes of Connecticut's voters.

The assistants, unlike the deputies, were chosen by a colony-wide constituency. Ability was a prerequisite of election. No man won a Council seat without demonstrating his talent for public service in some town office up to and including deputy in the General Assembly.[10] Recognition counted for just as much, perhaps more, in a society in which able and ambitious men outnumbered the available positions. A distinguished parentage and inherited wealth enhanced the possibility of election to local office and could generate voter appeal in a few contiguous towns. Though friends might nominate him each September, a favorite son could not win election merely on the votes of his hometown. Deputy service provided a way of earning recognition, but the odds were against a young man making his mark quickly when Assembly business was in the hands of experienced, almost professional, public servants. Some men labored for many sessions before they attracted sufficient attention to win nomination.[11] Most of the men with fewer than eleven years on the Council had worked their way up through the Assembly and were elderly when first elected. Those who served for twenty and thirty years generally entered when comparatively young.

Partial lists of returns for the September nominating elections for two years, 1737 and 1745, demonstrate some of the differences between the man still gaining in voter appeal and the man who had reached the limit of his popularity.[12] Of the fifty-seven individuals named in the 1737 return, only those who were popular in all parts of the colony had a chance of nomination.[13] The twelve incumbents and the six additional nominees were generally popular in all seven towns.[14] In some localities, however, the voters gave their ballots for the final six places on the slate to prominent local leaders unknown elsewhere. The only man outside the top twenty with a following in as many as four towns was Hezekiah Huntington of Norwich. In 1745 he won a substantial share of the vote in five of the six towns whose returns have survived, and he barely missed regaining the seat which he had lost two years before.[15]

Merely by virtue of his incumbency the man in office had an advantage over the popular, younger man eager for office. As long as the incumbent received enough votes to place in the top twenty, he won a position on the nomination list corresponding to his seniority on the Council. A popular newcomer therefore might appear fifteenth in the list were he not already an assistant. This could be a disadvantage since inertia — or popular pressure — might prompt the voter to select the first fourteen names in nomination, all of whom were familiar to him from the previous year's election.[16] If an incumbent did not voluntarily withdraw his name or commit some unpardonable act, he could expect continued support from the constituency that had elected him to office.

Some historians have argued that the ideology of deference democracy lay at the heart of Connecticut's political system. According to the interpretation of Jack P. Greene, voters believed that public affairs "should be entrusted to men of merit; that merit was very often, though by no means always, associated with wealth and social position; that men of merit were obliged to use their talents for the benefit of the public; and that deference to them was the implicit duty of the rest of society."[17] Patterns of service on the Council support this thesis. Connecticut voters consistently elected their most prominent fellow citizens as assistants and returned them to office year after year.

The stability characteristic of deference democracy does not imply, however, that the political structure was rigid or that issues had no impact. Connecticut voters reacted sharply to highly controversial issues, especially religion and the defense of charter rights, but they did so without discarding all of their traditional assumptions about the nature and function of government. The careers of two men — Hezekiah Huntington and Jabez Hamlin — demonstrate that this deferential political order could accommodate differences of opinion and emerge with ideas about officeholding substantially unaltered.

Hezekiah Huntington was born on December 16, 1696, the eldest son of Christopher Huntington of Norwich.[18] In May 1734 the voters sent him to Hartford to represent them in the Assembly. At thirty-eight, he embarked on a legislative career somewhat later in life than most of his influential contemporaries. Huntington must have been well prepared, for his spectacular rise in the next six years amply demonstrates the voters' confidence in him. At one point he served for seven consecutive sessions (May 1737 to May 1740, inclusive), a pattern not typical of service as a deputy.[19] At New Haven in October 1739 Huntington ranked seventeenth on the nominating list; with luck and good health, he could look forward to a seat on the Council when enough incumbents died or retired.

At the same session Huntington was appointed to one of the thirty-nine positions created when the Assembly reorganized the militia into thirteen regiments, each with three field officers. New London County was divided between the Third Regiment, containing New London, Norwich, and Lyme in the west, and the Eighth Regiment, combining Groton, Preston, and Stonington in the east. Apparently by tacit agreement one field officer was selected from each town. Thirty-nine-year-old Gurdon Saltonstall of New London, son of the late governor of the same name, became colonel of the Third. Huntington, at forty-three, the most prominent citizen in Norwich, ranked right behind Saltonstall as lieutenant colonel.[20] The newly appointed "Colonel" Huntington went as a deputy to Hartford in May 1740, only to relinquish this post upon election, in his first year of candidacy, to the twelfth and last seat on the Council.

Huntington won election in 1741 and 1742, but in 1743 his unpopular stand on the Great Awakening cost him reelection for six years. He favored this revival of religion and championed the evangelical and enthusiastic New Lights it spawned.[21] Unfortunately for his political career, the Awakening was not universally popular. Some voters, especially in western Connecticut, considered religious excess to be the work of the Devil and did not look favorably upon those who displayed it. Huntington's career on the Council appeared to have ended. For six years, though he received enough votes to remain in nomination, he was omitted from the Council. With his following in eastern Connecticut still intact, Huntington managed to survive politically until enough voters in the western half of the colony came to share his point of view. He returned to the Council in 1748 and served continuously for twenty-five years. He was Connecticut's senior assistant when he died on February 10, 1773.

Huntington was not the only assistant denied reelection for his rejection of Congregational orthodoxy. Because the Great Awakening forced religious differences into the political arena, proper beliefs became, for many voters, a test of the ability to govern. Samuel Eells, an assistant since 1709, was omitted in May 1740, shortly after he helped to found a Presbyterian society in his home town of Milford.[22] John Burr of Fairfield and Edmund Lewiss of Stratford were denied reelection in 1738 and 1739, respectively, about the time both men joined the Anglican church. Undoubtedly some voters penalized these men for following the dictates of their consciences. Though stripped of policy-making power, both Burr and Lewiss — like Huntington — retained their appointive militia posts and continued to receive judicial responsibilities. The men the voters had rejected continued to hold other positions because the Assembly realized that the government needed the support of locally prominent "magistrates of known ability and approved faithfulness."[23]

One further aspect of Huntington's career warrants mention. Concurrent service in all three parts of Connecticut's leadership structure — legislature, militia, and judiciary — was common among the assistants. Almost all elected to the Council in this period (thirty-six of thirty-eight) were appointed at one time or another to a number of judicial posts. Huntington was named one of New London County's twenty-four justices of the peace in 1737. The next year he moved up to become one of four justices of the peace and quorum, a position on the county court which he retained during his six-year absence from the Council. In October 1748 he was appointed judge of the Court of Probate for the newly created Norwich District; three and a half years later he became judge of the New London County Court. Huntington held both the probate commission and the county court seat concurrently for the remainder of his life.

Huntington demonstrated that a man could rise quickly given the right circumstances. More commonly, men gave many years of yeoman service before receiving a Council seat. On the face of it,

Jabez Hamlin of Middletown had more impressive credentials than Huntington, but he unaccountably had to serve a long apprenticeship as a deputy. Born on July 28, 1709, Hamlin was the son of Judge John and the grandson of the Honorable Giles.[24] His pedigree was impeccable, and he reinforced it with a bachelor of arts degree from Yale College in 1728. The men of Middletown's First Company of militia gave ample evidence of his stature when they elected him their ensign in October 1728, almost before the ink was dry on his diploma. Three years later, this precocious twenty-two-year-old was elected to the General Assembly in New Haven. After such a quick beginning, his career thereafter lagged. His name did not appear in nomination for the Council until 1754, and not until 1758 could he claim the twelfth seat in that body. But his appeal to the voters of Middletown never wavered. In the twenty-seven years between 1731 and 1758 he won a seat in the Assembly an astonishing fifty times out of a possible fifty-four. Rarely indeed did one man command such respect from voters. His position in Middletown was secure, and, though officeholding was not his profession, he certainly assumed more than his share of public service.

For all his popularity with the Middletown voters, however, Hamlin lacked appeal in other parts of Connecticut. His peers recognized his abilities and gave him appointments in the militia and the judiciary. Beginning in 1736, he accepted judicial responsibility each year for well over fifty years: justice of the peace in 1736, justice of the peace and quorum in 1744, probate judge of the Middletown District in 1752, and judge of the Hartford County Court in 1754. He held the last two positions concurrently for almost thirty years. All these offices were appointive — including that of major in the Sixth Regiment of militia — and all were gained initially before Hamlin's name first appeared in nomination for the Council in October 1754. This record clearly demonstrates that a locally prominent individual could wield extensive influence but lack the colony-wide popularity required for election to the Council. Hamlin received unprecedented assistance in demonstrating his talents to the greatest number of voters. Despite his ancestry, education, and record of service, Connecticut voters, apparently well satisfied with their incumbent assistants, were in no hurry to elevate him to the Council.

Hamlin served as an assistant for seven years before his stand on the Stamp Act caused the voters to deny him reelection in May 1766.

He shared Gov. Thomas Fitch's opinion that the act was a valid if unconscionable exercise of imperial authority. If the colony defied this act of Parliament, Great Britain would likely revoke Connecticut's charter and impose a royal governor.[25] Other leaders believed that the promulgation of stamp duties constituted a greater and more immediate threat to the colony's rights than did the distant prospect of losing charter privileges. This group took the unprecedented step of organizing the popular sentiment against the act in order to ensure the defeat of the incumbents who were prepared to accept its enforcement. Hamlin was one of four assistants who administered to Fitch the oath to uphold the act, and for this stand he was ousted with his like-minded colleagues in May 1766.[26] While no single issue created this response among the voters, it is clear that the essential and indispensable impetus came from the extraordinary sensitivity of Connecticut voters to erosion of their privileges of self-government.[27]

Fitch and the former assistants nonetheless retained popularity with a considerable number of voters. All five received a place in nomination for at least a few years. The rising generation of leaders drew enough votes away from Benjamin Hall and Ebenezer Silliman to remove them from the lists in 1767 and 1773, respectively. Both John Chester and Thomas Fitch remained in nomination until they died in the early 1770s.[28] Hamlin, more fortunate than his colleagues because he probably possessed a larger core of support, returned to the Council in May 1773 and served continuously until 1785. His return to office, like that of Huntington twenty-five years earlier, resulted from a change in the political climate. Tempers had cooled by 1773 and, though the connection with Britain remained unsettled and potentially perilous, the tension and the danger seemed less than during the Stamp Act years.

Though dropped from the Council in May 1766, all four former assistants were elected to the Assembly the following October. Two, Chester and Hamlin, served in every session until they either died or moved up again to the Council. All four were appointed justices of the peace for the rest of their lives and two, Silliman and Hall, actually received additional judicial responsibilities, Silliman as probate judge of the Fairfield District and Hall as judge of the New Haven County Court. All four, moreover, retained their high ranks in the militia. Perhaps these men owed their continued tenure in appointive offices to an attempt by the Stamp Act insurgents to conciliate their oppo-

nents and to consolidate their own position. Regardless of their motives, the victors honored a long-standing political custom in Connecticut. Whether the cause of the alteration was religious nonconformity
or apparent political blundering, defeat for reelection to a seat on the
Council carried no mandate to remove the individual from other
offices held concurrently or from consideration for other high posts.
Loss of popularity was not sufficient to deprive the government of the
talents and support of the colony's ablest citizens.

The voters continued to entrust the Council to men of long-
proven ability, all of whom had risen to power through careers of
service essentially indistinguishable from those compiled by the men
whom they displaced. For example, four of the six men first elected in
1766 had served for upwards of a dozen terms as deputies in the
General Assembly.[29] The fifth, William Pitkin, Jr., son of the new
governor, had been one of Hartford's deputies for nine terms since
1762.[30] The sixth, William Samuel Johnson of Stratford, was a prominent leader of the colony's Anglican minority. The upheaval of 1766
did not reflect an alteration in ideas concerning political officeholding. All six new men enjoyed the trust and confidence of Connecticut's voters for many years. Roger Sherman and William Pitkin, Jr.,
were elected to twenty consecutive terms until the General Assembly
forced them to choose between a place on the Council and election to
Congress. Except for a year (1778) when he was employed as a major
general in the Continental Army, Joseph Spencer of East Haddam
remained an assistant until 1788. William Samuel Johnson lost his
place in 1776 because he was suspected of loyalty to Great Britain.
Out of office for ten years, he managed to come back in 1786 and
served for two additional years.[31] Lengthy tenure continued to be
characteristic of membership on the Council. Though government
might have lost much of its paternalistic character, it was still conducted by men of merit whom the people trusted.

Any analysis of Connecticut politics must include the deputies as
well as the assistants. Patterns created by the voters each time they
sent their representatives to the General Assembly were free from the
stability-inducing constraints of a large electorate and so reflect more
directly the attitudes about political officeholding then current in the
society. Deputies were elected for a term of service, either from April
to the following September or from September to the following April,
and were expected to attend any special sessions called during their

tenure in office. The names of the deputies who attended each session were entered at the head of the record of business transacted at that session. These lists have been used to construct Table Two, presenting data on the prior service of the deputies elected to each regular session of the Assembly.

The number of deputies continually increased as newly settled towns in northeastern and northwestern Connecticut found the need and the wherewithal to elect representatives (Columns 1 and 2). Nevertheless, individual sessions could contain far fewer members than the average, depending upon the weather, the press of personal business, and the frequency of special sessions. During the Great War for Empire, for instance, the number of issues requiring Assembly attention mounted to the point where the number of special sessions exceeded the number of regular sessions for 1755–59. This placed a considerable burden on those individuals who could not afford to put the colony's business ahead of their own. Legislative business for 1755 began in January with ninety-eight members present. Ninety-five came to the March special session and one hundred to the May regular session. Ninety-six or more were present in August and October 1755 and in January, February, and March 1756. With so many meetings and the work they required attendance fell in May 1756 to seventy-nine, the lowest figure for a regular session in twenty years. Attendance increased sufficiently thereafter to produce an average of 101.4 men for the period (or eighty-three percent of the maximum possible). All things considered, the deputies took their responsibilities seriously when they were needed most. The drop in 1756 and the recovery through 1759 probably reflected a purge under great stress of the men who could not or would not devote the necessary time to Assembly business, and their replacement by men with fewer personal commitments.

The data in Table Two establish the general patterns of participation in the Assembly. Usually, between fifty-one and sixty percent of the deputies served for two consecutive terms (Column 4), a figure substantially lower than the comparable average of ninety to ninety-seven percent for the Council. Retention of incumbents was lowest (forty-four percent) — that is, turnover was highest (fifty-six percent) — during 1755–59, the height of Connecticut's involvement in the Great War for Empire. Like the assistants, the deputies constantly welcomed new men into their ranks. An average of between 9.2 and

TABLE TWO
Deputies

	1	2	3	4		5	6		7		8		9		10	
Years	Towns	Total Deputies Average Number	Percent of Theoretical Maximum	Deputies with Immediate Prior Service Average Number	Percent	Turnover Percent	New Deputies Average Number	Percent	Total Deputies with Prior Service Average Number	Percent	Deputies with 1 to 10 Years Prior Service Average Number	Percent*	Deputies with 11 to 20 Years Prior Service Average Number	Percent*	Deputies with 21 or More Years Prior Service Average Number	Percent*
1725–29	43	79.9	95	40.5	51	49	11.7	15	68.2	85	41.7	61	22.2	33	4.3	6
1730–34	44	81.5	95	44.6	55	45	9.2	11	72.3	89	44.9	62	22.3	31	5.1	7
1735–39	44	84.2	98	45.7	54	46	9.3	11	75.1	89	43.3	58	22.7	30	9.1	12
1740–44	48	88.7	94	49.6	56	44	9.9	11	78.8	89	44.3	56	25.2	32	9.3	12
1745–49	50	89.9	92	52.7	59	41	12.0	13	77.9	87	43.2	55	22.7	29	12.0	16
1750–54	53	100.2	96	52.1	52	48	15.8	16	84.4	84	49.9	59	24.1	29	10.4	12
1755–59	62	101.4	83	44.4	44	56	18.6	18	82.8	82	49.9	60	20.6	25	12.3	15
1760–64	66	116.4	90	68.0	58	42	14.7	13	101.7	87	64.2	63	22.3	22	15.2	15
1765–69	69	126.7	93	72.3	57	43	15.3	12	111.4	88	67.7	61	27.8	25	15.9	14
1770–74	69	134.7	99	81.2	60	40	15.4	11	119.3	89	69.7	58	34.3	29	15.3	13

*Percentages in Columns 8, 9, and 10 are based on Column 7 equaling 100%

18.6 individuals entered the Assembly for the first time in each session (Column 6); in other words, from eleven to eighteen percent of each Assembly was new. This pattern of constant renewal coupled with the high rate of turnover enhanced the stature and influence of men like Jabez Hamlin and Zebulon West who were returned to session after session with minimum interruption.

These trends must be understood in terms of the average number of men in each session who had previously served in the Assembly. Between eighty-two and eighty-nine percent of the deputies were drawn from a pool of men who knew some of the intricacies of legislative business (Column 7). The contrast with the Council is striking: interrupted careers were rare among the assistants but the rule among the deputies. As might be expected, only a relatively few men — an average of between six and sixteen percent per session — remained in consideration for upwards of twenty-one years (Column 10). More than half the deputies (fifty-five to sixty-three percent; Column 8) began and ended their careers within ten years, which again increased the prestige of those who served longer or with fewer interruptions.

These figures show clearly that Connecticut's voters constantly rotated the honor and burden of Assembly service among the leading freemen of their community. While some towns undoubtedly fell prey to factional infighting, the data do not reveal the extent to which the choice between candidates was free or limited by an influential individual or group. Perhaps, in those towns where more men thought themselves capable and worthy of a place in the Assembly than there were seats to fulfill those ambitions, politics was lively and contentious. Perhaps, in other towns, the leaders agreed among themselves to rotate the office so that each aspirant could prove his ability and share the responsibilities of office.

Participation in the Assembly differed considerably from participation in the Council. Turnover between sessions was higher, the number of men introduced to service was larger, and the ability of men to move into, out of, and back into office was much greater among the deputies than among the assistants. Patterns of service in the Lower House nevertheless show a remarkable consistency. Though issues undoubtedly altered the way in which people viewed their government, the voters accomplished the desired changes without disrupting the orderliness and stability of service in the Assembly.

Except for a slight increase during 1755–59, turnover between sessions averaged from forty to forty-nine percent. Though the fifty-year trend tends toward lower turnover, no drastic or abrupt shifts occurred in the patterns of deputy elections. The percentage of men with some experience never dropped below eighty, and the distribution of that experience generally inclined, by sixty to forty percent, toward men with fewer than ten years of service. The bitter controversies which wracked Connecticut during these fifty years are not reflected in these data.

An upheaval comparable to the one the Stamp Act caused in Council membership was absent in the Assembly. Indeed turnover for the years 1765 and 1766 was lower than that commonly experienced during 1755–59. The voters achieved an admirable balance among participation, renewal, and experience. Rotation in office ensured many men an opportunity to share in the decision-making process and prevented any single individual from gaining too great a share of power. Renewal was guaranteed because new men, presumably with new ideas, encountered few difficulties in winning seats in the Assembly. All these changes were orderly because enough men understood legislative business. The most conspicuous characteristic of the political structure in the Assembly was its flexibility in accommodating new political perceptions within the same basic framework.

The foregoing analysis can be refined by studying the data from Table Two in terms of the six counties existing in Connecticut before 1775. This method is somewhat artificial because county lines had no special significance for representation in the legislature, but it does furnish a convenient way to express certain patterns of settlement and economic activity.

The four original counties — Hartford, New Haven, New London, and Fairfield — were established in 1664 and lay like an inverted T along the dual axes of Long Island Sound and the Connecticut River valley. Hartford County contained towns on both sides of that great river from the Massachusetts border south almost to Long Island Sound. Age of settlement varied directly with distance east or west of the river, ranging from the three ancient river towns of Hartford, Windsor, and Wethersfield to some of the most recent settlements on the fringes of Litchfield County in the west. New Haven County existed as a separate colony until 1664, when it united with the river towns to create the larger Connecticut colony. Most of the towns in this south-central region were founded before that un-ion. New London County extended along the shore from New Haven County eastward to the Rhode Island border, reaching inland from New London along the Thames River to Norwich, a focal point for much of the commercial activity in eastern Connecticut. Fairfield, the last of the original counties, stretched along the shore to the west of New Haven County; Greenwich, its westernmost town, abutted the royal colony of New York.

The northeast and northwest corners of the colony were settled after the turn of the eighteenth century. Settlement proceeded haphazardly in the northeast, where many conflicting claims created an atmosphere of bitter competition for land ownership.[32] These dis-putes, plus the lack of direct access to water-borne transportation, undoubtedly contributed to the hunger for western lands that cen-tered in the region — Windham County — during the 1750s and 1760s. The colony government sought to regulate settlement more carefully when it put the public lands in the northwest up for sale in the 1730s. The land was surveyed, divided into townships, and sold at public auction for fixed minimum prices, all under public control and at public expense.[33] The towns thus created, along with a few settled previously, were organized into Litchfield County in 1752. While it included a few large and prosperous towns, most of the county's communities were small, poor, and thinly populated until after 1765.

The economic life of the colony was based almost exclusively on agriculture and associated trades.[34] Lacking direct commercial links with Britain, Connecticut's merchants conducted most of their busi-ness through middlemen in New York City, Boston, and occasionally Providence, Rhode Island. These merchants bought up surplus ag-ricultural produce, sold it in one of the middlemen's markets, and then purchased imported manufactured goods to retail in their hometowns. Patterns of economic activity seemed to divide the colony along the Connecticut River: the region to the west of the river de-pended largely on the port of New York, the region to the east, on Boston.

Historians have shown that an east-west dichotomy existed on most of the issues in the period 1725–74.[35] While no hard and fast lines can be drawn, it does seem that the people of eastern Connecti-cut approached issues more restlessly, more energetically, and more "radically" than their western neighbors. Eastern Connecticut, roughly New London and Windham counties, favored abundant paper money in the 1720s, revival of religion in the 1730s and 1740s, expansion into western lands in the 1750s and 1760s, vigorous opposition to the Stamp Act in 1765/66, and independence from Great Britain in the early 1770s. The people of western Connecticut, on the other hand, apparently were reluctant to risk measures which might upset the orderliness of society or tempt the wrath of the mother country. Western Connecticut — New Haven, Fairfield, Litchfield, and most of Hartford counties — generally took a conservative stance: against paper money and the excesses of revival enthusiasm, and in favor of greater cooperation with the mother country. Tables Three through Eight test whether patterns of deputy elections reflect any trace of this east-west division.

Column 2 in each table indicates the average number of deputies that the towns in each county sent to the General Assembly. These attendance figures tend to hide the fact that older towns were more conscientious about participation than were younger ones. In New Haven and New London counties, neither of which gained any additional towns in this period, attendance generally approached the maximum of sixteen deputies for the eight towns in each county. In Hartford and Litchfield counties many smaller and poorer communities tended to participate only infrequently in Assembly deliberations. During the Great War for Empire, for instance, Hartford County's seventeen towns sent an average of 24.1 deputies (seventy-five percent of the maximum of 32), while Litchfield County's ten towns sent only 12.9 men (sixty-five percent of 20). Average attendance declined in five of the six counties for these years almost certainly because of the additional burden imposed on the manpower pool. The sharpest drop apparently occurred in those towns with fewer leading citizens to bear the increased responsibilities.

Patterns of turnover between sessions vary from county to county. Hartford and New Haven counties generally mirror the colony-wide trends, though New Haven towns reelected a higher percentage of incumbents than the towns of Hartford County — evidence supporting New Haven County's reputation as a conservative bastion. In neighboring Fairfield County, however, fewer men were elected to consecutive terms in the Assembly. Turnover in western Fairfield and eastern Windham counties followed a similar course after 1740, rising above fifty percent only in 1755–59. All five counties

TABLE THREE
Hartford County: Deputies

	1	*2*	*3*		*4*	*5*		*6*	
	Number of Towns	Total Deputies	Deputies with Immediate Prior Service		Turnover	New Deputies		Total Deputies with Prior Service	
Years		Average Number	Average Number	Percent	Percent	Average Number	Percent	Average Number	Percent
1725–29	11	18.9	10.8	57	43	2.7	14	16.2	86
1730–34	11	19.5	11.2	57	43	2.0	10	17.5	90
1735–39	11	19.2	12.6	66	34	1.4	7	17.8	93
1740–44	11	20.5	12.7	62	38	1.7	8	18.8	92
1745–49	12	19.8	12.5	63	37	2.5	13	17.3	87
1750–54	15	25.9	15.7	61	39	4.2	16	21.7	84
1755–59	17	24.1	11.5	48	52	4.4	18	19.7	82
1760–64	18	29.3	19.5	67	33	3.4	12	25.9	88
1765–69	20	33.9	19.7	58	42	3.6	11	30.3	89
1770–74	20	39.4	27.0	69	31	2.8	7	36.6	93

TABLE FOUR
New Haven County: Deputies

	1	2	3		4	5		6	
	Number of Towns	Total Deputies	Deputies with Immediate Prior Service		Turnover Percent	New Deputies		Total Deputies with Prior Service	
Years		Average Number	Average Number	Percent		Average Number	Percent	Average Number	Percent
1725–29	8	14.8	10.0	68	32	1.3	9	13.5	91
1730–34	8	15.8	10.6	67	33	1.7	11	14.1	89
1735–39	8	15.6	10.7	69	31	1.2	8	14.4	92
1740–44	8	15.2	10.3	68	32	1.3	8	13.9	92
1745–49	8	14.7	10.0	68	32	1.6	11	13.1	89
1750–54	8	15.8	8.6	54	46	2.8	18	13.0	82
1755–59	8	14.7	6.7	45	55	1.9	13	12.8	87
1760–64	8	15.1	9.6	64	36	1.5	10	13.6	90
1765–69	8	15.2	9.7	64	36	1.8	12	13.4	88
1770–74	8	15.7	11.6	74	26	1.4	9	14.3	91

TABLE FIVE
New London County: Deputies

	1	2	3		4	5		6	
		Total Deputies	Deputies with Immediate Prior Service			New Deputies		Total Deputies with Prior Service	
Years	Number of Towns	Average Number	Average Number	Percent	Turnover Percent	Average Number	Percent	Average Number	Percent
1725–29	8	15.5	6.9	45	55	2.1	14	13.4	86
1730–34	8	15.4	6.9	45	55	2.2	14	13.2	86
1735–39	8	15.5	5.8	37	63	2.0	13	13.5	87
1740–44	8	15.8	6.4	41	59	1.9	12	13.9	88
1745–49	8	15.6	8.4	54	46	1.7	11	13.9	89
1750–54	8	15.6	5.3	34	66	2.9	19	12.7	81
1755–59	8	14.4	5.2	36	64	2.1	15	12.3	85
1760–64	8	15.9	6.4	40	60	2.1	13	13.8	87
1765–69	8	15.5	6.8	44	56	1.5	10	14.0	90
1770–74	8	15.7	7.6	48	52	3.1	20	12.6	80

Table Six
Fairfield County: Deputies

	1	2	3		4	5		6	
	Number of Towns	Total Deputies	Deputies with Immediate Prior Service		Turnover Percent	New Deputies		Total Deputies with Prior Service	
Years		Average Number	Average Number	Percent		Average Number	Percent	Average Number	Percent
1725–29	6	11.7	4.8	41	59	2.2	19	9.5	81
1730–34	6	11.4	5.3	46	54	1.4	12	10.0	88
1735–39	6	12.0	5.7	47	53	1.4	12	10.7	88
1740–44	7	12.8	7.9	62	38	1.1	9	11.7	91
1745–49	8	14.6	7.7	53	47	2.6	18	12.0	82
1750–54	8	15.3	7.7	50	50	2.5	16	12.8	84
1755–59	8	13.9	6.3	45	55	2.4	17	11.5	83
1760–64	9	14.3	8.4	59	41	1.9	13	12.4	87
1765–69	10	17.8	11.2	63	37	2.3	13	15.5	87
1770–74	10	18.7	11.0	59	41	2.5	13	16.2	87

Table Seven
Windham County: Deputies

| | *1* | *2* | *3* | | *4* | *5* | | *6* | |
| | Number of Towns | Total Deputies | Deputies with Immediate Prior Service | | Turnover | New Deputies | | Total Deputies with Prior Service | |
Years		Average Number	Average Number	Percent	Percent	Average Number	Percent	Average Number	Percent
1725–29	8	16.0	6.9	43	57	2.6	16	13.4	84
1730–34	9	16.5	8.9	54	46	1.6	10	14.9	90
1735–39	9	17.9	8.7	49	51	2.9	16	15.0	84
1740–44	11	18.7	9.3	50	50	2.7	14	16.0	86
1745–49	11	19.5	10.9	56	44	2.7	14	16.8	86
1750–54	11	21.8	11.8	54	46	2.2	10	19.6	90
1755–59	11	21.4	10.0	47	53	3.3	15	18.1	85
1760–64	11	20.9	11.4	55	45	3.0	14	17.9	86
1765–69	11	21.8	12.1	55	45	3.0	14	18.8	86
1770–74	11	21.7	11.9	55	45	2.7	12	19.0	88

Table Eight
Litchfield County: Deputies

	1	2	3		4	5		6	
	Number of Towns	Total Deputies	Deputies with Immediate Prior Service		Turnover Percent	New Deputies		Total Deputies with Prior Service	
Years		Average Number	Average Number	Percent		Average Number	Percent	Average Number	Percent
1725–29	2	3.0	1.1	37	63	0.8	27	2.2	73
1730–34	2	2.9	1.7	59	41	0.3	10	2.6	90
1735–39	2	4.0	2.2	54	46	0.4	10	3.7	90
1740–44	3	5.7	3.0	53	47	1.2	21	4.5	79
1745–49	3	5.7	3.2	56	44	0.9	16	4.8	84
1750–54	3	5.8	3.0	52	48	1.2	21	4.6	79
1755–59	10	12.9	4.5	35	65	4.5	35	8.4	65
1760–64	12	20.9	12.7	61	39	2.8	13	18.1	87
1765–69	12	22.5	12.8	57	43	3.1	14	19.4	86
1770–74	12	23.5	12.1	51	49	2.9	18	20.6	88

for which data are sufficient — excluding Litchfield County — again illustrate the impact of war on Connecticut politics. Turnover rates rose to well over fifty percent and in New London County to a remarkable sixty-four percent replacement from session to session. Patterns in New London County are unlike those in any other county. It is the only county where turnover consistently averaged above fifty percent, peaking at sixty-six percent in 1750–54 and declining slowly thereafter to fifty-two percent in 1770–74. No similar pattern is found in the figures for its eastern companion, Windham County. While the number of deputies from Litchfield County was too small to produce meaningful figures until at least 1760–64, northwestern Connecticut seemed to move through a period of political fluidity which stabilized during the last fifteen years before the War of American Independence.

Given the variation in rates of turnover, the average number of men with prior service (Column 6) might be expected to follow a similar pattern, but the percentage of experienced personnel in each county's contingent never fell below eighty. Towns in New London County might have rotated their deputies more frequently, but they persisted in selecting them from among men already familiar with legislative service. This group of experienced men was created by the practice — common in all counties — of steadily bringing new men into the system. While the number of men introduced per town was rather smaller in Hartford and New Haven counties and rather larger in New London County, none of these differences supports the case for an east-west split in political structure. New London County's peculiarities were not shared by Windham County, nor did the patterns in New Haven County parallel those in Fairfield County. Though the people in eastern Connecticut often disagreed with their neighbors in the west about what policies to pursue, voters in both regions held similar ideas about political officeholding.

By reworking the data, it is possible to give some indication of the character of politics in Connecticut's towns. Table Nine presents information on the forty-one towns which began sending delegates to the General Assembly before 1725. Wherever feasible, data from the period 1700–24 have been included to avoid basing conclusions on insufficient evidence. The records of service have been analyzed by using a measure called the midspan, derived by arranging the number of terms each man served in ascending or descending order

Table Nine
Average Number of Terms Per Deputy, 1700–1774*

Hartford		New Haven		New London		Fairfield		Windham	
Simsbury	3.7	Derby	2.9	Preston	2.7	Norwalk	2.1	Canterbury (1710)	2.1
Haddam	4.2	Waterbury	3.5	Stonington	2.7	Woodbury**	3.6	Pomfret (1715)	3.3
East Haddam (1710)	4.4	Branford	4.3	Groton (1705)	3.1	Stratford	3.6	Plainfield (1705)	3.5
Wethersfield	5.1	Guilford	4.3	New London	3.9	Danbury	3.7	Mansfield (1710)	3.8
Farmington	5.1	Wallingford	4.5	Norwich	4.5	Greenwich	3.8	Killingly (1710)	3.9
Glastonbury	5.3	Durham (1710)	5.1	Lyme	5.3	Fairfield	4.1	Lebanon (1705)	4.0
Middletown	5.3	New Haven	5.2	Saybrook	5.7	Stamford	5.6	Windham	4.8
Colchester (1705)	6.4	Milford	6.2	Killingworth	6.9			Coventry (1720)	6.4
Windsor	8.2								
Hartford	8.3								

* The five-year period during which a town sent deputies to the General Assembly for the first time is indicated in parentheses if other than 1700–1704.

** Woodbury was part of Fairfield County until 1752, when it became part of Litchfield County.

and calculating the average (mean) of the middle half. Because this measure omits both the extraordinarily high and the unusually low numbers, it pinpoints the central tendency in each town more precisely than would an average of all careers. Towns are entered in the table by counties, and counties are placed in order of seniority.

In seventy-five percent of the towns (thirty-one of forty-one), deputies served an average of between 3.0 and 6.3 terms, inclusive. Patterns in New Haven County most closely resemble those in New London County: both show a wide variation among neighboring towns. Western Fairfield County pairs with eastern Windham County. The five towns in each county which cluster together within a narrow range are sandwiched between towns with both high and unusually low averages. The distribution of towns in Hartford County is unlike that in any of its sisters. Deputies in Hartford and Windsor served an extraordinarily high number of terms per man (8.3 and 8.2, respectively), and their peers in the remaining towns averaged longer careers than those generally found in the other four counties.

A closer look reveals an east-west distribution of towns in New London and Windham counties. Killingworth, with the highest average in New London County, is the westernmost town, adjoining Guilford of New Haven County. Moving east along the shore, Saybrook is next, then Lyme, New London, Groton, and finally Stonington on the Rhode Island border. The pattern in Windham County is similar. Four of the bottom five towns are to the east of the top three. No such distribution occurs in the other three counties.

Data on Assembly service cannot explain these patterns or why politics in Hartford and Windsor apparently was less open and more oligarchic than in Stonington, Preston, Norwalk, and Canterbury. This material can serve as a foundation for further investigation. An example illustrates what can be learned about politics in a particular town through an examination of deputy service.

Lyme sent representatives to the Assembly 286 times out of a possible 300 terms (that is, two deputies twice a year for seventy-five years, 1700–74), a consistency typical of the forty-one towns in Table Nine. Forty different individuals served those terms, but to say that each man averaged a bit over seven times in office reveals little about Lyme's politics. More must be known: for instance, how many men served for an unusually large or small number of terms, how evenly was the service distributed among the forty deputies, and did some family names appear more frequently on the roster than others?

An indication of the distribution of service can be gained by comparing the average tenure of all individuals with the average of the middle half, the twenty men on either side of the median. The midspan average of 5.3 terms is considerably lower than the overall average of 7.2 terms, indicating that some men served a good deal longer than most. This trend was common in Connecticut's towns: usually a handful of individuals managed to monopolize more than their share of public office. Table Ten indicates the number of men elected to fifty percent of the terms in each of the forty-one towns included in Table Nine. Only eight men (or twenty percent of the total of forty deputies) represented Lyme in half the sessions between 1700 and 1774. Nonetheless, Lyme, along with the rest of New London County, shows a lower concentration of service than do most of the other towns. In Coventry and Stamford, for instance, careers were long (6.4 and 5.6 terms per man, respectively) and a few men (four in Stamford, only three in Coventry) dominated the political situation. In Derby the influence of a few must have been even greater, because the average tenure in office is shorter (2.9 terms). By contrast, in Windsor and, to a lesser extent, in Hartford, while fewer men got a chance to serve and those who did tended to remain for upwards of eight terms, careers of extraordinary length were rare. In Hartford six men (twenty-one percent of twenty-nine deputies) served for half the time and in Windsor eight men (twenty-five percent of thirty-two deputies), the highest percentage of the forty-one towns in Table Ten. Something both limited the pool of prospective deputies and prevented any one man from staying too long in office.

No single family in Lyme monopolized the office of deputy, though this does not preclude the exercise of a powerful influence on the selection by a strong family connection. Twelve family names appeared only once on the roster of Lyme's deputies. Three families sent two men, and another three supplied three men each. Two, Marvin and Lee, provided four deputies and one, Ely, put five men in the Assembly. Of these multiple-deputy families, perhaps three might be called influential. Three of the four Lees served for more than ten sessions each, and two of the five Elys split thirty-two sessions between them. The most important family in Lyme sent only three men to the Assembly. John Griswold was elected twenty-seven times in the thirty-seven years between May 1721 and May 1757. His eldest son,

TABLE TEN

Number of Deputies Serving Fifty Percent of Terms, 1700–1774*

Hartford		New Haven		New London		Fairfield		Windham	
Haddam	3	Derby	3	Norwich	3	Stamford	6	Coventry (1720)	3
Glastonbury	4	Durham (1710)	3	Killingworth	3	Danbury	6	Canterbury (1710)	4
Middletown	4	Milford	5	Saybrook	5	Woodbury**	6	Lebanon (1705)	5
East Haddam	4	Branford	6	Preston	6	Fairfield	7	Mansfield (1710)	5
Wethersfield	4	Guilford	6	Lyme	6	Norwalk	8	Pomfret (1715)	5
Hartford	6	Wallingford	6	Stonington	6	Greenwich	8	Plainfield (1705)	7
Colchester (1705)	6	New Haven	7	New London	7	Stratford	9	Windham	8
Simsbury	7	Waterbury	7	Groton (1705)	7			Killingly (1710)	9
Farmington	8								
Windsor	8								

* The five-year period during which a town sent deputies to the General Assembly for the first time is indicated in parentheses if other than 1700–1704.

** Woodbury was part of Fairfield County until 1752, when it became part of Litchfield County.

Matthew, began his Assembly career in October 1748 and left public service after two terms as governor in May 1786.[36]

The full story of government, politics, and political ideology in Lyme awaits the sifting of the raw materials of local history. Although this process is time-consuming, the rewards are often great. The careful study of genealogies, vital statistics, and church and court records can reveal the lives of scores of average men and women to historical investigation. Eventually, the structure, values, and beliefs of the society can be reconstructed, along with some sense of what it was like to live in that part of colonial Connecticut.

In the fifty years before 1775, the people of Connecticut questioned, evaluated, and reformulated inherited ideas about religion, politics, and the social order. New attitudes found expression through recognized channels: change was orderly, gradual, and democratic. Once the proper leaders had been chosen, the voters gave to them the same respect and deference once accorded their predecessors. Well satisfied with the framework of their government, the people rebelled against Great Britain to protect and preserve their remarkably flexible and congenial political order.

Notes

1. Oscar Zeichner, *Connecticut's Years of Controversy* (Chapel Hill: University of North Carolina Press, 1949) and Richard L. Bushman, *From Puritan to Yankee: Character and the Social Order in Connecticut, 1690–1765* (Cambridge: Harvard University Press, 1967).

2. Bushman, *Puritan to Yankee*, p. 268 and Preface.

3. The examples cited by Zeichner, *Controversy*, p. 9, illustrate how limited evidence is used to prove this important point. See Leonard Woods Labaree, *Conservatism in Early American History* (New York: New York University Press, 1948) and Jackson Turner Main, *The Upper House in Revolutionary America, 1763–1788* (Madison, Wis.: University of Wisconsin Press, 1967) for a more thorough analysis.

4. The records used to compile Tables One and Two were drawn from the lists of assistants and deputies in Charles J. Hoadly, ed., *The Public Records of the Colony of Connecticut* (Hartford: Case, Lockwood, and Brainard, 1872–87), VI–XIV.

5. The term *voter* is used in this essay to denote the men who cast ballots for the officers of the colony government. The problem of how many men voted — or had the right to vote — is not pertinent here.

6. Haddam and East Haddam were allotted one deputy apiece for the sessions between May 1713 and May 1769. See Table Two.

7. The best description of the mechanics of this procedure is found in Charles S. Grant, *Democracy in the Connecticut Frontier Town of Kent* (New York: Columbia University Press, 1961), pp. 122–27.

8. These men, with the years of their absence, were:

Thomas Fitch	Norwalk	1736 to 1739
Roger Newton	Milford	1740 to 1741
Hezekiah Huntington	Norwich	1743 to 1748
Jonathan Trumbull	Lebanon	1751 to 1753
Jabez Hamlin	Middletown	1766 to 1772

Both Fitch and Trumbull subsequently were elected governor of the colony.

9. The averages for the period 1725–29 have been calculated in the following manner:

	Began Service		
Year	*1 to 10 Years Previously*	*11 to 20 Years Previously*	*More Than 20 Years Previously*
1725	1715 to 1724	1705 to 1714	before 1705
1726	1716 to 1725	1706 to 1715	1706
1727	1717 to 1726	1707 to 1716	1707
1728	1718 to 1727	1708 to 1717	1708
1729	1719 to 1728	1709 to 1718	1709

The numbers thus obtained were averaged to create Columns 6, 7, and 8 of Table One. Because the pattern of service on the Council is overwhelmingly one of continuous reelection to office, the data in those columns can be taken to represent continuous terms of service rather than merely the years since first election. This identity does not apply to data on the deputies.

10. Only two of the thirty-eight men first elected between 1725 and 1774 never served as deputies. Daniel Edwards, an uncle of the distinguished theologian Jonathan Edwards, was a prominent lawyer who served as clerk of the Superior Court for twenty-five years (1729–53) before his election in 1755. See Franklin B. Dexter, *Biographical Sketches of the Graduates of Yale College,* first series (New York: Henry Holt and Company, 1885), pp. 216–17. Nathaniel Stanley, Jr., was a leading citizen in Hartford for many years before his election to the Council in 1725.

11. Zebulon West of Tolland served for forty-one terms between October 1748 and October 1769; in the last eight, he was elected Speaker of the House. He won a seat on the Council in May 1770 and did not live to be reelected.

12. These lists are published in the *Connecticut Historical Society Bulletin* XXXVI (3) (July 1971):94–96.

13. Fifty-nine names are listed, but the first two were Gov. Joseph Talcott and Deputy Gov. Jonathan Law.

14. The seven towns are Windsor in Hartford County, Derby in New Haven County, New London and Preston in New London County, Danbury in Fairfield County, and Lebanon and Mansfield in Windham County. In general this is a fair sample, for it includes towns in each of the five counties then in existence.

15. The six towns are Groton in New London County, Fairfield and Stratford in Fairfield County, Coventry in Windham County, and Kent and New Milford in what would become Litchfield County. This is a poorer sample than the one for 1737.

16. Charles Grant believed the arrangement of the ballot conferred an enormous advantage on incumbents (*Democracy in Kent*, pp. 126–27). The use of an open ballot was undoubtedly more important than the arrangement of the list.

When a former assistant won election to the Council after a year or more absence, his seniority was computed from the date of his first, *not* second, entry.

17. Jack P. Greene, "Changing Interpretations of Early American Politics," in Ray Allen Billington, ed., *The Reinterpretation of Early American History* (San Marino, Cal.: Henry E. Huntington Library and Art Gallery, 1966), p. 173. This definition has been applied to an analysis of politics in Windham. See William F. Willingham, "Deference Democracy and Town Government in Windham, Connecticut, 1755 to 1786," *William and Mary Quarterly*, third series, XXX (3) (July 1973):401–22.

18. Genealogical material is in *The Huntington Family in America* (Hartford: Huntington Family Association, 1915), pp. 228–29. Christopher Huntington (1660–1735) was the first male child born after the settlement of Norwich in 1660. (Ibid., pp. 78–79).

19. Most deputies were not elected to consecutive terms; see Table Two. The career of Joseph Kingsbury, Jr., Huntington's partner in May 1734, was typical. He waited four years before serving again in May 1738, waited again until May 1739, and won his final term in October 1742.

20. Huntington's election as ensign of the First Company of militia in Norwich was confirmed by the Assembly in May 1728. Exactly a decade later he received his commission as lieutenant in the same company. Five months later he was lieutenant colonel of the Third Regiment.

21. This reason for Huntington's failure of reelection is given in the *Public Records of the Colony of Connecticut* (Hartford: Case, Lockwood, and Brainard, 1874), VIII:512, citing Isaac Backus, *An Abridgement of the Church History of New England . . . .* (Boston, 1804), p. 171. Backus, the great Baptist itinerant, was in a position to know what people believed to be the truth about this event.

22. Frank F. Starr, *The Eells Family* (Hartford, 1903), p. 127.

23. Bushman, *Puritan to Yankee*, p. 268. See Bruce E. Steiner, "Anglican Officeholding in Pre-Revolutionary Connecticut: The Parameters of New England Community," *William and Mary Quarterly*, third series, XXXI (3), (July 1974):369–406.

24. A sketch of Hamlin is in Dexter, *Biographical Sketches,* first series, pp. 371–72. Giles Hamlin was an assistant from May 1685 until his death on September 1, 1689. John Hamlin served on the Council from May 1694 until after May 1729.

25. Zeichner, *Controversy*, pp. 56–57.

26. The same fate befell Gov. Roger Wolcott and Assistant Gurdon Saltonstall in May 1754. They had not taken sufficient steps to prevent a disabled Spanish ship from being plundered by some greedy New Londoners, and the case had expanded into an international incident potentially disastrous to Connecticut. The entire story is found in Roland Mather Hooker, *The Spanish Ship Case: A Troublesome Episode for Connecticut, 1752–1758* (New Haven: Tercentenary Commission of the State of Connecticut, 1934).

27. Christopher Collier, *Roger Sherman's Connecticut: Yankee Politics and the American Revolution* (Middletown, Conn.: Wesleyan University Press, 1971), pp. 56–57.

28. Chester died on September 11, 1771, and Fitch on July 18, 1774.

29. These four men were

Abraham Davenport	Stamford	25 terms
Joseph Spencer	East Haddam	14 terms
Robert Walker	Stratford	14 terms
Roger Sherman	New Milford/	13 terms
	New Haven	

30. The influence one family could wield is chronicled in Bruce Colin Daniels, *Connecticut's First Family: William Pitkin and His Connections* (Chester, Conn.: Pequot Press, 1975).

31. Robert Walker won election seven times before he died on July 13, 1772. Abraham Davenport was last elected in May 1783.

32. Bushman, *Puritan to Yankee,* pp. 73–103.

33. Grant, *Democracy in Kent,* pp. 9–11.

34. For a thorough examination of Connecticut's economy see Gaspare John Saladino, "The Economic Revolution in Late Eighteenth Century Connecticut" (Ph.D. diss., University of Wisconsin, 1964). For the career of a prominent merchant who later became governor see Glenn Weaver, *Jonathan Trumbull, Connecticut's Merchant Magistrate (1710–1785)* (Hartford: Connecticut Historical Society, 1956).

35. This theme is central in Zeichner, *Controversy,* and in Bushman, *Puritan to Yankee.*

36. Another Matthew Griswold, the father of John, served for five terms between 1704 and 1710. Glenn E. Griswold, comp., *The Griswold Family* (Rutland, Vt.: Tuttle Publishing Company for the Griswold Family Association of America, Inc., 1935), II:123–24.

PART TWO

Documents

T HE essays of Part One draw on primary material to make factual
generalizations. In Part Two the documents speak for themselves.

An intensive search of local, state, and national archives has provided some fifty documents, highly diverse in nature, relating directly to the Town of Lyme during the Revolution. Together they
reveal the day-to-day life of a small, rural town during wartime. Re-
curring themes are outrage over Parliament's impositions, consent to
quotas of men and food, fear of attack, courage and foresight in
response to danger, and hostility to loyalists. A number of documents
concerning Lyme's leaders — Samuel Holden Parsons, Matthew
Griswold, Samuel Selden, and others — demonstrate the considerable
contribution of individuals to the revolutionary effort.

Available primary material affords an incomplete record of the
revolutionary period. No documentation has been found for several
years, including the last of the war. The legendary visits of General
Washington in 1776 and of the Marquis de Lafayette in 1778 are not
substantiated, nor is the ride of Israel Bissel, the postrider who
brought to Lyme the news of the Lexington skirmish. Missing too is
mention of Ezra Lee, Samuel Holden Parsons' brother-in-law, who
manned the *Turtle,* David Bushnell's submarine built to destroy English ships. What is recorded is less dramatic but nevertheless valuable
insight into events and lives which must be considered in our reevalu-
ation of the War of Independence.

1760

Between 1755 and 1777 Ezra Stiles made many trips between North Haven, where his stepmother and half-brothers lived, and Newport, where he was pastor of the Second Congregational Church. On his way he visited his friend, Stephen Johnson, pastor of the Lyme Congregational Church, outspoken supporter of civil liberties, and fellow of Yale College. The men discussed topics of mutual interest: religion, politics, and Yale. Some measure of their friendship is evident in the decision of the fellows of Yale College to have Johnson inform Stiles of his election to the presidency of the college in 1777.

The map, drawn in November 1760, comes from Stiles's "Itineraries," a kind of journal he kept 1760–90. Note the detailed drawing of ships in Saybrook harbor, the Saybrook bar, the Lyme church on Meeting House Hill, and the "highways."

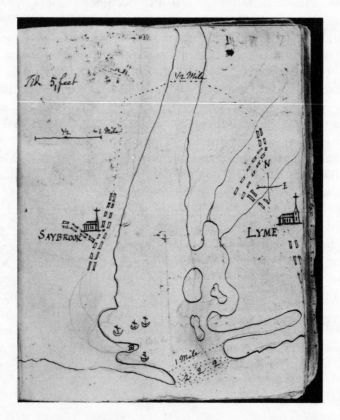

1761

This map, drawn over two pages of Ezra Stiles's "Itineraries" in October 1761, shows the shoreline from Saybrook to Black Point. Particularly interesting are the Indian settlements near Giants Neck and the marginalia about Benjamin Franklin's survey of mileage along the Boston Post Road. According to Stiles, Franklin in 1755 used a chain and wheel and measured the distance from the New London ferry to the Saybrook ferry as 14¾ miles.

In 1751 Franklin and William Hunter were appointed "Joint Deputy Postmasters and Managers of his Majesty's Provinces and Dominions on the Continent of North America." Because postage was determined by distance, Franklin contrived an odometer and calculated the entire Boston Post Road himself in the summer of 1753, not 1755 as Stiles has it.

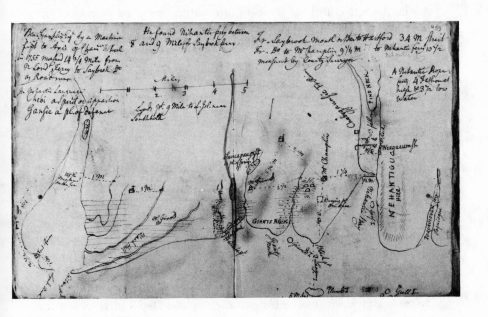

1765

In late summer and autumn 1765 Jared Ingersoll of New Haven was probably the most controversial figure in Connecticut. As the colony's agent in London a few years before, his nonsupport of the Susquehannah Company's interests had displeased some of the most powerful political leaders at home. Though he had advised British officials of the disadvantages of passing the Stamp Act, he agreed to become the colony's collector. This decision enraged many of his constituents.

On August 21, 1765, Ingersoll was burned in effigy at Norwich and the next day at New London. Five days later the ritual was repeated in Windham and Lebanon, and on the 29th in Lyme. Certainly the author of the account was a man of some learning, for he used allegory and historical and literary allusions to good advantage.

J——d Stampman is, of course, Jared Ingersoll; "one of his own brethren" is a fellow colonist; "other evil minded, wicked, and malicious persons" are British political leaders; Stampman's mother is colonial America; and the weapon, the stamp itself, is a symbol of the whole Stamp Act. The pun on "Bute-fied" is perhaps an allusion to the notoriously unpopular Scottish Earl of Bute, Prime Minister under George III in 1761–63.

The trial shows Ingersoll as a self-serving traitor of the colonies, and the choice of judges and councillors complements the satiric treatment of the whole incident. In Shakespeare's tragedy *Julius Caesar,* Brutus and Cassius are conspirators against the emperor, and Cato is their young friend. *Cato* was also a popular eighteenth-century tragedy by Addison concerning the hero's last stand for liberty. At the end of his *Gazette* article directly following the one presented below, Stephen Johnson quotes from a speech by Cato in the third act.

The names given the council for the prosecutor allude to two seventeenth-century English statesmen whose public support of civil rights made them heroes of American patriots. Algernon Sydney was a republican indirectly involved with the trial of Charles I and executed in 1683 for plotting war against Charles II. John Hampden was a famous statesman who led resistance in the 1630s in resisting the Court's attempt to raise revenue by imposing ship money.

Appropriately, the names given the council for the prisoner suggest two notorious seventeenth-century lord chief justices who were oppressors of justice. Sir William Scroggs was ultimately removed from the bench for corruption by Portuguese gold. George Jeffreys was the brutal judge at a trial in 1685 known as the "Bloody Assizes," which reputedly condemned 300 men to death.

New London Gazette, September 6, 1765[1]

Lyme, in Connecticut, Sept. 3, 1765

THE 29th of August last, came on here, the Trial of J——d Stampman, Esq., before the Proctors of Liberty. He was indicted by the good people of this colony: The accusations against him were: that not having the fear of God before his eyes, but being mov'd thereto by the instigation of the devil, he did, the 29th of Sept., 1764, kill and murder one of his own brethren, of the same family to which he belonged; and that still further pursuing his wicked designs, he did, on the first of June, 1765 enter into a confederacy with some other evil minded, wicked, and malicious persons to kill and destroy his own mother, *Americana,* an inhabitant of the northern parts of America.

And urged on by Satan, with the warmest zeal to perpetrate this wicked crime, he, by the help of those designing persons, in confederacy with him, obtained a weapon wherewith to commit the horrid fact. The weapon he obtained was called a stamp, which came from an ancient and lately Bute-fied seat in Europe. With this weapon his intent was on the 1st of Nov. following to have stamp'd his languishing mother, till she becoming unable to resist, and uncapable of supporting the grievous burden, should expire, for which he was to have been allowed 8 per cent per annum out of the rent of her estate. But whilst with these views his expectations were highly elevated, he was apprehended and arraigned before this Court.

— He pleaded not guilty upon his trial, and mov'd to be tried by his peers, but the Court finding that part of English privilege was, partly, by the instrumentality of the prisoner, cut

1. One newspaper is the source of all articles except the one dated January 24, 1766. From November 18, 1763, to December 10, 1773, this newspaper was published as the *New London Gazette;* from December 17, 1773, to February 26, 1823, as the *Connecticut Gazette;* and from [March] 1823 to May 29, 1844, again as the *New London Gazette.*

off, refused his motion. The fact being clearly proved, the counsel for the prisoner, in their defense insisted that the person said to be murdered the 29th of Sept. 1764 was but a servant of his father's family, and that the pride of his heart had prompted him to take many unjust measures to raise his fortune above the proper bounds of his station in life, and was justly suspected of a design to throw off his subjection; that it thereby became necessary and just to put him to death; and that by the manner he was executed, others might be prevented making such dangerous attempts.

As to that part of his indictment charging him with a design against his mother, 'twas urged in his defense that as her fate was absolutely determin'd, and could not possibly be avoided, he had good right himself to be the executioner, since he should by that means save 8 per cent out of her estate, to himself (which probably would be a living worth 5 or 600 per annum) which might as well be put in his pocket as another's; that he did nothing to urge on his mother's fate, but only stood waiting to make the best of every chance, which he had a right to do. In answer, 'twas said that as to the murdered person he had ever shown a proper subjection to the family he belonged to; that he was neither illegitimate nor a servant, but a son, and therefore ought to enjoy all the privileges that the other branches of the family did enjoy; that he had ever been ready to exert his power in defending the rights of the family, and had never disobeyed any lawful commands; that after the prisoner had thus been the cause of the death of his innocent brother, he was hurried on without any regard to the laws of nature or the family, consenting to and endeavoring to promote unconstitutional and unnatural measures, till now at last he was found going to execute, in the most inhumane and barbarous manner, his own natural mother; that no authority could justify so unnatural an act against an innocent person, never heard nor legally condemned; that his mother had always liv'd a virtuous life, nor was ever publicly accused of any crime, etc.

The cause being thus fully heard, and fairly debated, the Court, upon mature deliberation, found the prisoner guilty, and gave sentence against him, that he should be forthwith tied to the tail of a cart, and drawn through all the principal streets in town, and at every corner and before ev'ry house should be publicly whipped, and should be then drawn to a gallows erected at least 50 feet high, and be there hanged till he should be dead, and be then cut down by the common hangman, and buried at the meeting of three roads, and a monument erected over him, showing the cause of his ignominious death, that the infamy of the crime might be perpetuated to after generations.

— The said sentence was accordingly put in execution. The funeral ceremony was performed by the *Blacks* in the place, at which time there appeared a universal satisfaction in the countenances of all present, at the execution of one who had been often mentioned with distinction and respect, by people of all ranks in this colony, till by his treachery to his country and family the falacy of his heart was made perspicuous, in executing his plans to fill his own coffers with riches, by endeavoring to make miserable all those for whom he ought to have had the highest veneration and regard, bringing them to the subjection of slaves, or rather making them his beasts of burden. I will not omit to mention that this Court, with all the people who attended the execution and funeral occasion (which were very numerous) manifested the most loyal sentiments towards his Majesty and the present Royal Family. — The whole was conducted with the utmost decency and decorum.

Judges,   *Brutus, Casius,* and *Cato*

Council for }
Prosecutor } Mr. *Sidney* and Mr. *Hampden*

Council for }
the Prisoner } *Scroggs* and *Jeffries*

*   *   *

New London Gazette, September 6, 1765[1]

To the FREEMEN *of the Colony of* CONNECTICUT

My Dear Friends,

It is the most critical season that ever this colony or America saw, a time when everything dear to us in this world is at stake.

1. This paper by Stephen Johnson and the two that follow have been edited by Bernard Bailyn. Notes indicated by * are Johnson's, and are printed as they appear in the original publication.

The Stamp Act is passed, and officers appointed to carry it into execution. The courts of admiralty are vested with power to try and determine all matters relating to it, without JURIES. By the essential, fundamental constitution of the British government, no Englishman may be taxed but by his own consent, in person or by his representative — privileges extorted by the brave people of England from their monarchs by slow degrees and the effusion of rivers of blood. We have no representatives in Parliament; we never gave a vote for one, nor have we a right to do it: we know them not, nor do they know us. The tools of the ministry tell us we are *virtually* represented in Parliament. This is a *mysterious* representation, and of most uncertain signification. Whether we are *virtually* represented because the British Parliament are an assembly of men and of the same species with us, or because they are Englishmen, as we are, or because they represent the nation from whence we descended, or because we are under the same king, or in what other view, is uncertain. In any of those (views) the boroughs and towns in England are as virtually represented in our General Assemblies as the colonies are in Parliament. And all the Jews scattered throughout the world would be as virtually represented by a meeting of the rabbis of Hungary. I have no idea of our having a representative which we did not or might not choose for ourselves, or the Almighty choose for us. The colonies owe allegiance to King George the Third, and are as loyal and dutiful subjects as any in his dominions, and ought to submit to all such orders and acts of Parliament as are agreeable to the constitution of the English government and to the grants and privileges made to and conferred on them by royal patents and charters, which are *really* compacts and agreements with the colonists in consideration of services done and performed and to be performed by them for the crown and kingdom in the enlargement of the British dominions and increase of their commerce. If these grants and compacts are broke on the one side, can any obligation lie on the other? The colonists have no doubt of their being under the government of the British Parliament; no man questions their power of doing anything within the British dominions; but their right to do anything is not so extensive. They can't have right to govern the colonies in just the same manner as they have right to govern the isle of Britain because our distance renders it impossible for them to be so acquainted with our circumstances; because we have *really* no body to represent us there; and because we have by royal grant and compact certain privileges which the exercise of such a government necessarily vacates. If the B——sh Parliament have right to impose a stamp tax, they have a right to lay on us a poll tax, a land tax, a malt tax, a cider tax, a window tax, a smoke tax, and why not tax us for the light of the sun, the air we breathe, and the ground we are buried in? If they have right to deny us the privilege of trials by juries, they have as good a right to deny us any trials at all, and to vote away our estates and lives at pleasure. We are told very *gravely* of late that *the august body of the B——h Parliament will never exercise their power wantonly or unnecessarily.* If we could be assured that there never would be a corrupt and wicked m——r, or if there should be such a rarity that he never could find means to secure a majority in P——m——t to serve his pernicious designs, this might be some consolation; till then 'tis but cold comfort.

You ought, my friends, no doubt, and I know you are, most willing to do all in your power to contribute to the general good of the British empire in every way not inconsistent with the essential privileges of your charters, grants, and of Englishmen. These you ought not, you may not, give up. If you tamely part with them, you are accessory to your own death, and entail slavery on your posterity. "You have rights antecedent to all earthly governments — rights that cannot be repealed or restrained by human laws — rights derived from the great legislator of the universe," and to him are you accountable for their improvement. Be jealous of such as have lately attempted to fright you from your steadfastness and to lull you into security with insinuations that the sum to be raised by the Stamp Act is trifling and not worth such a stir, etc. You are also by the haughty dictator cautioned to suspend *"your judgments till you know a little more of the matter."* Let me add a word to this salutary advice: convince that G——n that you know *a little more of the matter* already than perhaps he is aware of or willing you should, or he might have tried his talents at vindicating the dangerous extension of the court of admiralty's power, of the new and extraordinary method of recovering the enormous fines and forfeitures annexed to the act. Let him know he has not touched the argument, that it is not the sum that affects you; no, you are willing to contribute your proportion in a constitutional way; you are not so ignorant as this wise man imagines; you do not account any illegal attempt against you inconsiderable or unworthy your notice, knowing a smaller will ever pave the way to a greater, and that to a greater still; and that it is not usual for a free people to lose all their liberties at once. Liberty once lost, how hardly, hardly regained.

It is in your power, Gentlemen, to choose your representatives at the approaching and at all your Assemblies. Let me humbly advise and entreat you, for God's sake, for your own and for posterity's sake, to choose men of wisdom, courage, and resolution — true Englishmen who will not be bought nor cowed into the tame submission of fawning placemen nor scared at the insolence of (our own) m——st——al tools who, as usual, begin their threats sooner than their masters. Give your representatives instructions how to act in this important affair. You have laudable examples of this before your eyes. The government of the Massachusetts have invited all their brethren on the continent to join in a humble, earnest petition for a repeal of the act of slavery. "Be not rash nor diffident." The brave people of Providence have also set a worthy example. It is not impossible to convince that august and venerable body, the B——sh Parliament, that it cannot be for the interest of the nation to deprive the American colonies of the privileges of Englishmen. Consider what Plymouth Colony got by being frightened to surrender their charter, or what the people of England have heretofore got by yielding an ace to arbitrary measures.

You have, my dear friends, as good a right to your privileges as Britain have to theirs, and you have as dearly bought them. If you should not do all that you can to preserve that inestimable jewel of liberty, your posterity in the anguish of their souls will load your memories with the bitterest reproaches. But I know you will.

Remember, O my friends, the laws, the rights,
The generous plan of power delivered down
From age to age by your .... forefathers,

Nor ever let it perish in your hands,
But piously transmit it to your children.
—Addison

New London Gazette, September 20, 1765

To the PRINTER

Sir:

Much has been said in Great Britain and America respecting the Stamp Act and duties for America, soon (if not happily prevented) to take place amongst us. And something has been done by the American governments to avert this calamity (the heaviest we ever felt from any earthly power); but far from enough, considering the nature and aspects of it, as it is perpetual, and strikes at our most important civil liberties, "such as our right of being taxed by our own representatives, and of trial by our own peers," with others, and especially as it will likely be followed with other taxes yet more heavy and ruinous (for what bounds can you set to the covetous and ambitious desires of a grasping ministry whensoever they shall be in power?). And if the scribbling, zealous advocates for these measures can have their will, the ruin of our liberties and properties will be completed in the most shocking manner, by a military force sent over and imposed upon us to force us to a slavish nonresistance and passive obedience, and rivet the chains of slavery upon us forever.

It is a serious and very affecting subject, and fills the minds of the most sensible people throughout America with great consternation: far greater than the Canada French ever did, in our fiercest wars, as that was like to be a short conflict, but this like to be irrecoverable ruin in our most valuable civil interests, to the latest generations.

Perhaps it may be seasonable to offer some thoughts tending to evince the propriety and importance of an union of the American governments in a general congress, according to the proposal of the late Boston Assembly, to come into some united measures (if possible) to prevent the impending evils which

211

threaten us, and the rather as CIVIS* seems to think it sufficient for our General Assembly only to determine for themselves and their constituents without other measures; and possibly some others may be of his opinion.

I would therefore, first, inquire into the evils apprehended from the late measures of the British ministry; secondly, what British subjects in America may do, and what, likely, they will do; thirdly, what the governments have done, may, and, we humbly conceive, would do well to do further. Lastly, conclude with some advices to my dear countrymen.

I will, first, inquire into the evils apprehended from the late measures of the British ministry. If there be no evils apprehended and to be feared from their measures then no congress is needful. But very unhappy for us, their measures (however intended) we think have been chiefly calculated to hurt us exceedingly, and in the end to hurt the subjects in Britain also.

It is needless to say, the late act of trade is embarrassing and impoverishing — lays a very unequal burden on Americans — and threatens the ruin of our trade. 'Tis already severely felt. But this STAMP ACT affects us much more nearly, and the consequences are likely to be far more fatal than the other would have been.

At first view, is it not a dead weight upon learning? Is it not a heavy burden and embarrassment upon all business? Are not the number of things charged, the severity of its penalties, and these to be adjudged by A COURT OF ADMIRALTY contrary to the constant and immemorable usage of our nation and this land, absolutely shocking? And, which is the worse part, does it not subvert our most important CIVIL LIBERTIES, such as, first, a right to tax ourselves, by our own representatives, which we esteem a fundamental birthright privilege?

It is well known, by common law, this is the birthright of Englishmen, and has been confirmed by acts of Parliament and sealed with the blood of thousands. In short, if we have not this right, we have no property: nothing to have and hold which we can call our own. But if, pursuant to the power exerted in this act, we may be taxed at pleasure by the will of others without

* [*torn*] the New-Haven Gazette, who sets [*torn*] of the Ministry, which may be [*line torn*   ].

bounds or limitations and without consent or representation, this birthright privilege is at an end with us. How have we it in America more than the slaves in Turkey?

To pretend we are VIRTUALLY represented by the members of Parliament is such a weak flimsy argument as deserves no answer. Pray by what members? Is it those chosen by the city of London, or any other city, shire, or borough? For we know not to whom to apply as our representatives. The particular members chosen by and for any borough or shire can say they are the representatives of such borough or shire (though all are not qualified and do not vote in their election) because chosen by the freemen of such shire, who, by constitution, act for the whole. But it is otherwise as to the Americans. Who of the members can say, I am the representative of the Americans, without the consent or vote of a single American? And if no one can say it, the right is in no one, and consequently not in the whole. Five hundred noughts can never make an unit.

How are we represented by any member of Parliament more than by the King? Or how is our case (in point of representation) better than if this act was imposed on us by ROYAL PREROGATIVE only, which all allow to be UNCONSTITUTIONAL?

'Tis ridiculous to common sense that two millions of free people can be represented by a representative who is elected by no one of them. Or that Americans have, or can have, a representation in Parliament in fact.

Another fundamental of British liberty is that of trial by our own peers — jurymen, after the manner of England. If there be any privilege in the common law it is this. If any in Magna Carta secure and sacred to the subject, it is this right of trial by our own peers.

It was one thing immediately in contest in the Baron War, which those sensible noble patrons of liberty asserted to be their right, for which they associated and fought, and which they would and did have secured as an indefeasible inheritance to themselves and posterity forever. No privilege, I think, is oftener repeated in Magna Carta. 'Tis express: "An earl and a baron shall not be amerced but by their peers; and according to the manner of the offense." And again, "No freeman shall be taken nor imprisoned, nor disseized, nor outlawed, nor exiled, nor destroyed in any manner: nor will we pass upon him, or condemn him, but by the lawful judgment of his peers, or by the law of the land." And it was fully provided as to what was passed where any had suffered in lands, or chattels, or privileges, etc., without lawful judgment of their peers; such judgments were annulled, and their rights to be restored. And for the future, 'tis brought over again and again with respect to the English and Welsh both: processes should be in England "by the lawful judgment of their peers, according to the law of England," in Wales "by their peers, according to the law of Wales." And 'tis made unalterable, like the laws of the Medes and Persians. So that this invaluable charter must be destroyed before we can be deprived of this precious privilege. 'Tis express in these golden lines: "We will not obtain of anyone, for ourselves or for any other, anything whereby any of these concessions or of these liberties may be revoked or annihilated; and if any such thing be obtained, it shall be null and void, nor shall ever be made use of, by ourselves or any other."

And after all this security, can any earthly power rightfully deprive us of this privilege? Is not every act of this kind declared in the charter to be absolutely null and void? Yet is not this inestimable privilege taken away from Americans by this act, as we are subject to a trial (in things relative to it) in a court of admiralty, or one admiralty, however unskilled, disaffected, or tyrannic he may chance to be? Yea, subject to be tried by them we know not where, nor how remote, whether in England or America, wherever jurisdiction is granted, at the will and election of infamous informers. What would a commoner and freeman in Great Britain think of this? Would they not (if their own case) resent it with high indignation? And shall Americans, as freeborn and good subjects as they, be deemed rebels if they absolutely refuse such trials, and claim their indefeasible birthright liberty to be tried by their own peers after the manner of England, and of America likewise till this surprising act?

New London Gazette, November 1, 1765

I proceed . . . to inquire what British subjects in America may do, and what likely they will do.

As to the first, they have doubtless a right of inquiry how their monies are to be disposed of, and whether such taxes are constitutional and equitable or otherwise. This liberty of free inquiry is one of the first and most fundamental of a free people, and where this is denied there is not so much as the shadow of *freedom* remaining. If upon examination they see plainly such taxation is neither constitutional nor equitable but a heavy grievance upon the subject and infringement upon their fundamental natural rights, they may lay their grievances before the King and British Parliament and humbly solicit a redress, and have an undoubted right to be heard and relieved. These have ever been the rights of *free Britons,* and since the grand struggle between Liberty and Tyranny in the reign of James the Second they are confirmed to us more strongly than ever, by the first Parliament in the reign of King William.

If such application should fail of redress, which is hardly supposable if properly made where the cause is so just and the grievances so evident and likely to be attended with so many and great evil consequences — but in case of such failure, they may publish and spread their grievances through the whole realm, and invite the compassion and friendly aid of their fellow subjects in Great Britain. The press is open and *free,* and how can it be better employed upon any subject of a civil nature than this, in which the trade, the liberties, the tranquility, and prosperity of Great Britain and her colonies are so nearly and deeply concerned. And our good and kind Christian brethren and fellow subjects in Great Britain may give us their friendly aid many ways — by instructions to their representatives in Parliament, or choice of new ones when the present Parliament is dissolved, etc., etc.

And were these measures pursued with wisdom and vigor, I apprehend we should not long have any room or occasion for a further question — whether we may not go on to enjoy and improve our rights and liberties as usual. If they are ours, are they not ours to enjoy and improve? And if they are our rights by the fundamental principles of the British constitution and the express letter and spirit of our charters, will not this same constitution and our charters fully vindicate us in such enjoyment and improvement of them? Or another question — whether relief failing, the American governments or inhabitants may not (after the example of the old barons and others) associate for the mutual security and defense of their birthright liberties and privileges. In general, does not this maxim, "That a person or people collectively may enjoy and defend their own," seem as plain as the law of self-preservation on which it is built? Is not the Glorious Revolution and the right of our sovereign and of all his royal predecessors of the House of Brunswick to the British throne founded and built upon this principle? And are not all our legal processes founded upon this maxim? It was a sensible saying of the learned Mr. Selden (who had the knowledge of twenty men, and honesty in proportion, says a smart writer upon the Revolution) "My penny is as much my own as the King's ten pence is his: if the King may defend his ten pence, why not Selden his penny?" But I say, if the proper measures of redress were suitably used, no doubt such questions as these would be entirely superseded and needless. But as to the other question —

What British subjects in America likely will do if this act is forced upon them (as forced it seems it must be, if ever it obtains, inasmuch as they have so great, so universal, and utter an aversion to it), I say, what they will do is not, perhaps, within human foresight to determine. Yet, when we reflect upon the violent efforts incident to human nature under the apprehensions of most heavy oppressions, and the tumultuous consequences of the Cider Act in England, not a thousandth part so hard bearing on the subject as this Stamp Act, and also consider the spirited resolves of the Virginians and some others, and especially how the hearts of Americans in general are cut to the quick by this act, we have reason to fear very interesting and terrible consequences, though by no means equal to tyranny or slavery. But what an enraged, despairing people will do when they come to see and feel their ruin, time only can reveal. However, this we may be sure of, that the importing of foreign forces further to insult and oppress us (as urged by the tools of the late m——y) will not prevent but increase and aggravate the evils manifold. For if we may judge by the experience of past ages, a free people will not continue under tyranny or military government any longer than till they can reassume their rightful freedom.* Such a measure would far more likely produce a distrust and hatred terminating in a hopeless, desperate, irreconcilable enmity than any good consequences. Nor can the forcing the act fail of producing great tumults and violences in England as well as America, when their trade, their woollen, and other manufactures fail for want of market. But I waive this as more immediately their own concern, and pass on.

Thirdly, to inquiry what the governments have done, may, and, we humbly conceive, would do well to do further. It is most justly expected that we use our utmost endeavors by all lawful means to retain and transmit our invaluable privileges full and unimpaired to our posterity. If we do not, we betray our country, and the true friends of liberty and people of sense and spirit in Great Britain and Ireland will laugh us to scorn for our dastardly meanness and tame servility, and succeeding generations will curse us to the latest posterity. And, which is worse, we shall have woeful torment in our own breasts while we live, and more so in a dying hour, under the crying guilt of such a great and irreparable wrong to our country.

Several governments have well stated and unanswerably defended their constitutional and essential rights infringed by the Stamp Act in their several tracts published. They sent them over to their agents (we take it) to be laid before our gracious King and the British Parliament before the passing of this act; but they failed, and, we understand, were never read in Parliament. But how it came to pass is to us a great mystery.

If seasonably offered, we conceive the Parliament could not refuse to hear them without contradicting the true spirit of the British constitution and the express resolves of Parliament in the first of King William and Queen Mary. If they were not seasonably offered by the agents, who well knew the rules of the House, were not the colonies very ill served by them in a case wherein their ALL is so nearly concerned? And on that supposition, have not this great, and greatly injured, people just cause of resentment? Let the fault be where it will, have not the colonies good reasons for loud complaints?

* See a pretty and very pertinent instance in Sidney, [*Discourses*] *On Government,* pag[es] 376, 377, too long to be inserted; and indeed we have very sufficient examples in the history of England and Holland.

As to what they may do further, we are very far from pre-scribing, and mean only friendly hints.

The measure of a general congress is evidently the most proper and important, and it is the joy of thousands that there is so general an union and concurrence in it. We doubt not every-thing which can be done for our relief by them will be done by the honorable commissioners in such humble petitions to our gracious King and in such a respectful, nervous, and convincing address to the British Parliament as becomes a free, most affec-tionate, loyal, and dutiful people. We trust they will also lay a foundation for another congress (in case this fails to gain us a redress) to consult of further measures. And is it not highly important that every government should modestly and loyally but most plainly and explicitly assert their own rights, now drawn into contest, that if the Stamp Act be obtruded upon us it may appear to be forced upon us wholly without our consent and against the explicit resolves of all the American colonies, that so our own and the hands of our posterity may be unbound and absolutely free to resume our inestimable rights and free-dom again, whensoever we are able? I will add, in case the Stamp Act be unrepealed and we fail of relief by the measures that are pursuing, I can't but think it highly important that the govern-ments spread our righteous cause and grievances before our Christian brethren and fellow subjects of Great Britain and Ire-land, and appeal to the great and good people of the whole realm by printing and dispersing many thousands of the tracts already published by them, or what may be drawn up by the general congress, or some other tracts fitted for the purpose, into various cities and parts of Great Britain and Ireland. It can't fail of a great and good effect. While the m——rs who contrived the act and the pensioners who hoped to riot in the plunder of it may have hearts as hard as the money they hoped to receive by it, the good people of the realm (rightly informed) will see and feel for us, or at least for themselves. To me it is a plain case, the American colonies can't be enslaved and ruined but by their own folly, consent, or inactivity; for if they use proper means with wisdom and vigor, such lights may certainly be thrown out, showing how the liberties, trade, and interest of Great Britain and Ireland are essentially connected with the colonies, as will gain a very great majority in those kingdoms into the interest and support of the colonies; for in truth it is their own best interest — the constitution by which they hold their ALL — that we are so earnestly and solicitously contending for. The Stamp Act at first view has a very plausible appearance of great good to the inhabitants of Great Britain. But I am bold to say it may be made evident that in its operation and effects it will hurt the interest of Great Britain far more than the colonies. The liberties of Americans, it is true, are most immediately affected by it, but in the conclusion it may equally affect the subjects in Britain and Ireland. If the colonies are enslaved, no doubt Ireland will soon be stamped and enslaved also. 'Tis already resolved, in the 6th of George II, they have a right to tax Ireland, and some other things have passed which have caused no small uneasiness in that kingdom.

It is allowed nothing but inexpediency now restrains from taxing Ireland; but greater weight of inexpediency is already overruled in this taxing of America. And if this succeeds, it will be so great an accession to the number of placemen and to the power of the m——y that the inexpediency will soon be got over as to Ireland also, and then I conceive the liberty of Great Britain will be worth very little and cannot long survive, after the number of placemen and power of the m——y becomes so prodigiously and enormously enlarged, as it necessarily will be in consequence of these measures. By reason of the number of placemen and some other things, the power of the m——y is already so great as seems not a little to endanger the liberties of Great Britain, without any enlargement of it. See it clear like the noonday sun in the instance of the late Cider Act. 'Tis generally complained of as an intolerable grievance. But all the loud cries and complaints with which the nation rings against it, seconded by the vigorous efforts of the great Mr. PITT and other worthy patriots, can't prevail for its repeal, so great is the power of the m——y already. And what then will it become with the enormous addition and weight of so many placemen as is necessary to effect the taxation and slavery of America and Ireland?

These things I do but hint to show the importance of laying the truth of the case open before the eyes of the good people of the mother country. For when once they see the measures of the late m——y against the colonies to be what they truly are — as bad as well can be against the trade, manufactories, and true interest of the mother country, and suited to no good national purpose but only to increase the number of placemen and power of the m——y, already too great, as they see and feel in the heavy grievances of the Cider Act and some others — the snare will then be broken by which we were to have been taken, ENSLAVED, and ruined. For suppose the spirit of the late m——y to revive, and in their very persons, too, and to attempt to force the Stamp Act upon Americans: were things rightly viewed, it would be impossible they could succeed. To say nothing of any opposition from America and of the resources which will be found in it when pushed to extremity, they would find such opposition and perplexity from the inhabitants of the mother country that they could not proceed. Those inhabitants would view it a procedure against the fairest warning from the wisdom of God: "A kingdom divided against itself cannot stand." They would see it directly against their interest, for trade must immediately stop; the merchant, the husbandman, and the manufacturer of every sort is immediately hurt by it; it could not be carried on but by an immense cost. But neither of these would do anything towards it by their representatives in Parliament, or by way of loan, to destroy their own interest. No, rather would they draw upon the exchequer for millions now due, sooner than risk their interest in the uncertain hazard of a bloody civil war in which, by sending away their men of war and forces against America, they would have everything to fear — from the sword in their own bowels, from the powers of France and Spain and the invasion of the Pretender, who would not fail to improve such an opportunity. And if any of the late m——y designed such a bloody and cursed revolution, would it be blacker treason against our rightful King George III and the British realm than this slavish scheme is against the colonies? And what have Britons to hope for as a balance to these tremendous evils and dangers? Why truly nothing at all from this most unnatural war with the colonies. If it should not succeed, they could never expect the affection and trade of the colonies as heretofore. Or suppose the colonies are overpowered, they cannot be more entirely Great Britain's than they now are, and so nothing is gained; and they would be most miserably impoverished in the struggle, and for many years could not possibly carry on trade again to the advantage of the mother country, in which a great and irreparable loss would certainly be sustained; nor would they have a heart to it, but as soon as they recovered ability for trade they would infallibly attempt their liberty again, at the expense of their ALL. In short, these measures of the late m——y may easily be shown to be most fruitless and most pernicious. And the true way in which the colonies will become of greatest service to the realm is not by taxation but trade, thereby increasing the manufactories and wealth of the nation. And for want of money, this trade has been and must be managed in a circle of great extent; and to encourage them to the toil and hazards of it their liberties must remain untouched and be secured to them as sacred, and their trade be as unembarrassed and free as possible. In this channel of trade, all the profits of North Amercia would, in an easy and gentle flow, naturally and almost necessarily terminate in the mother country; but this taxation, with the heavy duties on trade, necessarily turn Americans out of this channel, and drive them to such expedients as must hurt Great Britain in her trade and manufactures an hundred times more than the profits of these taxes.

The people of the mother country are mighty and have an endeared affection and concern for the people of these colonies; some for their children or grandchildren or other near relations or intimate friends amongst us — others for their virtue — and others for their trade, upon which thousands, I may say millions, have their subsistence. And did they see things in this true light they would soon have the duties on trade eased and this Stamp Act repealed, or the m——r who would force such destruction upon Americans and themselves would soon become as a great family who perished in Holland for far, far less provocation. In a word, if a spirit of true wisdom guides the affairs of Americans we have no reason to despair, but much to hope for —from the best of Kings — from the new ministry who are in favor of the colonies we hear —from the wisdom and righteousness of the British Parliament — and from the affection, justice, humanity, and even self-interest of the British inhabitants. And we have certainly very alarming motives to try our utmost, in our affection to our gracious King and to the general interest and welfare of the whole realm and particularly in our concern for ourselves, our country, and posterity to the latest generations, from the many and dreadful evils which are impending and which we have touched but in their general influence in the foregoing representation, and from the all-happy prospect in their removal. The duties on trade eased and the Stamp Act repealed — *the tumults in Britain die away and all the American colonies and West Indies are calmed and settled in perfect tranquility* — *a new spirit of love and harmony diffuses itself through the whole realm and cements all the parts of it in the firmest union* — *languishing trade by and by revives and flourishes. Nor is this all. Our most gracious King and the British ministry and Parliament are exalted* high, *higher than ever, in the affection and confidence of Americans for their most obliging readiness to redress our grievances as soon as known* — *fresh support, strength, and vigor is added to the British constitution* — *a general joy is spread through the whole realm, and in America it exceeds the joy of our most glorious military conquests. If these things will not rouse us, we must be dead to the most noble and best feelings of humanity.* — *I conclude with some advices to my dear countrymen.*

Your concern is great, universal, and, which is more, it is most just. I am an American born, and my all *in this world is embarked with yours, and am deeply touched at heart for your distress,* O my country!

My dear distressed country! *For you I have wrote, for you I daily pray and mourn, and to save your invaluable* rights *and* freedom *I would willingly die.*

Forgive my lamenting tears. The dear Saviour himself wept over his native country, doomed to destruction, and they most justly; but we — *may God give us repentance and pardon for all our sins against his most blessed Majesty. But as to man, we appeal to our supreme, righteous judge against the humane hand whence these evils are coming. Have we never offended, and have no pardon to ask? No, no, in this will we have comfort and triumph: if we perish, we perish being innocent, and our blood will be required at their hands* — *but how to conduct. The wisdom of God hath told us, "The wise man's eyes are in his head." Shut not yours to your danger, O my countrymen, lest your ruin be unavoidable. Yet be not rash, lest you precipitate into violences, which can do no good and which cannot be vindicated.* Do nothing to destroy your own or betray the invaluable rights of your posterity, but everything lawful and possible for the preservation of both. Do nothing to sully or shade the*

---

* *The author has reference to such plunderings of private property as was executed upon the deputy governor of Boston, and some others.*

memory of your noble-spirited ancestors: be virtuous, be pious, and, after their example, secure the favor of God in whom the fatherless find mercy, and the helpless salvation. Be loyal, yet free. *Indulge not a thought that our gracious King or the British Parliament designed your slavery. No, impute all these evils to the misinformations of a misguided m——y, to which they are undoubtedly owing. Yet be not decoyed and ensnared into slavery by the speciory and lovely names, "better security and protection," nor by the terrors of a temporary stagnation of trade and suspension of executive courts, which may display themselves to the imagination beyond what they may be felt, but at the worst can't compare with tyranny and perpetual slavery. Be frugal, be very industrious, use as little as possible of any foreign manufactures. Your heavy debts and the necessity of the present time absolutely require it. Yet make no sullen resolves to break off commerce with the mother country. No, rather determine according to your ability to trade as free as ever, but on this condition, and upon this only,* that the Stamp Act be repealed, and you can do it on equal terms, and not otherwise.

Finally, let all the governments and all the inhabitants in them unitedly resolve to sacrifice our lives rather than be disloyal to our rightful King George III or be rebellious to the equitable and constitutional orders of the British Parliament. Yet let all to a man determine, with an immovable stability, to sacrifice their lives and fortunes before they will part with their invaluable freedom; and let us all with a spirited, unbroken fortitude act up to these resolutions. It is the most likely way to keep you both loyal and free. It will give you a happy peace in your own breasts and secure you the most endeared affection, thanks, and blessing of your posterity. It will gain you the esteem of all true patriots and friends of liberty through the whole realm; yea, and far as your case is known it will gain you the esteem and admiration of the whole world. Amen.

By a Freeman *of the Colony of* Connecticut.

1766

Stimulated by the pleas of Stephen Johnson and the bitter resentment toward Jared Ingersoll, Lyme's opposition to the Stamp Act reached a peak as the new year began. Consensus in the community is clear in these resolutions, unanimously approved at what was very likely a meeting of the Sons of Liberty from throughout New London County. Although stamps were never sold in the colony, the presence in Long Island Sound of the British ship *Cygnet,* said to be bringing stamps, must have been an ominous reminder of the legislation.

Implicit in several resolutions is the role of leadership Lyme played in urging other towns to be vigilant and thwart any enforcement of the act. Maj. John Durkee of Norwich was an outspoken antagonist and leader of the angry group in eastern Connecticut who met Ingersoll on his way to Hartford and demanded and got his resignation. Also a prominent member of the Sons of Liberty, Major Durkee loosely organized patriots throughout the colonies to resist the Stamp Act. By persuading other colonies to correspond with Durkee, the people of Lyme were perhaps anticipating the general meeting of the Sons of Liberty held in March in Hartford, when a standing committee of correspondence was established to maintain direct communication with other colonies.

Connecticut Gazette, January 24, 1766[1]

At a meeting of the respectable populace held at *Lyme,* in the County of *New London,* on the 2nd Tuesday of January, 1766, the following resolves were unanimously agreed to and [are] to be inserted in the *New London Gazette,* viz.:

1. That we have an inviolable right by the God of nature as well as by the English constitution (which is unalienable even by ourselves) to those privileges and immunities which by the execution of the Stamp Act, we shall be forever stript and deprived.

2. That we are unalterably fixt to defend our aforesaid rights and immunities, against every unjust attack by every lawful way and mean.

3. That our aversion and threats to any person in public character or other in the colony is and shall be only on account and according as they are more or less engaged, and active directly or indirectly, to carry into

1. A *Connecticut Gazette* was published in New Haven between 1755 and 1768.

execution the detestable and oppressive Stamp Act, which would be an indelible stain to England's glory, and perpetual chains to American liberty.

4. That Mr. Ingersoll has made public and solemn resignation of his said office as stamp distributor, and confirmed the same by oath, as is inserted in the *Connecticut Gazette,* of the 10th instant, as also assures us by private letters, though not in every respect as we should have been glad to have heard, and as we have heretofore had reason to distrust his veracity; yet willing to extend charity as far as possible, do rely on and confide in his veracity, that he will preserve his said oath and engagements inviolate.

5. That whereas Mr. Ingersoll has resigned as above said, no copies of his letters or papers are desired, by the people of *New London* County, but that the gentlemen in whose hands they are take a copy of the whole and keep for the use of the public, and return the originals as soon as may be.

6. That whereas it is believed that the Stamped Papers for this colony are hovering on our coasts on board the *Cygnet* Man of War stationed in this colony, it is resolved that the Sons of Liberty keep a vigilant watch, and on any attempt to land the same, we engage our united assistance to take and secure them for his Majesty's use.

7. That whereas we conceive the general safety and privileges of all the colonies to depend on a firm union in support of the British constitution, we therefore do declare we will do our utmost to resist all such enemies to his Majesty and the British constitution, as shall attempt to dispossess the colonies of their most sacred rights, and will be ready on all occasions to assist our fellow subjects in the neighboring provinces to repel all violent attempts which may be made to subvert their and our liberties.

8. That Maj. Durkee, in the county of *New London,* be desired to correspond with the Sons of Liberty, in the neighboring colonies, and from time to time inform them of the sentiments of the populace there and re-

ceive and publish from them such things as shall be thought of general concern, and that the populace of *Windham,* and the other counties, are desired to appoint persons for the same purpose.

9. That the inhabitants of this colony are desired to be cautious in believing or adhering to any insinuations from designing persons who at times have endeavored to cast contempt and put false constructions on the meetings of the populace which are formed and kept up with righteous intentions and have had the most salutary effects.

10. That whereas the adjacent colonies proceed in business without regard to the Stamp Act, 'tis earnestly desired that the civil authority of this colony follow their laudable example, as the delay of business will be construed an implicit acknowledgment of the validity of the Stamp Act and a practical contradiction of the principal argument urged in our petitions at home for the repeal of the same, and for that purpose the eyes of all are upon the SUPERIOR COURT of this colony to give the example to the subordinate authority.

11. That another meeting of the respectable populace be held at the Meeting House in the 2nd Society in *Preston* on the last Tuesday of February next.

1768

Like other communities Lyme had its own Sons of Liberty, and this article may be an account of one of their meetings or what was called a dining in, a highly ceremonial event held in members' homes. Marksmanship was practiced and hospitality was generous. Sometimes there was a good deal of drinking, which may have been the case here.

Zebulon Butler, the host, had grown up in Lyme, engaged in the West Indies trade, and owned several sloops. In the French and Indian War he became a captain and at its end returned to Lyme for a short time before leading a group of Connecticut settlers to the Wyoming Valley of the Susquehanna River in 1769.

The toasts give a good idea of the interests of young patriots in 1768. After acknowledging allegiance to the king and mother country, they ironically hope she will not oppress them, then turn to protest. The figures in the sixth, seventh, and tenth toasts refer to the 92–17 vote by which the Massachusetts Assembly refused the demand of Lord Hillsborough, British secretary of state for the colonies, to rescind its circular letter sent other colonies refuting Parliament's right to tax the colonies. The negative tone of the eighth toast contrasts their own Sons of Liberty with the Grumbletonian Sons of Slavery, British politicians who opposed self-government in the colonies.

The ninth toast may be a satiric allusion to the notorious Scottish prime minister, Lord Bute, by comparing him unfavorably to an ordinary and formless soft hat.

The thirteenth and fourteenth toasts confirm the Sons' commitment to civil rights: to the Magna Carta and the Pennsylvania farmer, John Dickinson, member of the Stamp Act Congress and opposer of Parliament's right to tax solely for revenue.

New London Gazette, July 29, 1768

Lyme, July 15, 1768

At a meeting yesterday of the gentlemen who meet at Capt. Butler's, for the purpose of exercising the firelock in which they make great proficiency —— —— After exercise the following TOASTS were drank. Viz.:

1. Our Gracious Sovereign GEORGE the Third.
2. Our Mother Country.
3. May our Mother never oppress her dutiful children.
4. The loyal American Sons of Liberty.
5. May the present Union of the Colonies ever subsist.
6. Perseverance to the famous 92.
7. Immediate retractation to the infamous 17.
8. May the Grumbletonian Sons of Slavery ever be disappointed in their designs against our happy Constitution.

9. May the Temple of Liberty ever be founded on a better basis than a Scotch Bonnet.
10. 92 in every colony on the continent.
11. Success to military exercise.
12. Success to trade and navigation.
13. Magna Carta perfervid inviolable to the latest generation.
14. The glorious memory of the Pennsylvania Farmer.
15. Every asserter of liberty.
16. May freedom in the mind and trade throughout the Kingdom be displayed.

After which the evening concluded with the utmost decency and regularity.

*   *   *

In September 1768 Ezra Stiles included this map in his "Itineraries." It shows the organization of the town by parishes. The First Parish, under the charge of Rev. Stephen Johnson, was the oldest settlement, covering what today is known as Old Lyme. The Second Parish, led by Rev. George Griswold until his death in 1761, was established next in 1719 and incorporated what is at present East Lyme. The Third Parish, under Rev. George Beckwith, was formed last in 1724 and today covers Lyme. The Hadlyme parish, partly in Lyme and partly in East Haddam, was bounded on the west by the Connecticut River.

Stiles also indicated the presence of a separatist church and several Baptist churches spawned during the Great Awakening, as well as the formation of a new parish in the northeast, now known as Chesterfield. The five pyramids along the sound are Indian settlements.

1770

The colonists resented all forms of taxation without representation, but Parliament thought they might accept taxes on various commodities to help defray the cost of their government. In 1767 it instituted the Townshend Acts, setting duties on various items including

LYME

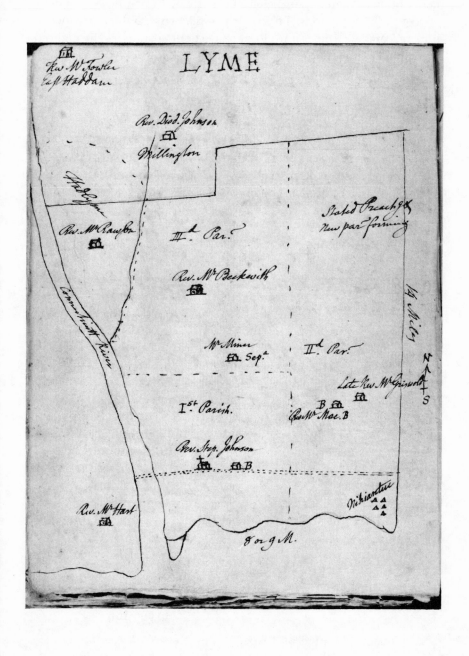

Rev. Mr. Fowler
East Haddam

Rev. Disd. Johnson
Millington

Rev. Mr. Rawson

III.d Par.s

Stated Preach.g
New par.g forming

Rev. Mr. Beckwith

Mr. Miner   Sep.a

II.d Par.s

Late Rev. Mr. Griswold

I.st Parish.

Rev.d Mr. Mac. B

Rev. Step. Johnson   B

Rev. Mr. Hart

Nihiantuc

8 or 9 M.

Connecticut River

14 Miles

N
S

tea. Colonial leaders, suspicious of Parliament's motives, urged a boycott of British goods. To ensure compliance with the nonimportation agreements, they set up local inspection committees throughout the colonies to monitor merchants' wholesale and retail transactions. Merchants also set up ad hoc committees to protect their own interests.

Although colonists in eastern Connecticut were some of the earliest and most outspoken advocates of the nonimportation agreements, those in New York were the first to resume use of British goods after the partial repeal of the Townshend duties in 1770. It is the conflict between the strict adherence to principle, self-respect, and keen sense of patriotism demonstrated by Elisha Merrow, John McCurdy, and their Lyme townsmen, and the flexibility or self-interest of New York colonists which is dramatically illustrated in these four documents.

Born in Southold, New York, Merrow moved to Lyme after his marriage to a native. Presumably he was a merchant, for in 1765 he bought a house, barn, and shop, and ten years later similar buildings on the bank of the Connecticut River. The indignant tone of his public letter makes clear Merrow's patriotic support of the nonimportation agreements and moral outrage at the unscrupulous behavior of the New York Committee of Inspection. John McCurdy, Merrow's alleged confederate in the importation of checks (a type of woven material), was Lyme's foremost merchant, an active patriot, and a friend of Stephen Johnson. Despite his Irish birth and recent arrival in Lyme, he had gained considerable wealth largely through foreign trade and privateering. Although the account of the town meeting resolutions, published several months after the indignant protests of Merrow and McCurdy, does not refer to them, it does mention New York. Perhaps McCurdy, himself eager for vindication, urged his fellow townsmen to take this public stand.

New London Gazette, July 20, 1770

To The Public

Lyme, July 12, 1770

The Committee of Inspection in New York has thought proper to advertise and hold up my name in a detestable light to all the friends of American liberty (in their public newspaper) for being a confederate and concerned with Mr. John McCurdy, merchant, of Lyme, and Mr. George Thomson, of New York, in clandestinely causing to be brought into and landed in the city of New York a parcel of checks, pins, ribands, knee-garters, tammies, etc., and for ignominiously fleeing from justice.

Now, had the committee related facts as they were, I should not have troubled the public; but it is far otherwise, as the sequel will show.

About the 29th ultimo, being at New York, and bound to Rhode Island, Mr. Thomson put some freight on board, and went passenger with me; put some trifles in my cabin in Rhode Island, and I came to Lyme, loaded with wood, and that day I sailed for New York. Mr. Thomson told me he had a few checks at Mr. McCurdy's; I took my horse and carried them on board my sloop (the checks were in two bags). Mr. McCurdy told me they were imported before the nonimportation agreement took place. As I was loaded with wood, I thought it not worth while to clear them out, or enter my boat at York, for such a trifle; but when I got to York, there was nothing but fire and sword, burning goods, knocking one another in the head, some for importing, others against it. Mr. Thomson was advised to run what trifles of goods he had, and being discovered, he and I waited on the committee, and confessed the whole truth. Mr. Thomsom showed the invoices, but all that we could say they would not believe us but that the checks came from Rhode Island. Mr. Thomson offered to deliver the goods to the committee, but they refused to take them. Their opinion was that the goods would be burned, as the others was the week before, and the vessel delivered to the custom house officers. On this some of the committee advised me privately to take care of myself and vessel. — Before I had time to get to her, sundry gentlemen in the street told me to make the best of my way, for there was information gone to the custom house against me, and every one that could get a hand to my vessel helped me out of the dock.

— Now was this ignominiously fleeing from justice? No, but rather from ravening wolves, from destruction and flames with which I was threatened. Had they took and stored the goods, as they ought to have done, I was ready to submit to any thing they thought proper for what offence I was guilty of. But for a committee that was chosen to do justice, to see what should and what should not be imported, to refuse to take me under their protection, but impose me to the mob, is of a piece with their tarring and feathering informers today, and turning informers themselves tomorrow; condemn and disclaim against their neighbor colonies for breaches of nonimportation agreement, and they themselves daily guilty of it (privately, and I dare say will be the first that will break it publicly); condemn goods to the flames that was imported before the importation agreement, as the checks were, must surely, in this era, distinguish the heroes of New York to the latest posterity.

— As for my being concerned either with Mr. McCurdy, or Mr. Thomson, or ever saw any of the goods (save the checks in the bags) is false and scandalous. And I must think it very hard to be so publicly exposed by the committee, for no other crime, that I know of, but only taking in a trifle of goods that brought me about five shillings freight, and never knew or inquired what they were.

— But not to tire the patience of the public — I despise any man, or set of men, whatsoever, that under pretence of protecting my liberty and property, would destroy both, and my reputation in the bargain. Therefore I am under no indispensible necessity of advertising and holding up in a detestable light, to all the friends of American liberty on this wide extended continent, the committee of New York, as enemies to the rights of mankind.

Elisha Merrow

New London Gazette, July 27, 1770

Lyme, July 12, 1770

To The Public

Whereas the Committee of Inspection of New York, *has advertised me in the public papers, for being concerned with Capt.* Elisha Merrow *of* Lyme *and Mr.* George Thomson, *merchant of* New York *in running goods into that place, contrary to the nonimportation agreement, it may reasonably be expected that I shall give the respectable public some satisfaction on the head. Therefore I take this earliest opportunity to acquaint all concerned, that I never was confederate with, or knowing anything of the above gentleman's running goods at the time I am accused with it, neither directly nor indirectly; nor never have had one article of goods in my shop, that I imported, either from* Great Britain *or* Rhode Island, *since the nonimportation took place, or ever concerned with them that did; and this I stand ready to make appear to a demonstration, to any committee in this colony, or* New York.

— *As to the committee of* New York, *many of them are gentlemen, and well known to me to be such, and from whom I have received many favors; others of them I am unacquainted with. But for them or any set of men to expose me to the public, in a contemptible light, without reason, or being heard, appears to me very extraordinary, and must be attributed to the disration of the times at* New York. *Which is all at present from the public's*

> *Humble servant,*
> JOHN MCCURDY

New London Gazette, July 27, 1770

COPY *of a* LETTER *from Mr.* John McCurdy *to the Merchants' Committee in* New London.

> Lyme, July 12, 1770

GENTLEMEN:

This day I was greatly surprised to see a piece in the *New York* papers, addressed to the public, wherein my name is held up in a detestable light, for being a confederate and concerned with *Elisha Merrow* and *George Thomson,* in causing to be brought into that city a parcel of checks, etc. imported into the neighboring colonies, contrary to the nonimportation agreement, as the preamble to the piece sets forth.

Now gentlemen, the truth of the fact is this, that on August 20, 1767 I had shipped on board the ship *Providence, Thomas Clark,* Master, at *Liverpool,* a quantity of checks. The ship went to *Ireland,* and lay long there, so that I did not receive those goods till towards the spring 1768. Since that time the sale of checks failed in this place, for which reason I had a few pieces by me, more than to supply my shop. — Mr. *Thomson,* who had been settled in *New York* in the Mercantile Way, as I understand, ever since last fall, came to see me, as he had formerly lived with me as a tutor to my son (not as a clerk) and seeing the checks, proposed to buy a few pieces. We soon agreed on terms. I delivered him the checks, told him that he knew they were legally imported to his knowledge (as he then lived with me) and to tell the committee of it.

Now if my letting a merchant in New York have a few checks out of my store, imported at the time aforesaid, be a crime worthy of such treatment, I leave to your judgment, to whom I appeal. And as wrong information, or the over-heated zeal of the good gentlemen of the committee at York, has caused them, without reason, to make my name public, and especially as they call on you to see that I and the other offenders be brought to justice, I insist on your coming over and making strict inquiry into the whole matter. The checks are brought back, and are at Mr. Merrow's. I have the invoices from Liverpool, and can make it clear to the satisfaction of every man that I never have had one shilling worth of goods in my shop that I imported from Great Britain or Rhode Island, since the non-importation took place. And if I had it in my power, no man else on the continent should import till all the acts were repealed that we complain of.

— It sits ill on my stomach to be impeached with those things that are contrary to my well-known principles, by all those that are acquainted with me. Therefore, as a Son of Liberty, I expect to be judged by my peers and neighbors in this affair, and that immediately, before my friends in this colony are prejudiced against me by wrong information, as no doubt the committee of New York were, or they would not have censured me so rashly, without being heard. That I was concerned with Thomson and Merrow, or ever thought of their running the goods, is false and without foundation. There was no occasion for it. The checks was landed at New York, entered in the Custom House, and reshipped to me.

I am, Gentlemen, with esteem,

Your most humble servant

JOHN McCURDY

Documents

New London Gazette, September 7, 1770

The following are the sentiments of the Town of LYME, *expressed in Town Meeting on the 31st of August last, to* SAMUEL SELDEN, *Esq. and Dr.* ELEAZER MATHER, *agreeable to which they were desired to conduct at the general Congress of the Merchants, to be held at* NEW HAVEN, *on the 13th of September instant.*

This town being fully sensible of the necessity of union and harmony among the American colonies at this time, especially when our liberties are attacked in a most unjust and high handed manner by the wicked influence of a haughty and tyrannical minister, and our destruction threatened, our privileges and properties rendered very precarious, the legal and constitutional barriers thereof being broken, and the hand of power exalting itself over the principles of law and justice.

That as the most effectual and prudent measure (under the present circumstances of the colonies) the nonimportation agreement entered into throughout the colonies, became expedient and necessary; and the principles on which it was founded were truly virtuous and patriotic: That the reasons on which the same was entered into continue to operate with equal force.

That any province or particular person, who have or shall recede from, or counteract the same until all our grievances are redressed, ought to be considered as unworthy [of] our confidence, and perfidious violators of public faith and honor. — That the late alarming conduct of New York, in breaking through said agreement, deserves the severest censure. But as our connections have heretofore been so great in that city we cannot undertake to point out to you those measures which will be most effectual to lessen our dependence and connection on them for the future: But must refer the same (as an object worthy your particular attention) to the consideration of the General Meeting.

1773

As legislator, patriot, and officer in the Continental Army, Samuel Holden Parsons was undoubtedly one of Connecticut's foremost leaders during the Revolution. Born in Lyme in 1737, the son of Jonathan Parsons (who had become pastor of the Congregational Church in 1731), he graduated from Harvard in 1756 and five years later married Mehetable Mather, the daughter of Capt. Richard Mather, a Lyme merchant. He studied law with his uncle, Matthew Griswold, later governor of Connecticut, and in 1762 was elected to the General Assembly in Hartford. He was then reelected continuously until he moved to New London in 1774 and held several other responsible positions throughout the period.

Parsons also belonged to the Connecticut Militia and as a colonel of the Sixth Regiment was in charge of a company of local men at the battle of Bunker Hill. In August 1776 he became a brigadier general, and in December 1779 succeeded Israel Putnam as commander of the Connecticut Division of the Continental Army. Congressional vote made him a major general in 1780. General Parsons retired to the practice of law in Middletown in 1782 and drowned in a canoeing accident in the Western Reserve in 1789.

Parsons's letter to Samuel Adams is significant for several reasons. Some historians believe it contains the initial suggestion for a gathering of colonial representatives which materialized in the first meeting of the Continental Congress in Philadelphia several years later. When Adams received this letter he was clerk of the House of Representatives of the General Court of Massachusetts and an outspoken adversary of Governor Hutchinson, who defended the supremacy of the Crown and Parliament. A few months earlier, in autumn 1772, Adams had persuaded the town meeting in Boston to organize, as the Sons of Liberty had in 1765, and to form a Committee of Correspondence. Doubtless familiar with Adams's insistence on independent government and political success, Parsons perhaps hoped the legislator's organizational abilities and enlightened thinking would produce action. Certainly the letter was timely, and its solid defense of "charter privileges" demonstrates well his imaginative foresight.

Documents

[To Samuel Adams]

Providence, March 3, 1773

Sir:

When the spirit of patriotism seems expiring in America in general, it must afford a very sensible pleasure to the friends of American liberty to see the noble efforts of our Boston friends in the support of the rights of America as well as their unshaken resolution in opposing any the least invasion of their charter privileges. I was called to my father's on a very melancholy occasion & designed to have seen you before my return, but some unforseen difficulties prevented.

I therefore take the liberty to propose to your consideration whether it may not be advisable in the present critical situation of the colonies, to revive an institution which had formerly a very salutary effect; I mean an annual meeting of commissioners from the colonies to consult their general welfare. You may recollect this took place about the year 1636 & was continued to the year 1684 between the united colonies of New England. Although they had no decisive authority of themselves, yet here everything was concerted which needed the joint concurrence of all the colonies. Many matters, which will be easily suggested to your mind, if we were not to take our connection into Great Britain into consideration, would render the measure convenient, as at present our state of independence on one another is attended with very manifest inconvenience.

I have time only to suggest the thought to you who I know can improve more on the subject than is in my power had I time. The idea of unalienable allegiance to any prince or state is an idea to me inadmissable & I can't see but that our ancestors when they first landed in America were as independent on the Crown or King of Great Britain as if they had never been his subjects. And the only rightful authority derived to him over this people was by explicit covenant contained in the first charters. These are but broken hints of sentiments I wish I was at liberty more fully to explain.

I am, Sir, in haste with esteem
your most humble servant
Samuel H. Parsons

1774

Parliament imposed the Tea Act in 1773 to bolster the profits of the flagging East India Company. The legislation required direct shipment of tea to the colonies and caused elimination of American wholesalers. By reducing the price of the commodity, the British expected to increase demand as well as profits. The colonists construed this maneuver as another means to force their acceptance of Parliamentary taxation. Loss of a lucrative enterprise and curtailment of rights also annoyed them. On December 16, 1773, a group in Boston dumped East India Company tea into the harbor, and several months later their compatriots in Lyme made a similar gesture of defiance. Both incidents illustrate the strong feeling about the act, especially evident in the smug tone of the *Gazette* article. The act gave the East India Company the privilege of appointing its own agents in the colonies, and Lamson evidently tried to establish the legitimacy of his tea by attributing its source to two officers at Newport.

Connecticut Gazette, March 18, 1774

Lyme, March 17, 1774

Yesterday one William Lamson, of Martha's Vinyard, came to this town with a bag of TEA *(about 100 wt.) on horseback, which he was peddling about the country. It appeared that he was about business which (he supposed) would render him obnoxious to the people, which gave reason to suspect that he had some of the detestable tea lately landed at Cape Cod; and upon examination it appeared to the satisfaction of all present, to be part of that very tea (though he declared that he purchased it of two gentlemen in Newport, one of them 'tis said is a custom house officer, and the other captain of the fort). Whereupon a number of the Sons of Liberty assembled in the evening, kindled a fire and committed the bag with its contents to the flames, where it was all consumed and the ashes buried on the spot, in testimony of their utter abhorrence of all tea subject to a duty for the purpose of raising a revenue in America.*

A laudable example for our brethren in Connecticut.

*   *   *

Documents

In May 1895 the legislature in Hartford resolved that "every town clerk in this state shall . . . make a true copy of all that relates to the revolutionary war in such records, between the year 1774 and the year 1784, inclusive . . . and mail the same to the state librarian at Hartford."[1] Although these documents are neither complete nor entirely reliable, they are invaluable for anyone studying Lyme history because the town's own volume of meeting records for these crucial years is missing.

The Committee of Correspondence in Boston, which first spread the alarm about the Tea Act, served as a model for others throughout the colonies. Their purpose was to communicate violations of rights and to consolidate resistance. The account of the establishment of Lyme's Committee of Correspondence at the June 20 meeting expresses loyalty to George the Third and concern for Lyme's Boston neighbors, the object of the Coercive Acts passed in March and April. Primarily punitive, they closed Boston harbor to commerce, gave the king power to appoint the governor's Council, ordered certain officials awaiting trial removed to England or Nova Scotia, and stationed British soldiers once more in Boston. Lyme and other towns set up committees to organize relief. The powder house voted in the September 13 meeting was probably built near the juncture of what are now Sill Lane and Saunders Hollow Road.

At a meeting of the inhabitants of the Town of Lyme in New London County by legal notice convened and held in said Lyme June 20, 1774, Eleazer Mather Esq. was chosen moderator of said meeting.

At the same meeting it was voted and resolved that we sincerely profess ourselves to be true and loyal subjects of his Sacred Majesty King George the Third.

— Also voted — that we are heartily concerned for the difficulties attending the Town of Boston in consequence of the late extraordinary measures taken with them by the British Parliament that affairs appear to us with a threatening aspect on the liberties of all British America.

Also voted — that we will to the utmost of our abilities assert

1. *Special Acts and Resolutions of the State of Connecticut* (Hartford, 1897), XII:329.

239

and defend the liberties and immunities of British America and that we will cooperate with our brethren in this and other colonies in such reasonable measures as shall in general congress or otherwise be judged most proper to relieve us and our brethren in Boston from the burthens now felt and secure us from the evils we fear will follow from the principles adopted by the British Parliament respecting the Town of Boston.

— Also voted that Ebenezer [Eleazer] Mather Esq., Mr. John McCurdy, John Lay, 2nd., William Noyes, Esq., & Mr. Samuel Mather, Jr., be a standing committee for the purpose of keeping up a correspondence with the towns of this and the neighboring colonies and that they transmit a copy of these votes to the Committee of Correspondence for the Town of Boston.

At a meeting of the inhabitants of the Town of Lyme by legal notice convened and held in said Lyme on September 13, 1774. — At the same meeting Capt. Richard Wait is chosen moderator of said meeting.

At the same meeting the question was put to the said town whether they think it expedient to do something for the relief of the inhabitants of the Town of Boston under their distressed circumstances. Resolved in the affirmative. At the same meeting the question was put to the town whether they would proceed to grant relief as aforesaid by a rate or tax upon the inhabitants or by a subscription. Resolved and voted that they will do it by a subscription.

At the same meeting Samuel Selden, Esq., Samuel Ely, Esq., Capt. Elisha Marvin, Mr. John McCurdy, Capt. Richard Wait, Elijah Smith, Capt. Jonathan Gillot, Benjamin Lee, Esq., and Joseph Way were chosen and appointed a committee to proceed directly to procure and forward subscriptions to and among the inhabitants of said Town of Lyme for the relief of the poor inhabitants of the Town of Boston and to collect and receive of the inhabitants the particular sums or specie by them subscribed, and deliver the same to the Committee of Correspondence in said Lyme to be by them transmitted to the Committee of Correspondence for the Town of Boston.

At the same meeting the question was put to the said town

whether they will proceed to build a powder house to keep the town stock of ammunition in. Voted in the affirmative.

Also voted that the said house shall be set upon the highway on the hill near Mr. Nathaniel Matson's dwelling house. Also voted that the selectmen of said town do take care & build said house with stone or brick.

1775

The Boston Port Bill, passed in March 1774 and made effective June 1, inhibited loading and unloading of ships in the harbor. Such interference with commerce caused immediate economic hardship for the residents of the city. At the town meeting on June 20, 1774, the people of Lyme resolved to cooperate with their brethren in Boston and elsewhere to resist the increased burdens of British legislation. In September the town established a committee of relief for Boston. Evidently it was slow in mobilizing, for the zealous Higgins family sent its contribution directly to Colonel Jackson, a member of the Committee in Boston designated to receive and distribute donations from other towns.

Born in Eastham, Massachusetts, Capt. Joseph Higgins moved to Lyme in 1740 and lived there until his death. He owned a wharf and warehouse on the Connecticut River and traded with West Indies merchants. Both his sons, Christian and Joseph, were mariners of some kind, and the latter probably served in the Revolution.

Lyme, January 31, 1775

Col. Jackson
Sir:

As there has been gentlemen chosen in this town for to make a collection for the Town of Boston, but it seems to be in slow motion, my father and my brother and myself concluded to take this opportunity to send in our mite by the post, which we should be glad if you would receive the same, and give it to your Committee for the use of our poor brethren in Boston. My father desires to be remembered to you and all friends there.

This from your humble servant,
Christian Higgins

P.S. My father sent   £2
      My brother Joseph   1   16
      I have sent   1   10
                     ———
                 5   6

N.B. I did not know who was the Standing Committee, or I should sent to them.

C. Higgins

Capt. Joseph Higgins
Mr. Joseph Higgins, Jr.
Capt. Christian Higgins

[To Capt. Christian Higgins]

Boston, February 7, 1775

Sir:

By the hands of Col. Jackson, we received a kind donation from your worthy father, your brother Joseph, and yourself, amounting to five pounds, six shillings, lawful money, for the use of your poor brethren in Boston.

The Committee of Donations, who are appointed the distributors of those charities, return their sincere thanks to the benevolent donors. The conduct of the said Committee respecting the monies, etc. with which they are entrusted, may be collected from the two printed publications they have been called upon to make since they engaged in this important business. We now enclose them, not doubting they will afford satisfaction to all the friends of true constitutional liberty.

Our troubles are many, our oppressions great, our opposition mighty, and our conflict sharp; but patience and fortitude have been communicated from above, and if God shall continue to favor our cause, which we indeed think is a common cause, and the cause of truth and righteousness, we shall finally rise superior to those who, we think, are seeking the destruction of our civil and religious liberties. It was a frequent saying of the late venerable Doctor Sewall's "That civil and religious liberty always go together."

The Christian sympathy our fellow countrymen have expressed from time to time in their letters, and their generous donations for the relief and employment of the people in this town, suffering by means of the Boston Port Bill greatly refresh our spirits, and encourages us to persevere in the noble cause, and by the divine blessing we may hope for the desired success.

I am, with due respects to your father and brother, Sir, your obliged friend and humble servant.

D. J., { Per order of the Committee of Donations

*   *   *

Shortly after the first shot was fired at Lexington on April 19, Israel Bissell, a postrider, left Watertown, Massachusetts, to carry the news southward. Passing through Worcester, Norwich, and New London, he arrived at Lyme at 1 A.M. on April 21, where his message was endorsed and the time recorded. The men of the town immediately enlisted and marched to Boston.

These names are transcribed from the official muster roll for Lyme, which is remarkable for its detail. In addition to rank and time of service, it records each soldier's wages and amount due for billeting. If he had a horse, he was paid two pence a mile and nine pence a day for forage. On June 20, 1775, Marshfield Parsons, the older brother of Gen. Samuel Holden Parsons, received for distribution to Lyme men who fought at Lexington "an order on Colony Treasurer for the sum of one hundred eighty five pounds, one shilling and two half penny."

Marched from Lyme for the Relief of Boston
in the Lexington Alarm
April, 1775

Men's Names and Quality		Number of Days Served
Joseph Jewett	Captain	31
David F. Sill	Lieutenant	9
Lee Lay	"	29
Daniel Lord	Ensign	29
Elisha Wade	Sargeant	8
Ichabod Spencer	"	8
John Anderson, Jr.	"	8
Adriel Ely	"	29

Men's Names and Quality		Number of Days Served
Elijah Selden	"	29
Josiah Ely	"	25
Abraham Perkins	"	25
Josiah Ely	Corporal	3
Abraham Perkins, Jr.	"	3
William Beckwith	"	8
Joseph Sterling	"	29
Stephen Otis	"	29
John Saunders	"	25
Ezra Sill	Private	29
Edward Dorr		29
Job Tucker		29
Silas Marvin		18
Stephen Dewolf		29
Christopher Leach		29
Martin Wade		29
Elisha Merron, Jr.		29
William Lord		29
John Coult, Jr.		29
George Rowland		29
Robert Denison		29
Isaac Sill		29
Adriel Huntly		29
Joseph Minor		29
Benjamin Gale		29
Jonathan Miner		29
Andrew Ely		29
Micah Sill		29
Stephen Ransom		29
Daniel Havens		29
Elijah Phelps		29
John Congdon		29
Thaddeus Phelps		8
Jasper Griffin, 3rd		8
Timothy Brainerd		8
Levi Luther, Jr.		8
Stephen Mosier		8
Allen McKnight		8
Samuel G. Dorr		8
William R. Hyde		8
Samuel Dewolf		2
Giles Gilbert		8
Simon Dewolf		8
Reynold Peck		8
Joshua Saunders		8

Men's Names and Quality	Number of Days Served
Jacob Comstock	8
Abner Brockway	8
Lawrence Johnson	8
Thomas Way, Jr.	9
John Johnson	9
Samuel Griswold	9
Elisha Lee	30
Andrew Griswold	9
Enoch Smith	30
Stephen Sawer	30

* * *

Following the skirmish at Lexington, there were preparations for war at every level. In Hartford the General Assembly established the Council of Safety, an emergency standing committee with power to legislate when it was not in session. Like those elsewhere, the people of Lyme set up their own Committee of Inspection, which was responsible for patrolling the coast and planning against enemy invasion. These two brief *Gazette* articles report the presence of British ships in the neighborhood. The first illustrates the delight the patriots took in harassing the enemy and the second the sense of alarm as the news of plundering spread then abated.

Connecticut Gazette, July 14, 1775

New London, July 14

Last Lord's Day afternoon, a barge was sent with two swivels and a number of small arms, from the KING FISHER *Man of War (which was laying in the sound off the mouth of Connecticut River) in chase of a schooner belonging to Rocky Hill, who was bound into the river; — the schooner grounding on Saybrook Bar, she was boarded by the people from the barge, who attempted to get her afloat, but finding they could not, left her. — On sight of the barge, numbers of armed people immediately collected on the points each side the river, when a number of shot were exchanged on both sides. Our people received no damage — what damage was done to the people in the barge we don't learn, but upon receiving our fire they immediately rowed in great haste further from shore.*

A Lyme Miscellany

Connecticut Gazette, August 25, 1775

About 1 o'clock last Tuesday morning an express arrived in town from Black Point, about 7 miles from hence with intelligence that a Man of War, the evening before, had arrived there, and anchored very near the shore, and it was thought intended to take off stock in that neighborhood: — A detachment from the troops here were immediately dispatched for said place; but before they arrived, intelligence was sent to them that the said ship had weighed anchor and stood to the westward, whereupon the troops returned.

*   *   *

As the summer progressed, the British need for provisions prompted them to ravage the coastal towns, and the next three letters show how the people of Lyme used all available means of communication to get adequate protection. As chairman of the Committee of Inspection, Joseph Mather wrote to Governor Trumbull and was answered within two days by Gurdon Saltonstall, a prominent civil and military leader from New London.

Apparently the conciliatory gesture at the end of Saltonstall's letter did not assuage the troubled people of Lyme, who were upset by the governor's refusal to grant their request. On September 2, two days after Saltonstall drafted his letter, they asked their fellow townsman, Matthew Griswold, deputy governor and a member of the Council of Safety, to write to the governor. Griswold's standing brought action. At a meeting of the Council in Lebanon on September 4, his letter was read, and the Council voted that "one company, *viz.* Capt. Rowlee's, be sent to Lyme, and under the direction of the Dep. Governor and civil authority of that town keep up and maintain proper watches and guards in such manner and places as they shall direct, for the present."[1] Thereafter, until the end of the year, the Council of Safety voted to continue or strengthen military protection to the town.

1. J. Hammond Trumbull and Charles J. Hoadly, eds., *The Public Records of the Colony of Connecticut* (Hartford: Case, Lockwood, and Brainard Co., 1850–90), XV:123.

To the Honorable Jonathan Trumbull, Esq., at Lebanon

Lyme, August 29, 1775

Honored Sir:

The distressed circumstances of the country in general fills us with anxiety, but especially our sea coast at present seems more immediately to draw our attention, as there has lately been a fleet in our neighborhood ravaging the islands, and a larger fleet now sailed from Boston which we apprehend is coming this way on the same errand.

And as there is a great number of cattle, sheep, & swine in this town within about the distance of one mile from the sea shore which we apprehend are exposed to be taken by such a fleet, if attempted, therefore we the Committee of Inspection for the town, at the request of a great number of the principal inhabitants of the town, beg leave to request of Your Honor that you would order one or two companies of soldiers that are now stationed at New London to be removed to this town for the purpose of guarding the sea coast where this stock is situated, to take the advice of the authority in, or the selectmen of the town, or of this Committee, or any other man or set of men, with regard to the most convenient places to keep their guards, that Your Honor in your wisdom shall think fit. Your Honor's compliance with this our request will greatly oblige Your Honor's most obedient

humble servant.

Signed per order, Joseph Mather, Chairman

N.B. The bearer is able to inform Your Honor with regard to the number of the stock & other matters that Your Honor may see fit to inquire after.

[To the Town Officers]

New London, August 31, 1775
8 P.M. o'clock

Gentlemen:

This morning I am honored with Governor Trumbull's letter of this date relative to an application you made to him desiring that one or two companies of the troops stationed here be removed for the purpose of guarding the coast at Lyme and observes that "the present aspect of the affair doth not admit a compliance; those companies will be employed in the best manner for the defence of the whole coast," and adds, "possibly if the Capts. Dan Marvin, James Huntley, and George Chadwick were ordered to set and keep a watch of a suitable number of men each, it is all that can be beneficially done till further danger appear, and is noticed that you give them orders accordingly," and leave the matter to my discretion.

The towns of New London, Groton, and Norwich have, by their civil authority and selectmen, appointed watches in their several towns, and the law appears to me has made most ample provision in the case; and should the three companies aforesaid be ordered to watch and ward would they not think hard for them to do the whole duty in the case for the town? Nor would it be possible for me to know what number of men would be proper or where to station them. —— And since the law has made such ample provision, and the authority in Lyme so much better able to conduct the affair than I am, make no doubt they will instantly. —— However, if you think my assistance will be advantageous [I] shall be glad to confer with any proper persons of your town on the subject.

> I am, Gentlemen, your humble servant.
>
> G. Saltonstall

[To Governor Trumbull]

Lyme, September 2, 1775

Sir:

The danger of being robbed of our stock on the sea coast near the mouth of Connecticut River has induced the people of that neighborhood to keep a watch for some time to prevent that mischief, but as few people live near the place of danger it is found greatly inconvenient to call people some [about?] distance of 5 or 6 miles to attend that service, which we have been obliged to do. Many at present seem to groan under the burden.

I am desired by sundry of the selectmen & civil authority of this town (all indeed who are present) to request that Your Honor would please to order & direct that some of the soldiers at New London might at present be stationed at Black Point about 6 or 7 miles from New London & another small party near Connecticut River on the east side. With submission to Your Honor's better judgment I apprehend if the party near Connecticut River should consist of about 12 men, 3 or 4 to watch at a time, might be sufficient to give the alarm and give timely assistance to the people to remove themselves & stock out of the way of danger. Such a small number might be taken into the few houses there without much trouble. The number on Black Point I should think ought to be greater as the access to that place is easier, deep water near the shore, the point long & narrow and so situated as easier to discover the approaches of any ships towards New London in the way they would undoubtedly go, & not so far distant but that they might afford timely assistance & serve New London to better purpose than if they were actually on the spot. Our people esteem it a hardship to be obliged to travel watch and do the service the soldiers are paid for. I don't doubt that Your Honor will do justice in the affair.

I am with great esteem Your Honor's most obedient & humble servant.

Mr. Gr.

*   *   *

Connecticut Gazette, September 22, 1775

NEW LONDON, September 22

At a meeting of the Committees of Inspection for the towns of Saybrook, Killingworth, and Lyme, convened and held at Saybrook, on September 5, 1775:

BENJAMIN WILLIAMS, Esq., Chairman

This meeting taking into consideration the necessity we are under, at this critical day, to preserve all the gun powder that we have in our hands (and all further supplies of that article that we may obtain) to use in our defense against our common enemies. And as there are a number, in the towns aforesaid, that do frequently make use of this necessary article, for fowling and

other game, which practice (in the opinion of this meeting)
ought to be laid aside, for the present: Therefore, RESOLVED,
that it be recommended, and it is hereby recommended to all the
inhabitants in the towns of Saybrook, Killingworth, and Lyme,
not to make use of any gun powder, for fowling or any other
game, from and after the date hereof, until the first day of April
next, as they would preserve to themselves that honorable
character of being friends to their country.

Signed per order

BENJAMIN WILLIAMS, Chairman

Saybrook, September 5, 1775

1776

After the British evacuated Boston in March 1776, General
Washington, expecting a major attack on New York, sent an urgent
request for 2,000 men from Connecticut to help protect the city until
his arrival. During its May session the Assembly devoted a good deal
of time to expediting Washington's orders and organizing its own
defense of the colony.

James Wadsworth, the writer of the first letter, was a native of
Durham and long a member of the Assembly. He fought at Lexington
and led troops at the siege of Boston. In January 1776 he was com-
missioned a brigadier general and in the spring made responsible for
recruiting Connecticut troops bound for New York.

Samuel Selden was a native of Lyme and like his superior officer
fought the British at Boston. He was the town's representative at the
May session of the Assembly in 1776 and subsequently was made
commanding officer of the Third Battalion of Connecticut Militia
under Brigadier General Wadsworth.

Joshua Huntington of Norwich also fought at Lexington and
Boston. Although he later was an agent of Jeremiah Wadsworth in
the colony's Commissary Department, in 1776 he was a captain in the
militia and led his troops to New York and New Jersey.

The letters, all written within a few days, show clearly the chain of
command from Washington to the colony's legislature to the local

commanding officers. The tone of urgency in each document is especially evident in Colonel Selden's of July 6th, in which he exploits his remarkable rhetorical powers to prod action to prevent "the ruin of America for ages to come." Although the correspondents' insistence on haste was undoubtedly a function of their sense of duty, it may have been related to the widespread difficulty of obtaining troops. In May the Assembly voted to raise the fine from two to ten pounds for men who failed to march on orders.

[To Col. Samuel Selden]

Durham, June 29, 1776

Sir:

In consequence of orders received from General Washington, you are hereby directed to give the necessary orders for expediting the march of your regiment in manner heretofore directed as soon as they can possibly be mustered & equipped; and direct that your men are all furnished with arms & that none are suffered to go without, as it will be impossible to procure them at Head Quarters, & their service will consequently be rendered useless.

James Wadsworth, Jr., Brig. Gen.

Copy: Brig. Gen.'s Orders

[To Col. Samuel Selden]

Sir:

As the greatest expedition is required in raising & forwarding the regiments to be under your command for the New York department, you are hereby ordered to give your earliest & utmost attention to the raising and forwarding said regiment & to give proper orders to all officers necessary for that purpose & that the soldiers be well provided & equipped & that there be no delay in marching forward as soon as they or any of them to the number of twenty five of a company are ready & mustered, & that a proper officer or officers of the company according to the number marching go forth with them & also a field officer or

officers according to the number marching from each regiment take the command of such parties, march forward to New York & give notice two or three days before their coming to the general or other proper officers in the army that provisions may be made for subsisting & disposing of them in proper places.
Hartford, June 23, 1776

James Wadsworth, Jr.
Brig. Gen.

N.B. Muster masters appointed are Maj. St. John, Mr. Pierpoint Edwards, Capt. Lynde Lord, Col. Gurdon Saltonstall, Col. Erastus Wolcott, Maj. Brown of Coventry, Col. Matthew Talcott.

Copy General Orders

[To Col. Samuel Selden]

Durham, June 30, 1776
Sunday morning

Sir:

Last evening by an express, I received another letter from General Washington requesting in the most pressing manner not to lose a moment's time in sending forward the regiments designed for New York. Must therefore direct that you give all possible attention to the raising, equipping & immediately sending forward your regiment in manner before directed, as the safety of our army may under heaven depend much on the seasonable arrival of the Connecticut regiments.

James Wadsworth, Jr., Brig. Gen.

To Capt. Joshua Huntington at Norwich

Sir:

Enclosed you have copy of Gen. Wadsworth's pressing orders to me for the raising, equipping, and marching the regiment under my command designed for New York. You are therefore directed and ordered to conform thereto and make no delay but give all possible attention and diligence to the raising, equipping, and mustering the company under your command designed for New York. And you are to see to it that your men are all well provided with good fire arms and not to march without. And as soon as you have enlisted to the number of twenty-five men of your company and have them equipped and mustered you will give immediate notice thereof to the commanding officer of the regiment that some proper officer or officers may be appointed to take the command of them to New York.

Given under my hand in Lyme this 30th day of June, 1776.

Samuel Selden

Capt. Huntington

N.B. Sir: I have the general liberty for the regiment to go by water if it shall be thought best and if your men go by water you will take care that there be no delay on account of transports to transport them.

From your humble servant,

Samuel Selden

For Capt. Joshua Huntington, Norwich

Lyme, July 6, 1776

Sir:

Enclosed you have the express of Gen. Wadsworth to me & the commands upon him from the head general to forward the Connecticut regiments designed for York department without a moment's delay. You are therefore desired, entreated, directed, and ordered by all that is desirable and precious to free men to give all diligence and suffer not a moment delay if it be possible raise equipment and muster your company. Rouse the people to see their danger. Stir them up by all that is dear in this life. Our wives, our children, our prosperity, our liberty is at stake; but above all social enjoyments our religion, for which our forefathers left their native land, fled to this wilderness, suffered cold, hunger, nakedness, and many of them were tortured and bothered in the most inhumane manner that they might leave to posterity freedom of religion and masters of their own property. I fear some strange intimidation or infatuation has seized the minds of people that they are no more spirited to venture in the glorious cause we are engaged in; for if we can't defend ourselves at New York I fear all is gone, for if they conquer the united strength of the continent what an easy prey will our little towns & ports become to them.

Pray, Sir, lose not a moment's time. As soon as you have raised 25 men, equip and muster them and you shall have orders to march immediately. I expected returns long before this time. A moment's delay may prove the ruin of America for ages to come. Pursue the orders of the Gen. and conform thereto & let me hear what success you have. Send me the number you have enlisted and in what forwardness they are that I may report to the Gen.

From, Sir, with respect your most humble servant.

Samuel Selden

Captain Huntington
I this day sent off between 60 & 70 men from East Haddam.

1777

Poor pay, inadequate care of the sick and injured, and demands at home accounted for declining enlistments and desertion. Many towns such as Lyme nevertheless took seriously their obligations to supply their quota of troops and assure care of soldiers' families through appointed committees. At the same time the Continental Army's enormous need for provisions caused shortages of essentials on the home front. To counteract the resulting inflation the Assembly put limits on the prices of basic commodities and labor, which local governments tried to enforce.

At a meeting of the inhabitants of the Town of Lyme in New London County by legal notice convened and held in said Lyme on March 31, 1777. — At the same meeting Richard Wait, Esq., is chosen moderator of this meeting.

— At the same meeting voted that in the present alarming

state of our country, occasioned by the cruel and unnatural and unjust war begun and prosecuted by the King of Great Britain with circumstance of unexampled barbarity against the laws of nations and the rights of humanity, it's the undefensible duty of every person who prefers the freedom and happiness of himself and posterity to the shackles and misery of the slaves of tyrants to exert themselves in the defence of the just rights of their country in opposition to the arbitrary claims of foreign powers: for this purpose this town will do all in their power to promote and encourage the filling up the batallions ordered by Congress for opposing the army of the King etc.

— At the same meeting voted that Mssrs. Joseph Coult, William Noyes, Abraham Perkins, Andrew Griswold, Jesse Beckwith, William Brockway, and Richard Wait, all of said Lyme, be a committee to supply (in their absence) the families of such as shall volunteer by enlistment into said service — with all necessaries which they may need for their support, so far as the soldiers shall deposit moneys with the committee for that purpose.

— At the same meeting voted that the committee be enabled to procure such sums on the credit of the town as are wanted to furnish necessaries for the families of the soldiers in their absence and who are not able to deposit moneys, which are to be supplied on the soldiers' soldiering order on the payments of the regiments for repaying the same.

— At the same meeting voted that this town will exert themselves to condign punishments all those who shall transgress the law of this state regulating the prices of the necessaries of life, and to expose to public notice all such as shall withhold those necessary articles.

*　　*　　*

Throughout the war General Washington requested from Connecticut provisions for the Continental Army. Towns were given quotas for the often small supply. Privateering, legalized in 1775 and 1776, was especially popular on Long Island Sound, where the British navy and merchant marine gave ample opportunity for attack and spoils. As a loyal patriot John McCurdy sold to the army as well as to the privateers goods from his store in Lyme. The recipient of his letter, Jeremiah Wadsworth, was a Hartford merchant, commissar of supplies for Connecticut troops, and later commissary general of purchases for the Continental Army.

> To Capt. Jeremiah Wadsworth
>   at Hartford
>
>   Lyme, July 5, 1777
>
> Sir:
>   I have 60 barrels of beef of the best kind, that I put up for my own use. You may have it for the army if wanted. The privateers that I put it up for, all got into the eastward, where I could not send it. I am, Sir, your very humble servant.
>   John McCurdy
> N.B. It is all repacked & pickled.

*   *   *

These minutes show the town's scrupulous conformity to the law. At the time Elijah Hubbard of Middletown was "Commissary and Superintendant of the stores of supplies and refreshments" for Connecticut troops. Royal Flint, a merchant from Windham, was assistant commissary.

> At a meeting of the inhabitants of the Town of Lyme in New London County by legal notice convened and held in said Lyme on October 1, 1777. At the same meeting Capt. Joseph Mather is chosen and appointed moderator of this meeting.
> At the same meeting the said town by their vote appointed and ordered the selectmen of said town for the time being to procure immediately one shirt, either linen or flannel, one hunting shirt — or frock, one pair of woolen overalls, one or two pairs of woolen stockings, and one pair of good shoes for each man, commissioned officer, or soldier in the Continental Army belonging to the said Town of Lyme; and deliver the same to Mssrs. Elijah Hubbard or Royal Flint, Superintending Commissaries, to be by them conveyed to said officers and soldiers in

manner and form according to the resolves of the governor and Committee of Safety at Lebanon in the State of Connecticut, September 12, 1777; and transmit to the General Assembly to be holden at New Haven in October instant: an account of such articles of clothing as they shall have delivered to said commissary according to the direction given in said resolve.

1778

Congress adopted the Articles of Confederation on November 15, 1777, forwarding them to local legislatures for approval. Upon final ratification on March 1, 1781, the country was governed by them until November 21, 1788, when Congress declared that the federal Constitution had been duly ratified. The eighth article of confederation, which would determine taxation solely by land evaluation, was generally unacceptable to Northerners because it gave an unfair advantage to Southerners, many of whom owned slaves, another form of property.

At a meeting of the inhabitants of the Town of Lyme in New London County by legal notice convened and held in said Lyme on January 5, 1778.

— William Noyes, Esq., was chosen moderator of the meeting. At the same meeting the town, having taken into consideration the Articles of Confederacy of the United States, do approve the same and instruct & direct their representatives to give their assent thereto. Although the town, apprehending the general scope of this Confederacy to be adopted to suit the convenience of the Confederated States, and considering the general difficulties which may arise from delaying the matter owing to the local situation & other considerations; and on that ground do at present assent to them in full confidence that Congress will alter such parts thereof as may be grievous — but at the same time would direct and order our representatives to move in assembly that the delegates from this state move for the following alterations, viz.: in the 8th article that all the expense therein mentioned be defrayed from a tax on all the visible estate, real, personal, or mixed, upon an estimate to be made once in ten years, or such term as Congress shall direct. — And also that the lowest value of any lands be ascertained by Congress.

We further instruct our representatives that our delegates be directed to move that the yeas & nays on every question be entered in the Journal without special motion therefor. And as the town conceives this necessary in larger bodies, so it is equally convenient that the minds of the members of Assembly be known to their constituents, the representatives are therefore instructed to move that the yeas & nays on every important question be entered on the Journal of the House — and the debate be as open as possible.

— At the same meeting voted that there shall be a contribution in every parish or meeting in the town for the soldiers in the Continental Service that belong to this town, and that a committee be appointed to receive all that may be contributed and forward the same to said soldiers.

— Also voted that Col. Marshfield Parsons, Mssrs. Abner Lee, Ezra Selden, John Griffing, Stephen Smith, Samuel Selden, Jacob Tillotson, Samuel Griswold, James Huntley, and Nathan Peck be a committee for the purpose aforesaid.

*   *   *

David Fithen Sill, who was born in 1733, served in the French and Indian War and in 1775 was appointed captain in Colonel Tyler's Connecticut regiment. Present at Lexington, Sill later became a lieutenant colonel of the First Regiment of the Connecticut line. Samuel Mather was born in Lyme in 1742/43 and became a physician as well as captain of the Sixth Company in the Third Militia Regiment.

When he wrote the letter Sill was probably encamped at White Plains, where General Washington had arrived on July 30 to set up a land blockade of New York. During the next few weeks there were several encounters nearby with the British.

Sill seemed to be well informed. He knew that the French fleet, which had arrived in New York earlier in July, had left for Newport

for the pending Franco-American campaign to rout the enemy. Sill
was familiar also with the unsuccessful efforts of the British peace
commissioners under the Earl of Carlisle and with the notorious trial
of Gen. Charles Lee, who actually had been found guilty of disobedi-
ence and misbehavior when the letter was written.

To Capt. Samuel Mather, Lyme

Camp, August 9, 1778

Dear Sir:

Yours of the 25th duly received. I am pleased to find you
have at last broke the way for a correspondence. You know my
sentiments are not to begin but ever to answer all letters in a
friendly way. Our expectations with respect to the present campaign are equally great with yours. We see the prospect of ending the war and are as anxious to have it speedily ended as you
possibly can be.

I am sensible [of] the effect the extravagancy of the times
will have on many and pity the thousands of middling farmers
(as well as army) that must fall a sacrifice to the avaricious.

I have little in the news way. We lay about fifteen miles from
Kings Bridge but keep out large parties scouting near their lines
to whom deserters daily come out, six or seven one day, with
another notwithstanding. They are on an island etc. etc.

I rather think the General will not make a general attack till
the fleet etc. returns from the eastward unless they should appear to be going off. I hope the expedition against Newport will
prove successful & that a few days will put our troops in the
possession of the place. What then will hinder the fleet and army
at New York falling into our hands? Nothing, it appears to me,
but a speedy arrival of a superior English fleet. You will see by
the commissioners' letters that they are panicky struck. They
have made use of every artifice to bring about a reconciliation of
dependency which seems to be the only thing they make a point
of which is a sufficient bar.

The court has not determined concerning Gen. Lee, but I
expect that with some acknowledgement to His Excellency he
will be discharged. This moment orders are come to strike tents

at 5 o'clock, tomorrow morning, where we are to march, we are not told.

> I am, Sir, your friend & humble servant,
> David F. Sill

1779

At a meeting of the inhabitants of the Town of Lyme in New London County by legal notice convened and held in said Lyme on April 12, 1779, Col. Marshfield Parsons was chosen moderator.

— At the same meeting voted that the selectmen prepare a petition to the governor and Council of Safety praying that the militia of this town be excused from detachments to do service within the state the present year considering the distressed circumstances of the people for want of provisions having their crops almost entirely cut off the last year.

* * *

As deputy governor, Matthew Griswold served also as chief judge of the Superior Court, which held sessions in each county twice a year. Perhaps he alluded to the principle of common law and by implication the relative importance of the Superior Court to justify his absence from the Council of Safety. Or he may have feared the possibility of chaos should the court system break down while the colony was in revolution.

For His Excellency, Jonathan Trumbull, Esq., Governor of Connecticut, at Lebanon

Lyme, July 28, 1779

Sir:

The frequent alarms we have had & being indisposed with a

bad cold prevented waiting on Your Excellency as I proposed. A few days past the enemy landed in our neighborhood and since that at Black Point carried off sheep from both places. By the protection of a kind Providence we have hitherto escaped the ravages of the enemy. One of their ships & two tenders have for several days been lying in the sound here till yesterday they sailed eastward and went out of our sight. The threatening danger we are in has engaged my attention to assist in regulating & disposing of the guards along this shore for the safety of the people & their property & have endeavored to take every necessary precaution for that purpose. — The time is so short before the session of the Superior Court begins that Your Excellency will excuse my attendance on the Council of Safety till after the circuit begins.

Your Excellency is sensible of the importance of holding the reins of government by keeping up the common law courts. That part of the trust committed to me shall endeavor to execute with all possible care.

The guards here want flints. The bearer will apply to Your Excellency for supply. I have enclosed a request in which have made myself accountable & to see them properly applied.

I am with great esteem
Your Excellency's most
obedient and humble servant
Matthew Griswold

1780

At a meeting of the inhabitants of the Town of Lyme in New London County by legal notice convened and held in said Lyme on June 26, 1780, Capt. Richard Wait is chosen moderator of this meeting.

At the same meeting voted that the chief commanding officers of each company in this town are hereby empowered forthwith to hire fourteen able bodied and effective men to enlist into the Continental Service until the last day of December next, as they can agree, and at the cost of this town.

— At the same meeting the town by their vote to direct the selectmen of said town to hire so much silver or paper money as will be sufficient to pay of those 14 men that may be hired by the commanding officer of each company in this town to enlist into the Continental Service until the last day of December next and the same to pay accordingly.

* * *

For His Excellency Jonathan Trumbull, Esq., at Lebanon

Lyme, August 9, 1780

Sir:

Your Excellency from the enclosed papers may see in some measure the distressed situation we are in. The enemy in sight from day to day, seeming ready to wreak their vengeance upon us, the guard destitute of provision, our family store exhausted with other melancholy circumstances renders our case gloomy indeed. In regard to the Irish beef mentioned in Mr. Richards' letter, I dare not presume to give order to deal out any part of it that belongs to Your Excellency & Council of Safety. If it was thought expedient to order out one or two barrels of it for this guard, it would serve for supply of meat for the present. Whether it would be advisable or not I submit — . If a few fat sheep were forthwith sent to my son for the use of the guard & some flour or meal of any kind sent to the Commissary at New London, it would relieve the present difficulty. My son will take particular care of the sheep and render the Commissary a particular account according to the order & direction he shall give.

Your Excellency & Council are sensible of the importance of keeping up this guard at this critical juncture, preventing all communication with the people on Long Island that whatever is carried from the main goes directly to the enemy. I expected Your Excellency call before now to attend the Council of Safety: stood ready to pay obedience. Setting out tomorrow to attend the circuit. Our selectmen have procured a whale boat for the use of the guard. I don't doubt but Your Excellency will pursue proper measures in this critical state of affairs.

> I am with great esteem Your
> Excellency's most obedient &
> humble servant.
> Matthew Griswold

1781

At a meeting of the inhabitants of the Town of Lyme in New London County by legal [notice] convened and held in said Lyme on April 27, 1781, John McCurdy was chosen moderator.

— At the same meeting the town by their vote do direct the selectmen of said town to hire money sufficient to purchase meat for to support the guard or soldiers stationed on the sea coast in said Lyme between the mouth of Connecticut River and New London for about two months till further provision can be made for them.

— At the same meeting Mr. Frederick Mather was chosen and appointed collector to collect the wine, wheat, and rye flour, and Indian corn and see that the same is good and marketable and to procure casks for and pack and store said flour and Indian corn that may be brought in by the inhabitants of the Society of Chesterfield in said Town of Lyme (and to collect the tax granted for the purpose aforesaid on that part of the town) pursuant to an act passed by the General Assembly of this state at their session held at Hartford on November 29, 1780.

* * *

A meeting of the inhabitants of the Town of Lyme convened and held in said Lyme according to adjournment on July 3, 1781.

— At the same meeting the town by their vote did release and exempt Mr. Samuel Griswold from serving as a collector and receiving the 4 penny tax to which he was chosen and appointed at their last meeting which was holden on June 28, 1781, and made choice of Mr. Seth Smith in the room of said Griswold to be a collector and receiver of said four penny tax and to do and act therein according to the Act of the General Assembly passed at their session in May last.

At the same meeting Mssrs. Samuel Mather, Jr., Joseph Smith, and Ezra Selden, Esq., were appointed receivers to procure barrels, receive and salt pork, and secure the beef & pork that shall be brought in and necessary to be salted, as also to store such other articles as shall be delivered in payment of the last tax mentioned in the act of the General Assembly of the State of Connecticut, passed at their sessions in May last — and to do and act therein according to the directions of said statutory.

*   *   *

When this letter was written, Col. William Ledyard of Groton was the commanding officer of troops in the area, and Adam Shapley was a captain of a company of musketry. Two months later, at the battle of New London, Ledyard, in command of Fort Griswold, was brutally killed by the British attackers. Shapley, who commanded the garrison at Fort Trumbull, also was killed.

To Lt. Col. William Ledyard

New London, July 4, 1781

Sir:

Agreeable to your order of June 29, I proceeded as far as Branford to view the guards. I found the guard at Black Hall under the command of Lt. Josiah Burnham and Ens. Marvin, to consist of 3 corporals, one drum, one fife, and 11 privates. They keep their guards at Black Hall, and when the weather permits they keep out a [rear ?] guard. The men are very poorly equipped with arms and ammunition.

[from Capt. Adam Shapley]

*   *   *

To His Excellency Governor Trumbull

New Haven, September 7, 1781

Sir:

At three of the clock this morning we had the disagreeable news that New London was attacked by the enemy. The judges of the court with sundry of the inhabitants immediately convened to consult what measures should be taken. We sent an express to the westward without loss of time with the intelligence directed to the civil and military officers in the western towns and to be forwarded to Gen. Mead, requiring them to exert themselves to the utmost of their power in their several departments to put the people in the best posture of defense and transmit the intelligence to the adjacent towns.

I also sent an order to Brig. Gen. Ward to fix posts of intelligence between New Haven and New London, also an order to Col. Cook who commands the Tenth Regiment to detach one hundred men out of his regiment to repair to New Haven for the defense of that place, also similar orders to Lt. Col. Sabin to call in one hundred men for the same purpose out of the regiment to which he belongs with further orders to those officers to cause those under their respective command to hold themselves in constant readiness to march at a moment's warning to any place that may be attacked.

> I am with great respect & esteem
> Your Excellency's most obedient
> & humble servant.
> Matthew Griswold

*　　*　　*

According to his own testimony Elisha Beckwith of Lyme joined the British when they invaded New London in September 1781 and accompanied the enemy to New York. In November he returned to the town via Long Island to retrieve his family and take them to settle in Penobscot, a small village on Penobscot Bay in Maine. After his arrest Beckwith was taken first to prison in Norwich and later to Hartford. From jail he wrote insulting and threatening letters to Governor Griswold and finally took his case to the General Assembly, which denied his petition for release. Strictly speaking Beckwith was not a refugee but a recalcitrant prisoner of war and therefore subject to harsh treatment by the legislature.

Connecticut Gazette, November 30, 1781

Last Friday a guard under the command of Ensign Andrew Griswold, stationed at Lyme, discovered a whale boat in a fresh pond near Black Point; and suspecting it came from Long Island, they set a guard of five men over the boat, and the night after four others of the guard with Ensign Griswold went towards the house of the noted Elisha Beckwith. One of the party named Noah Lester, advancing faster than the rest, was challenged by Beckwith's wife, who was near the house. This alarmed ten men who were in the house, well armed, and they immediately siezed upon and made prisoner of Lester, and carried him into the house. Soon after the other four of the guard came to the house (not knowing Lester was a prisoner) and went directly in, where they discovered the ten persons in arms. A scuffle immediately ensued between them, and after some time the guard secured six of the party, among them was Elisha Beckwith. The other four made their escape into the woods, but they were all except one taken the next day. They came in the above boat from Long Island, and were under the command of Thomas Smith, formerly of Middletown, who had a captain's commission under the British King. Elisha Beckwith went off with the enemy September 6 last, when they made their descent on this place. The above culprits are secured in Norwich jail.

1782

To the Honorable the General Assembly convened at Hartford, January 10, 1782.

The memorial of Elisha Beckwith of New London now in

the jail in Hartford humbly showeth — That he hath been viz. in sentiment attached to the British government, that in consequence he went off with the British troops in their late invasion at said New London — that he returned to New London again in the month of November last to carry off his family, but was taken in his own house by the guard — that he claims the benefit of a prisoner of war & that he may be the subject of exchange & not held upon any other footing — he humbly hopes Your Honors will not consider the line he wrote to His Honor Governor Griswold in the light of insult or threat, for he can sincerely say that he had no such intention, however it may be worded — he begs Your Honors not to be offended or take umbrage at the undisguised or coarse manner of his writing, or to take any severe measures thereon, without a hearing.

— But that Your Honors would candidly consider of what avail or real public advantage it will be to retain in prison a man, who from first to last considers himself a British subject & chooses to live under British government — will it not be better for this community to be rid of all such atones, rather than retain them a[t] public expenses, especially, as by allowing open exchange Your Honors will recover one of your well attached subjects, now confined in the same circumstances, & will be until the memorialist is released. The memorialist thus prays Your Honors, upon principles of policy as well as humanity, to allow the memorialist to be exchanged & to take with him his wife & family to trouble no more, & he as in duty bound shall pray. Dated at the jail. January 10, 1782.

Elisha Beckwith

In the Lower House
    The prayer of this memorial is negatived.

Jedidiah Strong, Clerk

In the Upper House
    The prayer of this memorial is negatived.

George Wyllys, Secretary

1832

John Ely was born in Lyme on February 28, 1758, and at the age of seventeen joined the militia. After the war he became a schoolteacher and lived in Philadelphia. In 1832, as an old man, he applied to the government for a recently instituted pension granted to surviving soldiers of the Revolution.

These paragraphs, taken from Ely's pension application, contain a remarkably full account of his military career. Time and memory have served him well and provide us with a coherent and lively tale. Through reference to many names and incidents appearing in earlier documents, Ely's application is also a review of Lyme's involvement in the Revolution.

A short time after the battle of Lexington I enlisted as a soldier in the Connecticut line of the army, then forming. The first year of the war I served in Col. Samuel H. Parsons' regiment (at that time some of the commanders of regiments had also a *company* of their own). I belonged to Colonel Parsons' company. David F. Sill was our captain, Christopher Ely of Lyme was lieutenant, and Elisha Wade ensign. We assembled at New London & being properly organized marched in haste to join the army near Boston, where we arrived on June 18, 1775, the next day after the battle of Bunker Hill, and encamped on the high grounds of Roxbury, the smoking ruins of Charlestown lying there before us.

Capt. David F. Sill was the recruiting officer who enlisted me. [John] Tyler was our lieutenant colonel and [Samuel] Prentis our major. The names of some of the officers of our regiment I remember: Capt. Chapman of New London, Capt. Ely, Capt. Coit; Ezra Selden of Lyme was then a sergeant in our company. He was afterwards a lieutenant and was severely wounded at Stoney Point. James Day, a deserter from the enemy, was our adjutant — a *strict* and *severe* disciplinarian. I also remember Lt. Richards, Lt. Lee, Ens. Elisha Ely, Nevins, Waite, and others I could name if necessary. Dan Lee of Lyme was one of our sergeants; he was afterwards a pensioner, till his death.

The place where I was mostly on duty the first campaign and where we mounted guard, was on the lines in Roxbury near Boston Neck. That place I cannot forget: there I was first terrified with the noise of cannon balls flying over and the bursting of shells. But when I found they did not kill me, the distressing sensations of fear were soon over, and no longer troublesome during my soldiership. Towards the close of this campaign, which ended with the year, I again enlisted as a soldier for another year, in the same regiment, commanded now by Col. Tyler, Parsons being made our brigadier general. [Samuel] Prentis was our lt. colonel, and Capt. James Chapman, major, with some other change of officers. We remained encamped on the same ground, and continued much the same round of duties until the month of March 1776, when I was attached to that part of the army which took possession of Dorchester Heights. There, during a cold, windy night, with much labor and fatigue, we constructed a fort, which by the first morning light appeared formidable, and greatly astonished the enemy who were, partly, encamped on the Boston Common, their ships of war riding at anchor in the harbor below us, at a short distance. A very few days after this the whole British army and navy, Tories and all, commenced their retreat. That day I remember well. It was the seventeenth of March: to them a day of sadness and chagrin, but to us a most jovial St. Patrick's Day.

Soon after the British had evacuated Boston, our army took up its line of march for the city of New York, and it was not many weeks before we again faced the enemy, on Long Island. And I had my full share in some of the battles and skirmishes which took place in that vicinity. But the enemy being now greatly superior to us in numbers, we were in turn compelled to give ground. And Washington, who never did wrong, deeming it imprudent longer to contend against such odds on that bloody arena, ordered a retreat. Which retreat, so far as my knowledge extended, was performed in excellent order. We were commanded to rest on our arms, and be ready at a moment's call; and not knowing that a retreat was intended, everyone expected hard fighting the next day. My own mind was made up and prepared for a terrible conflict. But, during the stillness and dead of night, while the enemy was yawning, we were quietly paraded and drawn off, so that by sun rise our whole army had crossed over the East River, at and near Brooklyn, and were again at our quarters in the city of New York. Not many days after this, however, we were forced again to retreat before a powerful enemy. It was in the month of September, and we were much harassed both in our flanks and rear. Many were killed. Our beloved Major Chapman here fell very near me, being shot through the body. He had been very kind to me and I was sorely grieved, but had no time to weep, for the enemy pressed hard. We fought and retreated, first to Harlem Heights where we made a stand, then to Kings Bridge, to White Plains, to North Castle, and so on, counter-marching till we came to Dobbs Ferry, where we crossed over the North River (I think it was *Dobbs* Ferry) into the state of New Jersey, still retreating, with the enemy at our heels, till late in autumn when the cold winter was upon us, being fatigued and ragged enough, we encamped at the foot of Mt. Ramapo Mountains where, for a time, we were at rest. In this place, the upper part of New Jersey, at the close of the year my true *regular* campaign of nearly two years ended. And here, after delivering into the public store my arms and accouterments, I received in *Continental bills* the small balance of my pay, which was then due to me, together with an honorable discharge from the commanding officer: which *discharge,* not then knowing the value of it, is lost. I now returned home, a long journey, at my own expense of *time* and *rations.* But shortly after this, I was again in the service of my country, my occupation being changed for a time, from fighting to working. In the spring of the year 1777 I was engaged as an *artificer,* and was employed in assisting to do the cabin-joiner work of the frigate *Independence,* then building on the River Thames between New London and Norwich. It is proper here to note that at the time I first enlisted as a soldier I was then serving an apprenticeship to learn the occupation of a house-joiner. And in the business of this ship-joiner work I was in the Continental service about three months, more or less. Afterwards in the autumn of the same year, when part of the British at New York were moving up the river towards Albany, and Burgoyne was coming down from the north, I served as a soldier in the militia about six weeks or more. We marched to the North River, and I was stationed at

Rhinebeck Flats, at the time Esopus (now Kingston) was burned. And after Burgoyne with his army had surrendered, I was here, at Rhinebeck, discharged and paid off again in Continental money. About the commencement of the year 1778, when it was contemplated once more to invade Canada, I was again called out with the militia and marched as far as Albany. It was rumored at the time that the Marquis de Lafayette, a young French nobleman, was to be our commander. But the expectation was relinquished. From what cause it was relinquished, they never told me. In this tour I was in the service only about three weeks. Again, some considerable time after, in the summer of 1779, when the enemy invaded the coast of Connecticut, sacked New Haven, and burned several villages along the sound, I was once more drafted and served another tour as soldier in the militia, and was quartered among the ruins of Fairfield, a beautiful village which had been recently burned. Here, after six weeks' service, I was again discharged, and paid off as before. And here my whole military campaign closed.

Note on the Documents

The documents beginning on the pages cited below are published with the permission of the institutions in whose archives they belong.

202 Ezra Stiles, "Itineraries," I:67. Beinecke Rare Book and Manuscript Library, Yale University.

203 Ezra Stiles, "Itineraries," I:498–99. Beinecke Rare Book and Manuscript Library, Yale University.

229 Ezra Stiles, "Itineraries," II:418. Beinecke Rare Book and Manuscript Library, Yale University.

237 Samuel Holden Parsons's letter to Samuel Adams, March 3, 1773. Manuscripts and Archives Division, New York Public Library, Astor, Lenox, and Tilden Foundations.

239 "Extracts from Lyme Revolutionary Records: 1774–1784," pp. 1–2. Connecticut State Library.

240 "Extracts from Lyme Revolutionary Records: 1774–1784," pp. 2–3. Connecticut State Library.

243 "Connecticut Archives," Revolutionary War, first series, II:21a, b. Connecticut State Library

247 Joseph Mather's letter to Jonathan Trumbull, August 29, 1775. Jonathan Trumbull Papers, vol. IV, pt. 2:159a, b. Connecticut State Library.

247 Gurdon Saltonstall's letter to town officers, August 31, 1775. Jonathan Trumbull Papers, vol. IV, pt. 2:164a, b. Connecticut State Library.

248 Matthew Griswold's letter to Jonathan Trumbull, September 2, 1775. William Griswold Lane Collection, Yale University Library.

251 James Wadsworth, Jr.'s letter to Samuel Selden, June 29, 1776. Jedediah Huntington Letters, Connecticut Historical Society.

251 Copy, General Orders, from James Wadsworth, Jr., to Samuel Selden, June 23, 1776. Jedediah Huntington Letters, Connecticut Historical Society.

252 James Wadsworth, Jr.'s letter to Samuel Selden, June 30, 1776. Jedediah Huntington Letters, Connecticut Historical Society.

252 Samuel Selden's letter to Joshua Huntington, June 30, 1776. Jedediah Huntington Letters, Connecticut Historical Society.

253 Samuel Selden's letter to Joshua Huntington, July 6, 1776. William Griswold Lane Collection, Yale University Library.

254 "Extracts from Lyme Revolutionary Records: 1774–1784," pp. 4–5. Connecticut State Library.

256 John McCurdy's letter to Jeremiah Wadsworth, July 5, 1777. Jeremiah Wadsworth Papers, Connecticut Historical Society.

256 "Extracts from Lyme Revolutionary Records: 1774–1784," pp. 5–6. Connecticut State Library.

257 "Extracts from Lyme Revolutionary Records: 1774–1784," pp. 7–9. Connecticut State Library.

259 David F. Sill's letter to Samuel Mather, August 9, 1778. Ms. 72538. Connecticut Historical Society.

260 "Extracts from Lyme Revolutionary Records: 1774–1784," p. 9. Connecticut State Library.

260 Matthew Griswold's letter to Jonathan Trumbull, July 28, 1779. Jonathan Trumbull Papers, X:53a, b. Connecticut State Library.

261 "Extracts from Lyme Revolutionary Records: 1774–1784," pp. 11–12. Connecticut State Library.

262 Matthew Griswold's letter to Jonathan Trumbull, August 9, 1780. Jonathan Trumbull Papers, XII:204a, c, d. Connecticut State Library.

263 "Extracts from Lyme Revolutionary Records: 1774–1784," p. 15. Connecticut State Library.

263 "Extracts from Lyme Revolutionary Records: 1774–1784," p. 17. Connecticut State Library.

264 Adam Shapley's letter to William Ledyard, July 4, 1781. Jonathan Trumbull Papers, vol. XIV, pt. 2: 323a, b, c. Connecticut State Library.

265 Matthew Griswold's letter to Jonathan Trumbull, September 7, 1781. Jonathan Trumbull, Sr., Papers. Connecticut Historical Society.

266 Elisha Beckwith's letter to the General Assembly in Hartford, January 10, 1782. "Connecticut Archives," Revolutionary War, first series, XXIII:338. Connecticut State Library.

Selective Bibliography, Part Two

MANUSCRIPTS

The fullest repository of manuscripts relating to Lyme is in the Connecticut State Library in Hartford. Particularly useful are several series of "Connecticut Archives" (1629–1820): Civil Officers, Ecclesiastical Affairs, Industry, Militia, Revolutionary War, Towns and Lands, and Trade and Maritime Affairs. There is also valuable material in the Jonathan Trumbull Papers (Massachusetts Historical Society) and in the Judicial Department Records (Record Group 3), New London County Court Trials and Dockets. The surviving town meeting minutes are found in "Extracts from Lyme Revolutionary Records, 1774–1784."

Other documents relating to Lyme are found in the Jedediah Huntington Letters and Jonathan Trumbull, Sr., Papers at the Connecticut Historical Society in Hartford and in the William Griswold Lane Collection at the Yale University Library.

PRINTED WORKS

Acts and Laws of His Majesties Colony of Connecticut in New-England. New London: Timothy Green, 1715.

Acts and Laws Passed by the General Court or Assembly of His Majesties English Colony of Connecticut in New-England in America. New London: Timothy Green, 1750.

Burr, Jean Chandler, ed., *Lyme Records 1667–1730: A Literal Transcription.* Stonington, Conn.: Pequot Press, 1968.

Bushman, Richard L. *From Puritan to Yankee: Character and the Social Order in Connecticut, 1690–1765.* Cambridge: Harvard University Press, 1967.

Collier, Christopher. *Roger Sherman's Connecticut: Yankee Politics and the American Revolution.* Middletown, Conn.: Wesleyan University Press, 1971.

Connecticut Gazette. New London. December 17, 1773–February 26, 1823.

Deitrick, Barbara. *The Ancient Town of Lyme.* Lyme Tercentenary Committee, 1965.

Hoadly, C. J., et al., eds. *The Public Records of the State of Connecticut.* 11 vols. Hartford: Case, Lockwood, and Brainard, 1894–1919.

James, May Hall. *The Educational History of Old Lyme, Connecticut, 1635–1935.*

New Haven: Yale University Press for the New Haven Colony Historical
Society, 1939.

New London Gazette. New London. November 18, 1763–December 10, 1773;
[March] 1823–May 29, 1844.

Stark, Bruce P. *Lyme, Connecticut: From Founding to Independence.* Lyme: privately printed, 1976.

Trumbull, J. H., and Hoadly, C. J., eds. *The Public Records of the Colony of
Connecticut.* 15 vols. Hartford: Case, Lockwood, and Brainard, 1850–90.

Van Dusen, Albert. *Connecticut.* New York: Random House, 1961.

Zeichner, Oscar. *Connecticut's Years of Controversy, 1750–1776.* Durham: University of North Carolina Press, 1949.

Printed genealogies of Lyme families may be found at the Connecticut Historical Society in Hartford and at the Phoebe Griffin Noyes Library in Old
Lyme.

Note on the Contributors

JOHN P. DEMOS, a professor of history at Brandeis University, has written extensively about early American social history. Mr. Demos is the author of *A Little Commonwealth: Family Life in Plymouth Colony.*

Formerly the editor of *The Public Records of the State of Connecticut,* CHRISTOPHER COLLIER is now a professor of history at the University of Bridgeport. He has published numerous essays on Connecticut and early American history. His book, *Roger Sherman's Connecticut: Yankee Politics and the American Revolution,* appeared in 1971.

JACKSON TURNER MAIN, a specialist in American political and social history, has taught at San Jose State University, the State University of New York at Stony Brook, Columbia University, and Whitman College. He is the author of many works in his field, including *Political Parties before the Constitution.*

An associate professor of government at Connecticut College, MINOR MYERS, JR., teaches the history of political thought. His interests include church history and colonial furniture of Connecticut. *History of Graduate Education at Princeton,* written in collaboration with Willard Thorp, is forthcoming.

BERNARD BAILYN is Winthrop Professor of History at Harvard University and the author of many articles and books. His most recently published work is *The Ordeal of Thomas Hutchinson,* which won the National Book Award in 1975.

Colonial and early national history are the major interests of JOHN W. IFKOVIC, who recently completed a study of Jonathan Trumbull, Jr. Mr. Ifkovic teaches at Western Connecticut State College and at the University of Connecticut, Torrington Branch.

A specialist in Connecticut history, BRUCE STARK has published several articles in the field and a book, *Lyme, Connecticut: From Found-*

277

ing to Independence. He is at present working on an extensive study of Connecticut's Upper House.

HAROLD E. SELESKY is completing his doctorate at Yale University and is currently cataloguing the Ezra Stiles Papers at the Beinecke Rare Book and Manuscript Library, Yale University.

An associate professor of English and former department chairman at Connecticut College, GEORGE J. WILLAUER, JR., teaches American literature and has published articles on Anglo- and Irish-American Quaker history.

Index

Index

Guthrie, William, 55

Haddam, Conn., 17, 18, 50, 191, 194
Hadlyme, Conn., 228
Hadlyme Society, 41
Half-Way Covenant, 150
Hall, Benjamin, 145, 147, 153, 176
Hall, Elisha, 54, 62
Hamlin, Jabez, 145, 147, 153, 154, 157, 173, 175, 176, 180
Hamlin, John, 147, 149, 175
Hammonasset River, 15
Hampden, John, 204, 207
Hart, Levi, 125
Hartford, Conn., 10, 104, 105, 113, 124, 137, 138, 139, 140, 141, 143, 150, 151, 153, 154, 173, 175, 177, 181, 183, 184, 190, 191, 192, 194, 224, 236, 239, 245, 256, 263, 265, 266, 267
Harvard College, 54, 59, 61, 62, 236
Havens, Daniel, 244
Higgins, Christian, 241–43
Higgins, Capt. Joseph, 241, 242
Higgins, Joseph, 241, 242
Higginses, the, 241
Hillhouse, James Abraham, 155
Hillsborough, Lord, 227
Hitchcock, Enos, 52
Holland, 91, 221
Holt, Sir John, 58
Homer, 35
Hooker, John, 149, 150
Hubbard, Elijah, 256
Hudson River, 106, 107
Hunter, William, 203
Huntington, Christopher, 173
Huntington, Hezekiah, 105, 107, 108, 145, 146, 150, 151, 172, 173–74, 176
Huntington, Jabez, 145, 152
Huntington, Jonathan, 152
Huntington, Joshua, 252–54
Huntington, Samuel, 119, 157
Huntley, Adriel, 244

Huntley, James, 52, 60, 248, 258
Hutchinson, Thomas, 51, 236
Hyde, Phoebe, 97
Hyde, William R., 244

Ingersoll, Jared, 58, 82, 104, 111, 152, 204, 223, 225
Institutes (Coke), 101
Institutes (Wood), 101
Ireland, 88, 217–19, 233
"Itineraries" (Stiles), 202, 203, 228

Jackson, Colonel, 241, 242, 243
Jackson, Joseph, 242, 243
James II, King, 86, 90, 215
Jefferson, Thomas, 81
Jeffreys, George, 205, 207
Jewett, David M., 53, 60
Jewett, Joseph, 53, 243
Jewett, Nathan, 38, 60
John, King, 87
Johnson, Diodate, 62
Johnson, John, 245
Johnson, Lawrence, 245
Johnson, Stephen, 35, 48, 51, 54, 56, 57, 58, 59, 62, 99, 104, 202, 204, 223, 228, 230
Johnson, Sir William, 57
Johnson, William Samuel, 101, 102, 103, 106, 107–8, 111, 122, 123, 124, 155, 177
Josephus, 51

Kent, Conn., 151
Killingly, Conn., 191, 194
Killingworth, Conn., 15, 191, 192, 194, 249, 250
King Fisher, 245
"King George's War," 32
King Philip's War, 29

Lafayette, Marquis de, 201
Lamson, William, 238
Laud, Archbishop, 90
Lay, John, 52, 53, 60, 240
Lay, John, Jr., 36, 39

283